The Art & Science of the Hotel Concierge

Connecting Guests to Experiences Around the World

Holly Stiel
with Lin Ivice

Compliments of

CONCIERGE
THE LUXURY COLLECTION

The Art and Science of the Hotel Concierge

ISBN 978-0-7627-7852-2

9 8 7 6 5 4 3 2 1

Printed and bound in the United States of America.

gpp where

This book
is dedicated to all
Concierge Artists,
past,
present
&
future.

FOREWORD

Holly Stiel: Chronicler, Collector, Collaborator

Chronicler

Holly Stiel is "The Chronicler" of the World of Concierges in the same way that J.K. Rowling has been our guide to "Hogwarts" and "the World of Wizards" and I dare say that learning *The Art and Science of the Hotel Concierge* from Holly is no less magical and wondrous! She is passionate, witty, a keen observer of human nature and possesses the heart and soul of a gifted natural-born teacher.

Through her 17 years of practicing the profession before authoring her first book, *Ultimate Service*, she came up with creative, memorable descriptions of what concierges do and how they do it. Who can forget those early training programs? *The Neon Signs of Service* flashing through our collective minds: "The Wings of No," "Being Right is the Booby Prize," "Make No Assumptions" and "The Psychic Salary!"

Holly has inspired a generation of concierges and her new book will instruct future generations. Her artful portrayals of service issues and opportunities have shaped the profession of concierges and how it is perceived. She has created the cultural memes, acronyms and metaphors that have defined *The Art and Science of the Concierge* beginning with her hotel staff, her Clefs d'Or colleagues and then spreading the message around the globe after 1992, when she became a full-time speaker and consultant. Virginia Casale, First Vice President of the International Association of Concierges, and in line to be elected President this year, remembers her first international meeting in Singapore in 1992 and how receiving a complimentary copy of *Ultimate Service* influenced her development as a concierge.

Holly is indefatigable in advocating the mission of "Ultimate Service" – she writes articles, authors video training programs, blogs and creates workbooks. With Talent Mondial, Holly recently introduced a new program entitled *Becoming Extraordinary: The Magic of S.I.L.K.*℠ that she and her colleague Dorothy van Hoorn took to the call centers of 10 countries for American Express. Holly's name, brand and unique way of teaching based on the concierge, have become associated with the most prestigious global companies.

Collector

From her early days at the concierge desk, she collected stories and kept records that define the ultimate in service – the funny ones, the poignant ones and the heart-warming ones. At every networking opportunity, she can be found encouraging colleagues to share their stories which she skillfully uses to amplify and illustrate her service observations. As Holly travels the world, she collects these "tales from the front" providing color and depth to her speeches and training programs as well as archiving them for future generations of concierges and service professionals.

With these collected stories, she chronicles all aspects of the concierge job from the joys of being of service to the stress and how to handle it. One of my favorites is from her own concierge desk at The Grand Hyatt on Union Square in San Francisco.

Of course every visitor to San Francisco wants to have at least one meal in Chinatown. In the summertime, with so many tourists in town, the concierges tired of the question "Where should I eat in Chinatown?" Holly had the brilliant idea of taking the 5 or 6 restaurants that they usually recommended and having Fortune Cookies made. Each cookie conveyed the name of one of the recommended restaurants. The guests were delighted and the concierges were relieved of their boredom.

Collaborator

I have known Holly for 30 years and one of my favorite phone calls occurs at least once a month when I hear Holly's voice and she says, "I have a Great Idea!" She loves to share her ideas as well as hear those of others. That is what makes her one of the all time great practitioners of *The Art and Science of the Concierge*. These brainstorming sessions are so useful in advancing the Art of Collaboration. The best concierges are "seekers" and are always searching for the next best idea for a new service opportunity, a new way to train staff, or a networking option that we hadn't previously considered. Holly has always realized that service is a "collective endeavor" and the beauty and strength of the profession rests on this ability to network locally and internationally to achieve elegant solutions and create small miracles for our guests.

Holly and I were involved in the heady days when the profession was new in the USA and we had the opportunity to create our jobs as well as a new profession. We saw the organization grow from 28 members at our first meeting of LCD USA in 1981 to more than 600 today. That is a shared legacy of a professional lifetime bringing us back full circle to our beginnings and our search for collaboration to bring our message to the world.

The Beginning and the End of an Amazing Story: The Educational Institute (EI) of AH&LA and *Where* Magazine (Morris Visitor Publications)

In the mid-1980s, the concierge profession was barely known or recognized in the North American hotel world, let alone in the service world at large. Holly wanted to do a book and Les Clefs d'Or USA wanted her to do one. Jack Nargil was president and I was vice-president of Les Clefs d'Or USA, and we and our Board of Directors, considered that our mission to get the word out about concierges would be well-served by helping Holly to publish a book. Les Clefs d'Or assisted in collecting concierge training manuals at our meetings as well as collecting stories and hardest of all: finding a publisher and sponsor for the book.

One spring night Holly, Jack and I traveled to Lansing, Michigan to meet with the Educational Institute of the American Hotel & Lodging Association. We had prepared a proposal and wanted to partner with them to publish and distribute Holly's book (not written at the time but detailed in outline). All of our hotels belonged to the association we reasoned and even though there were fewer than 100 LCD members in the USA at the time, we knew that we would grow and prosper. We had a lovely meeting with EI and they listened carefully to our proposal but they could not justify training others for a profession that had such a small footprint at that time.

The book was published about 7 years later without their help but over the years, Holly kept in touch with the Educational Institute. Her dogged persistence has paid off and this time they will be involved in the distribution of *The Art and Science of the Hotel Concierge*. This educational imprimatur will be important to the success of the book and the advancement of the profession through certification using the text as a study guide.

On behalf of all concierges from around the world, our hearty congratulations to Holly on the accomplishment of this milestone and to repeat her four favorite words: "Thank You Very Much."

—Marjorie Silverman, *President d'Honneur*
Union Internationale des Concierges d'Hotels, "Les Clefs d'Or"

PREFACE

Planting the Seed

AS I WAS ON MY WAY TO REGISTER AT THE CONCIERGE CONGRESS in spring 2009, Jon Adler, a concierge at the St. Regis in New York, asked me if I planned to update *Ultimate Service, The Complete Handbook to the World of the Concierge* – a book I had written in 1992. At the time, I politely told him I didn't think it was necessary, as many of the chapters remained "evergreen." Though the section on technology was an exception, I felt that the bulk of the material in the book hadn't changed much. Plus, revising it would be a daunting task, and I wasn't sure if I could invest the required time and effort on a project of this magnitude again. Jon's reply came as a bit of a surprise: "Well, I'll help you with the high-tech portions if you ever change your mind – and I hope you do, change your mind, because our profession could really use a new book!"

I thanked him, but didn't think much about it again until early December of that same year when I got a call from John Pelletier, a professor in Boston, Massachusetts. John wanted to teach a class on the hotel concierge based on my book, but was reluctant to, because the school felt it was out of date. This was my wake-up call. In 1992, when I wrote Ultimate Service, I poured my heart and soul into the project and couldn't fathom allowing it to fade into oblivion because some of it might be a bit outdated.

I wasted no time springing into action. I immediately called Jon Adler. "Remember the offer you made to help me in Miami?" I asked him. "Well, I'm ready to take you up on it!" I then got busy eliciting the help of many concierge friends from San Francisco and beyond to reread the book and help me decide what material should stay and what should go. They worked hard to help me determine what had remained relevant and what needed to be updated and added.

I then enrolled my friend, Lin Ivice, a very talented writer, to be my co-author, explaining that the book needed a bit of renovation. I needed help in taking the old book apart and, much like Humpty Dumpty, putting it back together again. It is fair to say that Lin Ivice made this new book possible.

At this point, after close to twenty years of consulting, speaking and training – most significantly in the area of thinking like a world-class concierge – I had to do some soul searching. Did I have the willingness to commit to such an ambitious endeavor? As I told Jon in Miami, I never thought I would choose to devote the time and treasure it takes to create a comprehensive concierge text ever again. But upon closer examination, I realized that my passion and enthusiasm for the topic had actually increased over the years, and the very thought of an updated book began to excite me. After all, it still stops me in my tracks when I stand in awe of the artistry of a great concierge in action. Having worked with businesses as diverse as Nascar and the Bank of America, I have gained a new appreciation for the masterful work that excellent concierges perform and the rarity and wonder of all that it truly encompasses. Because my love of the profession had continued to expand after 30-plus years, I knew I had to make the effort and make it happen. It's my responsibility, my labor of love . . . and my legacy.

Legacy

In the last several years I have been thinking a great deal about the concept of "Legacy" and all that it entails. The proper definition of "Legacy" is "a gift of personal property or something handed down from the past." Perhaps it is something that one hopes to be remembered by. While I believed that *Ultimate Service* was a wonderful legacy in its time, I knew I could build upon it to leave something better to future generations of concierge and other service providers that concierge inspire. I love the concept of "a gift of a legacy" and it is because of it that not only this new book took shape, but other aspects of my business as well. To meet the challenge of building legacy expectations I have established a strategic partnership with Ann Buzzotta of Talent Mondial. Together, we will continue to bring new, exciting ideas and approaches that build upon the thinking of a world-class concierge.

As the revised edition evolved, I began taking the best from the original Ultimate Service and creating something even better for the future. As I got deeper into the project, I realized it wasn't only the technology that had changed. Other aspects of the job had evolved, too, so the book also needed to be different and called for a different name.

I chose the title, *The Art and Science of The Hotel Concierge*, for a couple of reasons. First, I wanted to clarify the true purpose of the book. Readers had told me that the original title, *Ultimate Service*, misled them to believe it was a "how-to" book on starting your own concierge business. Most importantly, however, I liked the new title because it captures what I know to be true about the unique work of a concierge. I believe there are several elements required to do the job well – some are technical, some are stylistic and others are spiritual in nature. They all come together to create a beautiful art form.

My friend Joanna Husk, concierge at The Grand Hyatt in San Francisco, sums up the artistry of the concierge this way:

> *"In the information age, anyone can ask a question and get an answer – whether it's through an Internet search or seeking the wisdom of a*

reference librarian. That is not why someone seeks a concierge. Yes, we are here to answer questions, but often the question a visitor asks is just the tip of a vast iceberg, underlying what they really need to know: How can they get the most from the limited time they have during their visit, and how will they fit it all in to make an enjoyable experience? It is up to the concierge to determine the size and shape of each guest's needs, convey a thoughtful response in a way that's most useful and suggest the best way to enjoy each moment. This calls for the art and science of the concierge.

As humans, we are like snowflakes – no two of us are exactly alike, and we don't do things in exactly the same ways. However, there are several distinct modes of operation that shine in the concierge's world. There is the problem solver who loves a challenge and takes joy in amazing each guest with an elegant solution. There is the hero, who swoops in during times of crises to rescue guests in distress and save the day (perhaps even an entire trip). There is the ultimate organizer, who categorizes each guest's disparate wish list items and finds the most efficient way to see and do it all in a very limited timeframe. Each of these modes constitutes the mindset of a great concierge.

I consider myself a Locative Artist Concierge. Locative art is a most intimate and personal form of art that creates a unique shared moment and cherished memory. San Francisco is my gallery and the concierge desk is my studio. Each guest is a patron who brings not only his or her request for a particular piece of my art, but the psyche and desires that color the unique experience I will craft for them. My guests experience a customized multi-sensory event of sight, sound, taste and smell that they will view and review in their mind's eye for the rest of their lives. It's an ensemble performance in which my beautiful city and its amazing residents are the stars."

Be a Gift

Many years ago, I was giving a workshop to concierges in San Francisco. One of the attendees that day was a man named Michael Thorburn. It turned out that it was Michael's first day on the job as a member of the concierge staff at The Mandarin, and his assignment was to attend my class. That day, I made a comment about always being a gift when you go to work. I remember that I had heard someone on a TV talk show say, "If you are going to bother showing up, be a gift." It was not something I typically said, nor do I particularly remember saying it that day, and may have never said it since. For some reason, however, it was fresh in my mind and I shared it with the class. Years later, Michael approached me at another event and told me that he has started every day at the concierge desk with those words and that intention: "If you are going to bother showing up, be a gift." It had colored his entire career.

One never knows what little word or action might inspire someone else to pay it forward. I retell the story now in the hopes that this book will be a gift to everyone who reads it, rereads it, and uses it to train new concierges and inspire experienced concierges. May the legacy of this book and corresponding workshops and certifications be my way of showing up as a gift in the lives of today's concierges and the concierges of the future.

A SPECIAL TRIBUTE TO TOM WOLFE

Founder of The Society of the Golden Keys USA
(Now Les Clefs d'Or USA)

TOM WOLFE helped us to innovate the concept of the concierge in the United States and continues to share remarkable innovations to this day. I like to think of him as the king of re-invention.

One of the most amazing aspects about Tom is that he always looks toward the future, while holding a healthy respect for the past. Today on YouTube.com, you can see videos created by Tom about the San Francisco he loves. He sends these videos to guests, instead of simply sending off a pre-printed itinerary. In this way and many others, he demonstrates his commitment to connecting with guests on a personal level.

While Tom uses the latest technology to forge these connections, you will also see him typing a confirmation card on an old fashioned typewriter in one of the video's opening scenes. Tom is the very epitome of the word "Legacy": To take the best from the past and work with it to design a better future. His old-fashioned type-writer sits comfortably alongside his iPad™. This is just one illustration of how Tom skillfully weaves together "The Art and Science" of the concierge profession.

I owe so much of my career to Tom's vision – and for the good grace that it all began in the beautiful city of San Francisco. A plaque, which sits proudly in the Fairmont Hotel San Francisco, denotes the history of Les Clefs d'Or USA and its humble beginnings in the late 1970s. I feel so fortunate to have been in the right place at the right time, enabling me to be a part of this wonderful legacy.

Link to YouTube video:
http://www.youtube.com/watch?v=btw6AW2SWm8
(As of this book's publication.)

CONTENTS

SOCIETY OF THE GOLDEN KEYS OF THE UNITED STATES

"LES CLEFS D'OR"

Minutes of Executive Meeting held on Thursday, June 23, 1977.

MEMBERS PRESENT

Thomas P. Wolfe	Fairmont Hotel
Larry Allport	Clift Hotel
Charles Martin	Holiday Inn, Union Square

MEMBERS ABSENT

Perry Ayers	Holiday Inn, Financial District

The meeting took place at Tom Wolfe's apartment, and was called to order at 7:00 p.m. Perry Ayers was unable to attend as he had not received his invitation, and had unavoidable arrangements.

The matter was raised as to whether or not female members should be allowed, in particular since the Hyatt Hotel Union Square has a female Concierge who is trying hard to provide first class service to their guests. It was therefore moved and carried that females should not be excluded, and it was further moved and carried that Holly should be invited to our next meeting as a guest (Holly is at the Hyatt Union Sq.).

It was resolved that meetings should take place once a month, the day to be the first Tuesday of the month. The next meeting will therefore be on Tuesday, July 5th.

Tom Wolfe said that he has ordered five sets of Golden Keys from Ted Cooper, Secretary of the Golden Keys of Great Britain. They should be arriving soon.

Howard Storm of the Stanford Court is to be invited to our next meeting as a guest.

The matter of a newsletter was discussed and it was agreed that a newsletter will be published in due course; all members are asked to contribute material that may be relevant and of interest.

Charles Martin noted that he had spoken to Mr. David Rose, General Manager of The San Francisco Guide, and that Mr. Rose expressed interest in our organization and would possibly be interested in an article about the Golden Keys and the Concierges. Charles will follow up on this and report at the next meeting.

I'm so happy I saved the early minutes from the creation of Les Clefs d'Or USA. It was a time when the idea of including a female concierge had to be "moved and carried." I believe the decision to include women proved to be an auspicious one.

CHAPTER ONE

1

Spirit, Characteristics, Values, Philosophy

OBJECTIVES

The following chapter will equip readers to:

Explore the essence of what it takes to be an exceptional Les Clefs d'Or Concierge.

Recognize that it's your "Spirit" that motivates you to exceed expectations and differentiates an extraordinary guest experience from an average one.

Observe the unique set of qualities and attributes required to maintain composure and perform to the high standards set by Les Clefs d'Or.

Consider ethical boundaries and identify the professional values and standards that are the foundation on which the legacy of the concierge rests.

See that the excitement and challenge of the concierge role lies in being able to find the impossible and deliver the unattainable.

A guest walks up to the concierge and says, "The cheeseburgers here are terrific. I want you to send one to my brother in Bahrain and I want it to arrive hot."

"The concierge calmly replies, "Will that be Bleu Cheese or Cheddar?"

SPIRIT

IT MAY SEEM ODD to think about the concept of one's spirit within the context of a textbook, but it is exactly this ingredient that is paramount in all service jobs – especially that of concierge. It is the spirit in which the job is performed that makes the difference and concierges need to understand this on a very deep level. It is the spirit behind the professional skills that motivates concierges to go the extra mile, perform the impossible and push themselves to the limit. The concierge is a curious partnership of idealism and realism that combine to create true hospitality. For years, concierges have been used as the service role model and rightly so.

Many times, I start my seminars by asking people why they would choose to be in the hospitality business and what characteristics they feel they bring to the profession. The usual responses I receive are: "I like people", "I love challenge", "Variety appeals to me", "I'm well organized", "I stay calm in a crisis", "I persevere", "I have a sense of humor", "I'm flexible", "I have endless patience" This type of bantering can go on for 10 minutes or so until finally someone says that the most important characteristic they bring to the job is their desire to help other people. Although the other characteristics are all a true part of the work, the bottom line is that this job is extremely personal, and the truth is – it is about understanding and fulfilling personal needs. I believe that it is about a deep-seated love of helping people. Without this, concierges would never be able to sustain the level of intensity that their job demands.

Job responsibilities and job descriptions cannot possibly give a true sense of the work performed by the concierge. There are so many intangibles, such as high visibility, prestige, a sense of personal power, a variety of business contacts and a deep sense of satisfaction. On the surface, it would seem that the motivation to become a concierge might be self-serving, but the primary motivation is actually based on a personal need to give, to nurture and to feel good about oneself by serving others. The passion to help others is a necessary ingredient that no concierge can be without.

"It gives me peace to know the people around me have nothing to worry about."

When I first came to the concierge desk, I loved it so much that I wanted to stay. I was a management trainee at the time, and knew I would be giving up a more established career in management if I were to become a concierge. I looked at the sacrifice in two ways: I wondered, if in ten years, I'd look back and wonder if I'd made a mistake. Then, I turned the question around. What if I became a general manager and ten years down the road, I wished I'd been a concierge? At that moment, I realized that the moment-by-moment experiences creating unforgettable memories for our guests were more important to me than a career in hotel management. I chose what I loved, rather than what I was educated to do and I couldn't be happier.

—"Barak" at the Four Seasons Hotel in Istanbul

CHARACTERISTICS

It takes a unique set of characteristics even to survive at a concierge desk. Of course, many of these characteristics are seen in other nurturing professions, such as nursing, social work, theatrical representation and even executive assistant positions, but they are at the very heart of being a concierge. The desire to give to others, to please and ultimately, to gain personal gratification and satisfaction are part of the underlying foundation that motivates and sustains concierges in their work. These, along with basic native intelligence ("street smarts") and the utmost professionalism, are the fundamental characteristics that enable the concierge to maintain composure day in and day out, year in and year out – but by no means is it the total picture.

This uniqueness was made very clear to me, early on in my career. In 1978, six concierges In San Francisco were taken on a familiarization trip with a new tour company. It was a private limousine tour that specialized in out-of-the-ordinary, off-the-beaten-track itineraries. We enjoyed a picnic lunch on a hilltop while being entertained by Japanese kite flyers and the melodious sounds of a child prodigy playing the flute. We stopped at artists' studios and at a jewelry warehouse. But the last stop was the most interesting. It was at a Victorian home in a cozy San Francisco neighborhood. The residents were a husband and wife team that specialized in numerology (very California, I know!). We all had our "numbers done" and the most curious thing happened: All of our numbers came out to be the same. We all had the same numerological type!

Begin with an outgoing nature and professional demeanor. Combine it with a deep desire to serve and be appreciated. Top it off with one's comfort zone at center stage, throw in a love for excitement, a voracious drive to organize, the patience of Job and the soul of a private eye. Combine these characteristics and you have the makings of a good concierge.

> *When I got my first job as a concierge, I thought I'd died and gone to heaven, for all my natural tendencies and quirks were not only accepted, they were appreciated and part of the job description. I got to talk all day and tell everybody what to do. I couldn't believe I would actually get paid to do what I'd always done anyway. I was always worried that I was a bossy person by nature and that I talked too much. Now, I was appreciated. My "liabilities" became my assets and I loved it!*

In the theater of the hotel lobby, a concierge is like an ER doctor or an air-traffic controller. It would be easy to become frustrated and "lose it" when asked to do three or four things at once, all the while being "on stage" in full view of the public. The ability to do multiple tasks without losing one's cool is paramount to being a concierge. If one cannot perform multiple tasks simultaneously, one should not even think about the concierge as a career choice. Multi-tasking on display is an aspect of the job that comes with the territory of having a desk in the lobby. There is no way around it.

THE SIX Cs

Marjorie Silverman, former hotel concierge and Honorary Past President, Union Internationale des Concierges d'Hotel, Les Clef's d'Or, has identified these six characteristics that define the top professional concierge:

Curiousity: Concierges are curious about people, the world, travel and tourism. They explore every nook and cranny of their locale – its history, restaurants, tours, architecture, culture and subcultures.

Creativity: Concierges are innovative and proactive. They anticipate guests' needs and generate new/fresh ideas for every challenge. They look for new and better ways to operate and constantly adapt to the marketplace, new technology and changing preferences of guests and management.

Confidence: Successful concierges are self-assured and confident, not tentative. Today's guests generally come to the concierge, having done their own basic research. They are looking for a local authority they can trust for accurate knowledge of the "up-to-the-minute" local scene.

Charisma: The word "charismatic" comes from the Greek definition and means that a person has the gift of grace. This is a beautiful way to describe the ultimate concierge, who projects an image of charm, poise and enthusiasm.

Competence: Concierges are effective and efficient. They understand their role and exactly how it fits into the hotel's service mission. Guests can put their full trust into the hands of the competent concierge.

Courteousness: Concierges are kind, understanding, gentle, diplomatic and giving. They always demonstrate civility in their interactions with guests, staff, management, vendors and their concierge colleagues.

PHILOSOPHY

The philosophy of the concierge embraces the concept of service with willingness and a sense of pride.

Webster's New World College Dictionary defines "concierge" as follows:

> **con·ci·erge**
> **Noun**, a doorkeeper, a custodian or head porter, as of an apartment house, a hotel employee who assists guests as by booking theater reservations or arranging for transportation
>
> Etymology: Fr, prob. ult. < VL *conservius < L conservus, fellow slave < com-, with + servus, slave
>
>

The part that stands out for most people in this definition is "fellow slave." The old adage; "It's all in how you look at it," is exemplified by a concierge. Concierges take pride in their work and understand the subtle difference between service and servitude. Over the years, they have turned the former into a work of art.

One must first thank the concierges in Europe for turning the tasks, such as booking airport shuttles, sending UPS and Federal Express packages, reserving rental cars, ordering amenities and giving out bus routes into an art form. The talent of the concierge, however, enables him or her to "gift wrap" even the most monotonous task in such a way that it appears very glamorous – much like an expert gift wrapper who transforms a power tool into a festive, elegant package.

MAKING MAGIC IN CONCIERGELAND

In the 1993 movie, *For Love or Money*, Michael J. Fox plays the leading role as Doug Ireland, a concierge at a ritzy New York hotel. Much of the movie reflects the fantasy world of Hollywood, but a good portion of it portrays the reality of what life is actually like in "Conciergeland," as I like to call it. So many of Fox's lines ring true, such as; "This hotel is a place where dreams come true." and "I'm a genie in a suit. Just rub me and get your wish." Concierges are in the magic-making business and it truly is an art.

COMMITMENT

The profession is demanding and requires a very high level of commitment. The level of responsibility and the demanding aspects are routine. Concierges are also required to "wear many hats" to get a job done, whether it's ironing shirts, polishing shoes or babysitting, when these services are unavailable through other means. The concierge understands that the job has to get done and it is the concierge's responsibility to figure out how best to accomplish it. Sometimes, this means doing it personally when there are no other alternatives.

The buck stops at the concierge

This should be emblazoned on the forehead of every concierge. If the concierge can't do it, it can't be done. This should be the overriding principle at a concierge desk. Some people in service jobs thoughtlessly pass people along to someone else, but not the concierge. When all else has failed, the concierge comes through with flying colors. He or she is the last stop, the end of the line. Yet from the other side – from the point of view of the guest – particularly the savvy traveler, it is the first and only place they need to go.

A large part of the concierge service philosophy is that the concierge will do anything, can do everything and never says "no." Of course, not all requests can be met all the time. Some restaurants are actually fully-booked at 8 o'clock and some shows really are sold out, but the dedicated concierge will exhaust all possibilities and always offer alternatives.

The concierge can do everything, with a very few exceptions…

> *At the Ritz Carleton in Cancun, a guest wanted to watch a film, privately, on the beach fronting the hotel. No problem. However, the guest didn't like sand, so asked the concierge to "cover it up somehow." Thinking quickly, the concierge dispatched a team to Mexico City to buy a panoply of rugs that were carefully rolled out onto the beach.*
>
> *At the Sagamore Resort in Lake George, New York, a guest asked a concierge to promptly send engineering to his room to replace the gas-burning fireplace with a wood-burning fireplace. Even the omnipotent concierge couldn't accommodate this request, but did refer the guest to a nearby lounge that warmly welcomed its patrons with a wood-burning fireplace.*

ETHICS AND VALUES

There are requests that simply cannot be met, not because they are impossible, but because they extend beyond the boundaries of the concierge's morals and integrity. The concierge philosophy condones only services that are legal and kind. Betting on a horse in the Kentucky Derby through a bookie or pulling practical jokes on another guest on April Fool's Day are examples of services that are inappropriate for the concierge.

Les Clefs d'Or [pronounced "lay clay door" – "keys of gold" in French] is a well-respected association of professional concierges. You will learn more about Les Clefs d'Or in later chapters, but it bears mentioning here, because one of this association's primary purposes is to establish and promote highly professional and ethical standards. Their motto succinctly expresses one of the primary values of the concierge: ***"In service through friendship."***

The foundation, on which the concierge rests, consists of rock-solid values. They are simple and direct and can help the concierge through his or her entire career. ***"In service through friendship"*** means we are consistently helpful and kind to each other. Concierges are a special breed – co-survivors of the completely unique work-days and experiences they all share. ***"My word is my bond"*** instills trust, and ***"My guest today is your guest tomorrow"*** describes how concierges all over the world collaborate to help each other. These core values are our legacy.

The following is the Les Clefs d'Or "Code of Ethics" and Professional Standards:

Personal Demeanor

- Always maintain a professional appearance. Unless told otherwise, wear professional attire to all Concierge related functions.
- Always use proper grammar.
- Stay poised and professional under all circumstances; remain polite, courteous and helpful.
- Honor all commitments to colleagues and others.
- Never practice nor permit discrimination of any type.
- Treat colleagues respectfully at all times.

Guest Relations

- Listen attentively to guests' requests. Always offer to provide guests with written confirmations of their requests.
- Return all correspondence in a timely manner.
- Always thank guests if they remember you in some way. Send thank-you notes whenever possible.
- Always maintain professional relationships with guests; address guests in a professional manner.
- Tactfully decline illegal or unethical requests from guests.
- Never promise guests results, unless you are positive you can deliver.
- Advise guests, up front, of surcharges or service fees on tickets or other requests.
- Always provide guests with detailed seat location information, including obstructions, when acquiring tickets for guests.
- Inform guests of dress codes at restaurants.
- Learn to evaluate guests by their manner, dress and preferences. What might be good for one guest may be unsuitable for another.
- Always respect and protect the identity and confidentiality of all guests.

Vendor Relations

- Never double-book restaurants for guests.
- Never accept goods or services from vendors for personal gain.
- A Les Clefs d'Or, USA, Concierge neither receives commissions from restaurants nor participates in incentive driven competitions.

- Always use reputable businesses and service organizations.
- Exercise objective and independent judgment in the evaluation of goods and services.
- Pay all invoices upon receipt.
- Never take advantage of restaurants that invite you for dinner by ordering the most expensive items on the menu or bringing uninvited guests along. Tip your server 20% of the estimated bill.
- Remember when you are invited to theaters, restaurants or other venues, you are an ambassador of your hotel and of LCD USA.
- Treat vendors with respect, professionalism and courtesy. Appropriate verbiage is imperative.
- Always thank your host(s) before you depart and send a note of appreciation afterward.

Use of Social Media

- Be aware of and abide by your company's policies when making personal statements about your company, its subsidiaries and/or any affiliates via any form of electronic media including, but not limited to Twitter, Facebook, YouTube, My Space, etc.
- In the course of your electronic communications, if you receive inquiries from any member of the press or media regarding Les Clefs d'Or, USA, you should refer the media to the current President or Vice President of Les Clefs d'Or USA.
- Do not share information you would not want repeated or photos you would not want publicized. Once you have posted anything electronically, it becomes public domain.
- Whether you are on company or personal time, you are *not* free to share information that is considered confidential to Les Clefs d'Or USA, including personal guest information or any company business of your employer.

Public Relations

- Always speak with your Public Relations Director before speaking to the press. This includes vendor endorsements.
- In the course of your personal statements or commentary to any media outlet, you may not present yourself as a representative of or spokesperson for Les Clefs d'Or USA unless you have been authorized in writing by the Board of Directors to do so.
- The use of the trademarked Les Clefs d'Or USA or UICH International logos/insignias for any public relations or marketing

usage is prohibited without prior written consent from the Board of Directors to reproduce said trademark.

SAYING "YES" TO CHALLENGE

"I don't know" is half the sentence for the concierge.

The other half is, "and I'll find out."

Nobody on earth knows everything. The concierge, however, must always know how to find out. The following is a perfect example of a really difficult request, alien to even the most knowledgeable concierge. It was handled brilliantly.

A Japanese gentleman approached an unflappable concierge and asked where he could find a slaughterhouse. She thought there was something more behind the simple request and asked further. It turned out, after some discussion, that he wanted to purchase a pound of ox gallstones. The concierge thought he meant the gallbladder of an ox, but after careful clarification, she understood and called the owner of a steak restaurant who was affiliated with a ranch that had a slaughterhouse on the premises. Within a few phone calls, the concierge located an ox with gallstones and the guest was able to procure his pound, albeit at a very dear price.

Believe it or not, the odd request such as the one described above is a request that the concierge enjoys most. The more difficult and obscure the request, the more challenging and fun the job becomes. The concierge thrives on challenge and values resourcefulness. Fulfilling the bizarre request is where the creative instinct of the concierge really kicks in, and after one has been a concierge for long enough, even the most bizarre situations begin to seem normal.

A concierge was approached by a gentleman frantically in search of twenty yarmulkes (a skullcap worn by men) for a Jewish wedding. The person responsible for bringing the yarmulkes had forgotten them and the wedding was about to begin. Thinking quickly as a concierge must, she called a Jewish funeral home, which had yarmulkes and sent them by messenger. The wedding went on as planned.

A concierge in New York had to assist a guest who left her wallet in the hotel limousine. She was headed for London, and by chance, another guest was leaving on the next flight to the same destination. The concierge arranged for the second guest to take the wallet with him and had it collected by a concierge friend at Heathrow Airport. The friend was able to deliver the wallet to the guest's residence before she actually arrived, and it was waiting for her when she walked in the door.

Doing the impossible is very exciting to a concierge. It is the challenge that keeps the concierge going – changing hats every few minutes, remembering even the smallest detail, appearing omnipotent, repeating common information without sounding bored, working with a myriad of cultures and personalities and responding to each guest in a professional, yet personalized way.

Concierges are lucky. They live in a "Yes" universe. When the next challenge confronts them, concierges figure it out. To them, the impossible becomes possible. Going above and beyond the call of duty is standard procedure – the "impossible" just takes a little longer.

A colleague of mine was asked to obtain a permit to land an advertising hot air balloon in Union Square (a public park in downtown San Francisco). My colleague managed to execute what the guest had not been able to do on his own. She was resourceful and determined and was able to obtain a balloon permit. (Just for the record, the guest didn't even say "thank you.") My colleague's payoff was the pure satisfaction of going through the process and accomplishing her goal.

If concierges only worked for tips, their lives would be a constant disappointment. Because the job is personal, it is the personal sense of satisfaction that is truly important. The opportunity to solve problems for others, in conjunction with the freedom to be creative, is the payoff. Beyond the rare request that cannot be met and the occasional illegal or unkind requests, most difficult situations are handled with a sense of adventure and determination. Concierges are satisfying their own desire to feel accomplished when they go out of their way to obtain the unusual for a guest.

When Michael J. Fox's character in For Love or Money *is confronted by a cynical guest who says, "He makes a living being nice to people, so he can get something in return," he doesn't waste a second in replying: "I don't do it for money. It comes from the heart." For the professional concierge, truer words have never been spoken.*

COMMON SENSE

Common sense is essential in the concierge profession. The concierge needs to have a double dose of it, one for him or herself and one for guests, as they can become disoriented when visiting a city that is strange to them. It is often the job of the concierge to help people regain their bearings, by providing knowledge about their cities and ways for maneuvering within them.

The application of some good old horse sense, infinite patience and a strong sense of humor are mandatory when confronted with questions, such as:

- Do you know that you are in a draft here?
- Can I get a cup of coffee in the coffee shop?
- How do you get out of room 912?
- Are the planes leaving from the airport?
- If it's raining today, will I get wet?
- Is Fishermen's Wharf indoors?
- Can I fly a kite from the balcony?
- Where is the bathroom? I can't find it in my room.

When faced with a multitude of tasks, the concierge must have common sense and be an expert at prioritizing. They perform a type of "triage." Triage is the system typically used by medical professionals to prioritize patients in an emergency situation in which there are a great number of injured or ill. While the severity of the situation is usually less dramatic in a hotel setting, a form of triage is used nonetheless. Is the box office closing, making it necessary to deal with theater tickets before making a dinner reservation? Is someone waiting for an answer? Is the Federal Express pickup happening in the next 10 minutes when there are five packages to be wrapped? The hotel lobby is not an emergency room, but it may well be that hotel guests will perceive their immediate needs as life-or-death situations. It's up to the concierge to use his or her common sense to prioritize guests' requests.

SENSE OF HUMOR

A sense of humor is probably the most valuable asset the concierge can bring to their job. Without it, life as a concierge would be difficult at best; and in many cases, relying on a sense of humor will save hours of aggravation.

> *I had three guests from New York approach the desk. The conversation went like this: "We are sick of Californian food, we have had it. We want food, you know, like you can get in New York." I responded by recommending the Palm restaurant. Without skipping a beat, this family replied: "The Palm? What do we want that for? We have that in New York." One reaction would have been to be aggravated or think people were ridiculous – my reaction was to laugh and come to the conclusion that people are funny.*

Without a sense of humor, the job of the concierge would soon become annoying – possibly even downright intolerable.

To maintain a sense of humor, we kept a red spiral notebook at the desk and when something amusing happened that we really wanted to remember, we wrote it in the "Red Book." It's great therapy and, if nothing else, it's always good for a laugh. The following are a few examples of our entries in the Red Book.

- *I was asked to make airline reservations for a Mr. Schmulivitz and a Mr. Custer. I asked, "How do you spell 'Custer'?" Mr. Schmulivitz loved it.*
- *A guest wanted to rent a tuxedo. When asked what size he wanted, he responded, "My size."*
- *A mother asked me if a show known for high satire would "go over her daughter's head." The child was four.*
- *A man once asked me how to get out of San Francisco. I asked which direction he preferred: north, south or east. He was furious and insisted that I just tell him where to go.*

SURFING IN THE ZONE

Many people who walk by a concierge desk and observe the concierge on two phones at once, while handling three or more guests, shake their heads in amazement and ask, "How do they do that?" They can do it only because they are energized and invigorated by the excitement. In the same way as a long-distance runner is at his peak during a race, the concierge is "in the zone" (though some of the stranger guest requests make it seem like the Twilight Zone!). Concierges love the feeling they get from managing chaos (when they are handling it all) and remaining in control, like the calm at the eye of a hurricane. They gain their greatest satisfaction from delivering the finest service they can when the pressure's on.

The hotel business is constantly changing, filled with pressure and ripe with opportunities to ameliorate dissatisfaction. To describe a typical day at a concierge desk, as being overloaded with situations and problems, is an understatement. A surfing metaphor is a great way to describe the experience. The professional surfer senses each wave, stands up, maintains his balance through the roughest of waters and successfully glides into shore – only to paddle out again and catch the next challenging wave, again and again. Such is the life of the concierge, mastering wave after wave of interactions – with guests, colleagues and the world at large.

During a particularly busy period, I once asked if any of the many guests at my desk had a question that could be quickly and easily answered.

A gentleman responded, "Could you give me a list of the names of all the chicken farmers and places to buy chicken farming equipment in northern California?" I had to laugh. My idea of a quick question was "Where are the cable cars?"

The concierge lives in a world where it's critically important that "everyone wins." It cannot be emphasized strongly enough how important it is to have a person with these basic philosophies, characteristics and motivations in the position of concierge. It requires a certain belief system, common sense and a sense of humor. Once that is established, one begins to think like a concierge. The rest can be taught, and one can then proceed to learn the more technical aspects of the role.

STORIES TO LIVE BY

I am including four stories from a book, *Words to Live By*, which was published by Simon and Schuster in 1959. This very special book was given to me, by my father, on my fourteenth birthday. I've taken four stories from the book that I think apply to the concierge profession. They are excellent reading and re-emphasize the philosophy needed to excel as a concierge.

How Not to be Bored

by Emily Kimbrough, Noted Traveler, Lecturer and Writer

"I have never met anyone who couldn't tell me something I hadn't known before."

—My Grandfather

Grandfather Kimbrough took me on a train from Muncie, Indiana, where we lived, to Indianapolis, where we could see a bridge he was building. I was nine years old, and I had been Grandfather's companion on many such trips about the state. At that time, I was anticipating this particular one because it was to include lunch in a big dining room at the Claypool Hotel, and the grand finale, before train time, of a chocolate soda at Craig's – a double one. I remember these things only because I have never forgotten Grandfather's conversation with the train conductor.

We had arrived in Indianapolis, the end of the line. Everyone got off the train except Grandfather. He stood on the steps of the parlor car, talking to the conductor. I tugged at his coat; he was so absorbed he paid no attention. When the conversation ended, he took my hand and said, as we walked along the platform, "That was a very interesting thing he told me."

I was cross. The shimmering day ahead – a bridge, a hotel lunch and a chocolate soda – was a long time getting under way. I quickened my step, tugging at Grandfather's hand. I said over my shoulder, "What could a conductor tell you that you didn't know already?" I was not relegating the conductor to a low status; I only considered it preposterous that anyone in the world know more than my companion and idol.

Grandfather stopped so suddenly I was jerked back and around so that I faced him. He wasn't angry – he was arrested by an idea. He looked down at me a long time in such a way that I was held quiet and silent.

"Why, Emily," he said, shaking his head a little in astonishment at his own discovery, "I believe I have never met anyone who couldn't tell me something I hadn't known before." And that is how it has been for me from that day to this.

Enthusiasm

by Samuel Goldwyn, *Hollywood Producer*

"Nothing great was ever achieved without enthusiasm."

—Ralph Waldo Emerson

Emerson was certainly right – but not right enough, for enthusiasm is the key not only to the achievement of great things, but to the accomplishment of anything that is worthwhile.

Enthusiasm is a wonderful word, but more so, it is a wonderful feeling. It is a way of life. It is a magic spark that transforms "being" into "living." It makes hard work easy – and enjoyable. There is no better tonic for depression, no greater elixir for whatever happens to be wrong at the moment, than enthusiasm.

No person who is enthusiastic about his work has anything to fear from life. All the opportunities in the world – and they are as plentiful today as ever despite what some people say – are waiting to be grasped by the people who are in love with what they are doing.

For as long as I can remember, whatever I was doing at the time was the most important thing in the world to me. Today, I look forward to my next picture with the same degree of excitement and anticipation and enthusiasm with which I went into my very first production.

I have found enthusiasm for work and life to be the most precious ingredient in a recipe for successful living. And the greatest feature of this ingredient is that it is available to everyone – within himself.

The Other Fellow

by Clifton Fadiman, *Writer and Lecturer*

"The worst sin toward our fellow creatures is not to hate them, but to be indifferent to them; that's the essence of inhumanity."
—George Bernard Shaw

Alone, no man can save himself. Alone, no man can find himself. Alone on his island, Robinson Crusoe was merely a highly ingenious animal. With the arrival of Friday, he became a man.

We cannot love all our fellow men, except in the most abstract way. But we can at least not be indifferent to them. We can cultivate awareness; we can try always to connect. What is civilization, after all? Surely it is man's effort to grow away from his original state of brutal separateness, or indifference. It is the bridge one man throws up to connect himself with another man; the sense of connection is like a muscle. Unused, it withers. Exercised, it grows. Look at the next strange face you see, in a train, a theater lobby, behind a counter – really look at it. Behind those eyes there is a whole life, as complicated, as mysterious as your own. If, for only a fleeting instant, you can feel the pressure of that life, you have hailed in passing that unique miracle – the other fellow.

The Looking Glass

by King Vidor, *Producer and Director*

"The world is a looking glass and gives back to every man the reflection of his own face."
—William Makepeace Thackeray

I had to live a long time before I found the courage to admit to myself that we all of us – make our own worlds.

The realization came to me in a very simple way. Though I am a Californian, I make frequent trips to New York, and I had decided that all New York cab drivers were impatient, bad-tempered or hated their jobs. And hotel employees and railroad personnel were the same. I found them all difficult to get along with.

Then one day in New York, I came upon the words from Thackeray quoted above. The very same day when a cabby and I were snarling at one another, this thought occurred to me: "Could this whole situation be the result of my own thinking and outlook?"

I began to live Thackeray's idea and soon it became a part of me. The result: On my next trip East, I encountered not one unpleasant taxi driver, elevator operator or employee! Had New York changed or had I? The answer was clear.

To abandon excuses for one's own shortcomings is like journeying to a distant land where everything is new and strange. Here you can't continue to blame someone or something else for failures or difficulties; you have to assume the responsibility for them yourself. Of course, outside pressures do influence our lives, but they don't control them. To assume they do is sheer evasion – it's so easy to say, "It's not my fault!"

Since that day in New York, I've come to believe that this idea is the basis of all human relationships. It doesn't matter whether it is your neighbors, your mother-in-law or the people of a foreign nation. The quickest way to correct the other fellow's attitude is to correct your own.

Try it. It works. And it adds immeasurably to the fun of meeting people and being alive.

THE ART AND THE SCIENCE

WHILE THIS TEXTBOOK is designed as a manual detailing the duties and job responsibilities of hotel concierges, such as booking restaurant reservations and other routine requests, it is equally concerned with the finer brush strokes that create the "magic" behind these everyday tasks. This book has been written in the spirit of both idealism and realism – the art and the science – needed to serve guests in a manner befitting the values and goals of Les Clefs d'Or and the profession as a whole. As mentioned earlier in this chapter, it's so much more than solving guests' problems and meeting their needs. It's about "gift wrapping" even the most mundane of tasks and exceeding your guests' expectations with a stroke of magic.

CHAPTER TWO

2 Thinking Like a Concierge

OBJECTIVES

The following chapter will equip readers to:

Appreciate the importance of positive attitude and the impact that it has on your ability to "Think like a concierge".

Recognize that paying attention to the detail and subtle nuances of every guest interaction opens up an opportunity to create a unique and memorable experience.

Observe the enormous benefit to all departments when the concierge assumes responsibility for sharing information across the organization.

Use their heightened intuition to "read the moment" and identify clues to anticipate what guests really need.

Manage the communication challenges with guests and see the importance of clarifying important information to avoid misunderstanding.

Differentiate the guest experience by using their extensive network to think out of the box and creatively overcome daily challenges.

Understand the need for improved security measures and their enormous responsibility during disaster management.

Anybody can have a menu translated into Braille, but the concierge can get it done in 30 minutes while handling 15 other problems, answering phones and serving guests.

That's the kind of service that separates concierges from the rest of the world.

ATTITUDE

THINKING LIKE A CONCIERGE is the essence of success. It is the foundation that makes or breaks the outcome of every encounter. All the other aspects of the job are icing on the cake. In the world of the concierge, there are no half-price sales for so-so service. Every minute of every day requires full-out excellence – the ultimate in service. The mystery, the magic and the solutions are created by thinking like a concierge. This is the glue that holds it all together. It is the reason the concierge has become a phenomenon across so many industries.

There are so many facets to "thinking like a concierge," but the principal aspect can be summed up in two words: Positive Attitude. A positive attitude makes it possible to endure the challenge of demanding guests, endless telephone calls and the drudgery of constant repetition, all swirling around you at warp speed. The concierge is both an advocate for the guest and ambassador for the hotel and his or her city. While professionalism is very important, one also wants to remain always warm and welcoming. Arrogance has no place here!

"Thinking like a concierge" also requires excellent communication skills, creativity, intuition, imagination and a burning desire to get the job done – whatever it may be. It boils down to one simple word: "on". The concierge is always "on" the phone, "on" the computer, "on" the job, "on" the front line, "on" call, "on" their feet, but most importantly, "on" the ball.

A concierge in Phoenix, Arizona, remembers a guest in a wheelchair who had checked in as part of an architect's convention. The group was going to visit a Frank Lloyd Wright school building and this guest couldn't be included because the bus had no wheelchair access. The concierge noticed that the gentleman was alone, so as a gesture of hospitality, she offered him tickets to a nearby museum. He reacted most peculiarly and shouted that she had no business feeling sorry for him or interfering. Although she was startled, she maintained a professional and calm approach and said, "I'm sorry if I offended you. I was trying to help, as it appears you haven't been confined to a wheelchair for very long. "The man's response was again unexpected. He asked how she knew that and being a concierge who is always 'on,' she explained. The previous day, he'd purchased stamps, at which time she'd noticed that his hands were smooth – not callused, as would be the hands of one continuously operating a wheelchair. She also noticed that his shoes were scuffed-simple deduction for one who pays attention to every detail. The guest was so impressed that he poured his heart out and told her an odd truth. He wasn't disabled at all, but his brother had recently been disabled and he'd wanted to experience it for himself in order to relate more genuinely. He'd found the task so exhausting and frustrating that his anger had overwhelmed him.

The next day, in full view of the entire group, he wheeled himself over to the concierge desk and told her, "I can't thank you enough for what you've done for me." With that, he pushed off, stood up and walked away, leaving his colleagues to marvel at the miracle performed by the concierge. The concierge calls that little tale "Lourdes of the Lobby".

Being able to think like a concierge requires three basic, but integral elements:

- **Integrity**
- **Responsibility**
- **Everyone-Wins Mentality**

In the life of the concierge, it might be tempting to become greedy and think only in terms of "taking care of number one," but the concepts of integrity and responsibility are always held in the highest regard. Concierges are not only responsible for themselves, the guests and the hotels they serve; they are also responsible to other concierges and to the overall reputation of the profession.

The concierge's job is filled with paradox. On one hand, there is the desire to serve, to "do good. "On the other hand, there's the wheeling and dealing necessary to get the job done. It is often difficult to maintain equilibrium within that dichotomy.

The principle that "everybody wins" is the key factor that brings everything into balance, and if the concierge keeps this in mind, decisions tend to come out right. In a situation where this is not the case, an incorrect decision has been made or faulty thinking has been applied. "Everybody" includes the guest, the hotel, the vendor, the individual concierge and the body of concierges within the profession.

Many people believe that because concierges can seemingly create magic, they can do it with no fees attached. While the concierge is indeed an invaluable service that the hotel provides to its guests without extra charge, some requests – especially the outrageous ones – do in fact cost money to accomplish.

I was at the gym when a woman, who knew I was a concierge expert, asked me about what she perceived to be an outrageous request asked by one of her real-estate clients. She wondered, "What do you do when someone asks for what is obviously over the top and outrageous?" I told her that as long as it is legal, kind and moral, we are delighted to accomplish it, but such requests will often require an additional cost. In hotels, you can't charge an upfront fee for doing the research (which is sometimes extensive), but you can absolutely charge a fee for accomplishing the task. I used this example: You want to have a pizza delivered to your yacht in the middle of the Atlantic, and you want it to arrive hot. Yes, we can make that happen, but at a cost.

Concierges are often required to handle tasks after normal business hours, such as retrieving an item for a guest from an airport late at night. Although the concierge cannot perform such services as favors on a constant basis, there are methods for accomplishing such tasks. Outside resources can be deployed to handle problems such as collecting a misplaced piece of luggage. Or, the owner of a florist shop may be encouraged to remain open past normal hours to accommodate a guest's special request. However, such services usually carry an extra charge, and whatever the charge, it should be fair. In other words, the concierge must never allow others to take advantage of the guest. The guest deserves value, and although there is a price for the additional convenience, it is up to the concierge to maintain integrity and constantly strive to keep pricing reasonable.

At the same time, it is important for the concierge to reward the people who assist them in handling special requests. The cost for those rewards are taken into consideration when quoting and later charging the guest. If, for instance, the florist reopens her shop for a guest late at night, it is appropriate to charge more for the flowers than would have been charged during normal business hours.

While it is appropriate for the concierge to maintain fair pricing, some special services carry a significant price tag. Tickets to a sold-out show, for example, are more expensive than tickets for a popular but available performance, and although the concierge has no need to apologize for the added cost, it is very important that the situation be carefully communicated to the guest. In determining price, it is imperative that the concierge bears in mind the "Big Three:" "Integrity," "Responsibility," and "Everyone Wins."

ATTENTION TO DETAIL AND GOING THE EXTRA MILE

The concierge needs to have a mind that can take in all the details of the situation, process them and choose the appropriate action. For example, when the president of Coca-Cola® is due to arrive, it would be advisable to remove any other brands of soft drinks from his suite or limousine and replace them with Coke® products. Thinking like a concierge means being sensitive to the details and the subtle nuances that dictate how to handle every aspect of the guest experience. There are a myriad of details involved in booking an airline reservation alone, and this is just one of many tasks that the concierge is asked to complete for their guests. One small detail can make or break a guest's day and quite possibly his or her opinion of the hotel. For instance, since Alcatraz is a federal park, a government-issued ID is needed to take the tour. Neglecting to inform the guest of this ahead of time would result in a great disappointment for the guest.

Attention to detail also means putting the icing on the cake and going the extra mile to provide a unique, authentic and memorable experience.

The following is a missed opportunity to "wow" a guest, who, in this case, happened to be me.

> *I was off to Puerto Rico to meet my sisters to celebrate my milestone birthday. The hotel was well aware of my visit well in advance. They knew it was a special occasion, as I had spoken about it directly to the public relations manager. Imagine my surprise, when the room I had requested for three women wasn't even big enough to squeeze in one suitcase. The bellman, thankfully, saved the day and moved us to renovated – and much more comfortable – accommodations. But here's where they really dropped the ball: I was a guest there for five days and not once did I receive a note or any acknowledgement whatsoever that we were celebrating something special. While I felt a little disappointed on a personal level, I kept thinking how unfortunate it was for them to miss such a perfect opportunity. A handwritten note with a few strawberries would have sufficed nicely to create a lasting memory, the likelihood of return visits and a glowing report about the hotel to friends and family back home. Instead, it resulted in a lackluster experience that felt impersonal and uncaring.*

The cost of making someone feel special is minimal. Attention is all you really have to pay, and the reward is . . . priceless.

SHARING INFORMATION

Thinking like a concierge also means considering other departments in the hotel when it comes to sharing information. Being the "eyes and ears" of the hotel, the concierge is responsible for passing along relevant and important information for the benefit of all departments. For instance, the executive departments should always be informed of any VIPs visiting in the hotel. A good concierge has top management's ear and is able to call matters to their attention that can only be handled at that level.

A concierge at a hotel on Fisherman's Wharf once spotted a famous cellist, but felt certain that no one else was aware of the gentleman's identity. He was able to inform his general manager in time to avoid his having to deal with the embarrassment of appearing uninformed.

The principle of sharing information applies to other departments as well. For instance, if the concierge is a guest at a restaurant in town and notices something new and intriguing, they can pass the good idea along to the food and beverage manager. There are additional details on sharing information with other departments in CHAPTER 5.

BEING A SLEUTH AND READING THE MOMENT

The concierge is a bit of a sleuth. When called upon to make decisions with very little information, the concierge must become skilled at reading the moment and speed reading it, at that. For instance, it is important to know when to make a fuss over someone and when to respect their privacy. The concierge must intuitively "read" a guest, looking for their "hidden agenda" to ascertain exactly what their wants and needs are – and all this in a matter of seconds. Funny as it may sound, it's often not what guests are asking for that matters, but what is hidden behind their request that gives you clues to what they really want and need. With only seconds to interact, the concierge is required to "read the subtext" to really "get" the guest, ask questions to zero in on what he or she really wants and then offer solutions in the manner in which the guest wants to hear them.

It's a lot like speed dating. The concierge often has only seconds to interact with each guest, ask questions and determine the subtext of what he or she is saying. In a short amount of time, the concierge "reads" who the guest is and deciphers what he or she really wants, while showing interest in him or her and the desire to help. Continuing with this analogy, it's not unusual for a concierge to "speed date" 70 to 150 guests a day!

Ask Questions

When possible, it's helpful to ask questions. More often than not, solving a guest's problem is more about asking questions than answering them. When a guest requests a pharmacy, for instance, it is a good idea to probe a bit deeper (discretely and politely, of course) and follow the "clues." Perhaps all they need is a Band-Aid®, which you can easily provide from your drawer of supplies. Providing ultimate service is not as much about giving guests what they ask for, but what they actually want and need.

A man asked me for directions to Reno, and when I looked at him, I somehow knew I needed to inquire further. I asked him why he wanted to go to Reno, and he told me that he wanted to get divorced and remarried in the same day. Such a feat is not possible in Reno, so through a concierge friend in San Diego, I was able to help him arrange for a lawyer in Tijuana who could handle the divorce and wedding without difficulty.

A man asked a concierge in New York for directions to the Metropolitan Museum of Art, and something told him to ask further. Sure enough, the man wanted to go that day and the concierge was able to inform him that the museum was closed and would reopen the following day, saving his guest from unnecessary disappointment.

The concierge needs to "go the extra mile" and ask the next logical question to figure out what the guest is actually requesting. Someone may be asking for a location or an item by a name that makes no sense, but the concierge should, with a little polite inquisitiveness, be able to decipher the true name. The following are actual examples of guests' requests and their proper "translations:"

If a guest asks for:	They might mean:
Good Cheese	Gucci
Louis Van Newton	Louis Vuitton
Frogup Café	Fog City Diner
The Banged Roof	The Slanted Door
Topless Bar	Tapas Bar
Dem Tings	Mints

A guest in a New York hotel asked the concierge where he might find yachting supplies. The concierge did a great deal of research, looking for a supplier of ropes, life vests, anchors, etc. To his dismay, the concierge later discovered that all the guest actually wanted was a store that carried Ralph Lauren clothing.

I remember when a guest asked me about "Freemont" and I packed him off on a train to a nearby town by that name. Unfortunately, he actually wanted the Fairmont Hotel, which was located three blocks away. Today, I know better how to ask questions to get to the truth.

Another great phrase to ensure you're on target is: "Let me make sure this is what you're really looking for."

SEEING THE WHOLE PICTURE

Good concierges don't simply answer and ask the obvious questions. The great ones answer questions that haven't even been asked. This requires observing details, thinking them through and making suggestions based on the information.

For instance, when giving directions for a walking tour in your city, you notice the guest is wearing shoes with a small heel. While this might be appropriate for a walk downtown, it is not suitable for the cobblestone steps that she will be taking on the tour. By mentioning this to the guest, you have ensured that she will have a more enjoyable time and possibly avoid twisting an ankle! Another example would be suggesting she wear a scarf, if it is a cold and windy day.

A SENSE OF NUANCE

A nuance is a slight or delicate variation in tone, color or meaning. In the case of a good concierge, he or she understands the nuances of body language and inflections of voice.

A married couple approaches the concierge desk and the husband requests information about a nearby nautical museum. While he speaks excitedly, his wife stands with her arms crossed, rolling her eyes and looking exasperated. It is a beautiful day and she is dressed in shorts and a sun hat. The great concierge quickly notices and processes the nuances and details. After providing the information about the museum, the concierge also tells them about a nautical museum on the shoreline, which is just as interesting and outdoors. As she speaks, she sees the wife's – and the husband's – faces brighten. This is a job well done.

COMMUNICATING

Communicating can be problematic. In San Francisco, for instance, the Palace of Fine Arts has no art, but houses a science exhibit. There are also several places with the title "Galleria": Galleria Apartments, Galleria Shopping Mall and Galleria Design Center. It is important to be quite clear at all times and verify information with guests to check for understanding.

Language may also be a problem at times and being multi-lingual is an asset. Some concierge desks are "well balanced," in that they are staffed by concierges who, between them, are conversant in many languages. A hotel in New York, for example, boasts a concierge staff that can communicate collectively in 14 different languages! While this is a definite asset and more in demand recently, some good concierges function admirably without being multi-lingual. About 70 percent of the members of Les Clefs d'Or speak more than one language, particularly in urban areas such as New York, Chicago, Los Angeles and Washington, D.C. It is advisable to have at least one multilingual person on staff, but it's also important to remember that all concierges speak a universal language: Service. With that in mind, it is possible to tackle language problems in a variety of ways.

Even having a multi-lingual concierge desk doesn't always prevent language issues, and it can work both ways. A concierge from France, who was fluent in English, asked a guest how he would like a package shipped. The guest, thinking he would make a little joke, replied, "A slow boat to China." The concierge, who was not familiar with this American idiomatic phrase, took it literally and didn't understand why she couldn't find it on the Internet.

A concierge from another country was working at a hotel in the U.S. While her English was quite good, she spoke with an accent. In response to a guest who had requested that she wrap a Christmas present for him, she replied, "I'll be right up to "rape" your present."

Many guests can speak English, but interpreters are not difficult to find, if needed. If one cannot be found close at hand in the hotel, a quick check with a local "native" restaurant will usually produce a friendly person willing to translate. Another source is the language department at a local university.

Sometimes, local expressions can be misinterpreted:

A guest asked the doorman at a hotel in San Francisco to have a hansom cab waiting. The poor doorman, not being familiar with the term "hansom" (a horse and buggy) hired a limo. When the guest complained, he replied, "But this is a much more handsome cab than the taxi that was just here."

Sticky situations can sometimes arise, when the concierge isn't sure how to address a couple or a group of people. Here are a few suggestions for overcoming potentially awkward situations.

- If a couple approaches, but you are unsure if they are married, use a general greeting, such as "Good morning. How may I assist you?"

- When a group of people is approaching, greet them with, "Good afternoon, everybody" or "Good morning, folks," for a more informal approach.
- If a couple conducts themselves very formally, one might say, "Good morning, sir, good morning madam."

Again, reading the subtext is crucial, but the most important point is that guests are greeted with a professional and pleasant salutation and a welcome smile. This works without fail, even if you stumble a bit.

Artful Communication

Clarity and proper form are not the only concerns when it comes to effective communication. Choosing words carefully and artfully is one of the many communication challenges that greet the concierge day in and day out. It takes finesse to present information in a way that each individual guest will find palatable, interesting – even exciting.

A concierge I know has a creative way of answering the question, "Is it safe?" when it comes to "marginal" neighborhoods in her city. If the area is generally safe, but requires a bit of caution, she likes to respond with, "It's a good idea to wear a city face in that neighborhood" or "Prepare for an urban adventure!"

The "No Problem" Problem

When I started teaching and writing about customer service in the 1980s, I remember thinking that "No problem" was a good way to respond to guests' requests. I first noticed it while out on a date. When my attractive companion greeted me at the door, he offered me a sweet compliment, to which I, of course, replied, "Thank you." His response to me was, "No problem." It made me smile all the more, so I decided to apply this response at work. I thought it was a good idea to assure people that it was "no problem" to serve them.

Over the years, I have learned many lessons and matured in my understanding of what "clicks" in terms of forming connections between people. I've subsequently been told many times that people actually hate when service providers use the expression, "No problem," as it implies a double negative. I now understand that bringing in the word "no," when attempting to take care of a request starts the process off on the wrong foot. Furthermore, introducing the word, "problem," when there may not be one (or if there is one, you don't want to emphasize it), just doesn't make sense. I've always believed – and still do – that the underlying sentiment behind

"No problem" is "Yes, it would be my pleasure." So why not just say that, instead? If your intent is to serve others and help make them happy, it makes good sense to couch one's responses in positive terms. Put this way, there should be no problem ridding our vocabulary of "no problem!"

YOU MAY HAVE BEEN THERE, BUT *YOU ARE NOT GOING*

It's critically important for the concierge to speak from experience whenever possible, rather than relying on what you've heard or read. This is particularly true when it comes to recommending restaurants. This topic is covered in depth in CHAPTER 7, but it bears mentioning here that concierges need to experience for themselves the restaurants, activities and services they recommend to their guests. They need to know their cities inside and out – from direct experience. It is one thing to read a menu, but quite another to taste the fare, absorb the atmosphere and experience the service at the restaurant.

There is, however, an important caveat: ***You are not going.*** In the case of a restaurant, it will be the guest who ultimately will be dining there, and while you may never want to step into the restaurant again, it may be the perfect spot for your guest. This requires "reading" the guest and paying close attention to both verbal and non-verbal communication to determine what will work ***best for them.*** For example: You are a vegetarian and the guest has just described a dining experience that sounds very much as if an Outback Steakhouse might fit the bill. In cases such as these, always remember: You are not going.

CREATIVE THINKING AND COLLABORATION

The concierge's unrelenting goal is guest satisfaction. In thinking like a concierge, when a request cannot be accomplished easily, creativity kicks in. The concierge begins problem solving by searching beyond the confines of the hotel operation and thinking outside the box.

A concierge was called upon to find a full set of mako shark's teeth and could only locate them in Rio. He arranged to have the whole head of the shark shipped in dry ice and had the teeth extracted by the hotel kitchen staff.

A concierge in Beverly Hills tells of an Italian movie director who'd been given a beautiful crocodile attaché case by his cast, which had great sentimental value. He wanted the gold-toned corners and lock replaced with 18-carat gold, and after many calls, she was able to find a jewelry store that could satisfy the request – for a mere $12,000. Done deal.

A concierge once had a foreign guest come to her with a handful of American coins and a look of utter bewilderment. Without a common language, she still managed to impart invaluable information by patiently sorting through the pile of change and taping the exact amount for the bus onto a file card. She also taped one of each coin with the numeric breakdown, so the guest would be able to make her own change during the day.

A concierge in Washington, D.C., was asked to find 30 copies of the morning newspaper from Frankfurt, Germany, for a breakfast meeting at 7:00 a.m. the following day. Copies from the Internet just wouldn't do. He needed the actual papers. Newsstand copies are one or two days old, and most newsstands don't even carry many foreign papers, so he had to think fast. He called a local Lufthansa representative, who in turn called a hotel in Frankfurt and arranged for 30 papers to be delivered via the next Lufthansa flight. The concierge hired a courier to pick them up and had them ready on time.

A blushing bride had purchased a gown that was a bit too snug. With her wedding guests waiting, taking a deep breath as she walked down the stairs, the zipper in the back of her gown gave way. She came to the concierge with tears in her eyes, asking for help. The concierge attempted to calm her down, indicating the damage was not that bad. (Inside, he was panicking, as it was Sunday afternoon and the bridal shops were all closed.) Quickly, he thought to himself, "A tailor is what I need!" He contacted a tailor, who was able to add mesh to the gown so it fit like a glove. The day of the wedding was saved. This concierge, who fondly remembers this incident has entitled it: "It is my right size, it's simply a bit tight."

The more challenging the request, the more the "on" concierge rallies to get the job done.

A dapper Scotsman staying at a hotel in San Francisco approached the concierge and showed her his beloved eyeglass pouch that he had purchased 20 years prior at a Mexican Market. Since it was falling apart, he asked if he could find one in San Francisco's Hispanic neighborhood. Knowing this would be an impossible task; she took a photo of the pouch with her cell phone and e-mailed it to a colleague in Mexico City. The colleague was unsuccessful in finding anything similar, so he commissioned two samples from a local seamstress. In the meantime the guest returned to Scotland, and shortly thereafter, received the eyeglass pouches. He couldn't have been more delighted. In his words: "Brilliant! Amazing! The concierge network brings a ray of optimism to this benighted world."

A concierge in Chicago was faced with a seemingly impossible problem. A large, formal wedding was to take place in her hotel in three hours, when she learned that the city had turned off the water in the neighborhood – with no certainty as to when it would be restored. Thinking quickly, she made arrangements with another hotel on the other side of town and rented panel trucks to transport the food, linen and china to that location. When the guests arrived, she ushered them onto busses, whisking them across town to the alternate hotel. The wedding went ahead without a hitch and the story made such an impression that it was picked up by local newspapers.

A pop star staying at a hotel in Montreal insisted on drinking raw milk – straight from the cow – for breakfast every morning. To accommodate the guest, the concierge made regular trips in the middle of the night to a farm a couple hours outside the city, so he could return to the hotel in time for the guest's breakfast. (He even milked the cow himself, decked out in his concierge uniform.) He had managed to barter with the dairy farmer, exchanging free milk for a night's stay in the hotel, so it cost the guest nothing.

As you can see, most of these "miracles" were accomplished by reaching out to others outside the walls of the hotel. Collaboration is key. My favorite line from Michael J. Fox in the movie, *For Love or Money,* says it all: **"I know a guy, who knows a guy, who knows a guy . . .** "

On the other hand, there are some requests that simply can't be met, as demonstrated in the example below.

A guest once wanted to land a helicopter on Alcatraz Island. When he was (politely) told this simply wasn't possible, he followed up with a second impossible request: "Can't you get permission from the Secretary of the Interior?" Even though concierges can make magic happen, there are limits.

THE FULLY-DEVELOPED CONCIERGE'S THINKING

Concierges who have been on the job for years love to play "The Game." Very often, guests approach the desk with only a vague idea of what they are looking for. They may have dined at a restaurant on their last visit and remember nothing more than red banquets in the entrance. Really savvy concierges can usually come up with the right place, and they love the challenge of doing it.

A gentleman forgot a suitcase on his trip home to Tokyo. The concierge knew that shipping companies would require at least two full days, but it so happened that the concierge himself was scheduled to leave that evening for a vacation in Japan. He telephoned the guest and informed him that the suitcase would be delivered in person the following morning. Even after experiencing this level of personal service, the guest didn't seem impressed, but the concierge didn't take it personally. He quite enjoyed his stay in the country and felt satisfied that he'd done exactly what had been appropriate.

A concierge in Las Vegas tells of the day that Penn & Teller were scheduled to perform. Thirty minutes before the start of the show, they called in a panic with news that they'd forgotten to pack their most important prop, a straightjacket. She first tried a hospital, only to discover that straightjackets have become obsolete. Then, thinking quickly and expertly, she contacted the University of Nevada-Las Vegas theater department. Success.

A concierge in Naples, Florida learned a valuable lesson in fully developed thinking when he helped a group booking through an incentive travel house. The group leader was adamant that everyone in the party be treated absolutely equally. For instance, he insisted that no person should be given an ocean view if the others were not. When the leader requested 40 "equal" rental cars, the concierge obligingly requested 40 of the same cars from his rental company and was rewarded with the delivery of 40 identical white Tempos. One has only to imagine the depths of confusion that resulted, as each guest approached the valet, requesting his or her white Tempo. Of course, this concierge now knows how to avoid such dilemmas, but he remembers the occasion vividly.

FOLLOW-THROUGH

The practice of checking back regularly and following through on guest requests is vital, because it provides the concierge the necessary assurance that their guests are 100 percent satisfied. Furthermore, it lets guests know the concierge has done all the necessary footwork and cares enough to take the time to follow through.

A guest called to ask for the bus route to a prominent location. I wasn't completely sure of the correct response, so I told the guest I would find the information and get back to him. (This was before the days of the Internet.) I immediately phoned the location, only to receive a taped message, so I then called the public relations office. They were unable to help me, but indicated that BART (The San Francisco Bay Area's Rapid Transit system) might provide a bus connection. Unfortunately, BART was in the middle of labor problems with an impending strike and reaching their offices was impossible. Finally, I decided to recommend that the guest drive to the destination and carefully prepared detailed directions to the site. When I called the room to give the guest the information, I discovered he had left the hotel without stopping by the desk to speak with me. Although

I then left numerous voicemail messages, it was to no avail. The guest never checked back with me, so he knew nothing of the work I'd done on his behalf. To him, it must have seemed as though I had done nothing at all. In such cases, perception is reality; and this guest's perception was, no doubt, "bad concierge service" – plain and simple.

Many concierges do complicated research on behalf of their guests – ranging from car-rental price comparisons to locating specialized rare antiques. After lots of time, many, many telephone calls and Internet searches, it's disheartening to find that the guests have checked out, without ever benefiting from the results of their work. Situations such as these are frustrating for everyone concerned. Fortunately, there are ways to help prevent them.

First, it's important to estimate the time it will take to locate the information and get back to the guests, so they know what to expect. It's also vital to ask when the guest plans to check out or leave the hotel and make contact with them prior to that time, even if you've not yet received a definitive answer. Lastly, it's always a good idea to get the guest's cell phone number, e-mail address to make contacting them as simple as possible. Lastly, be sure to log all the actions you've taken into the computer.

Whether the guest has requested a crib or an entire itinerary, it is the concierge's responsibility to ensure everything is accomplished and the guest is properly informed, every step of the way.

DEALING WITH DISASTERS

Different regions across the world pose different threats to the peaceful routine of the concierge. One threat that all hotels share is bad weather, which can ground flights and create all sorts of havoc. Usually, the concierge is faced with irate guests whose only option is to wait. Other situations are more threatening. The following stories describe events that range from the most tragic (9/11) to those where the "disaster" was, in reality, more of an inconvenience. Either way, concierges require the ability to remain calm, communicate precisely and act quickly.

Depending on their proximity to Ground Zero, each concierge in New York City had a unique experience on September 11, 2001, when the Twin Towers were attacked. Suffice to say, however, that each and every one has an indelible memory of that day that is even more personal than concierges elsewhere in the world. For most concierges, their primary responsibility was to help panicked guests, who were stranded in the hotel, to find transportation to their respective homes. One concierge told me that he found a driver to take a guest from New York City to Dallas. The overwhelming feeling in New York for many days was an eerie sense of silence, a horrifying smell and a city at a standstill. Soon, however, people began moving again. The hospitality community contributed by volunteering, along with local restaurants, to serve food at the Trade Center site, and many hotels hosted the police and firefighters from out of town, who came to help.

During the 1989 earthquake in San Francisco, hotels became the refuge, not only for guests, but also for local residents who could not get to their homes. The concierge became the focal point for everyone's problems. While chaos abounded, guests continued to be guests. They asked which stores were open, where they could find the best earthquake T-shirts and if they could rent a limo to see the wine country. It was important for everyone on the hotel staff to remain calm and exhibit patience. Not every guest could comprehend the gravity of the situation, and not everyone cared. The concierge desk was deluged, but they managed to keep order and still carry out their duties.

In 2004, during the blackout in New York City, hotels were left with minimal electricity (if they had a generator, that is). This meant no air conditioning, no refrigeration and no ability to cook food. In addition to the buffets that the hotel immediately supplied, concierges scrambled to find other restaurants that were able to remain open. They were also in charge of supplying flashlights and bottled water. This situation endured for two days, until power was restored, and concierges were called upon to soothe impatient and irate guests. Though it was obvious that the problem was intractable and widespread, guests (being guests) continually complained about not having hot food.

During Hurricane Andrew in Florida, the concierges were asked to evacuate an entire hotel and arrange for busses to transport all guests to Orlando. In addition, they were expected to secure hotel rooms and switch everyone's flights from a Miami to an Orlando departure. An elderly neighbor, who lived close to the hotel, heard that the hotel was sending people to Orlando and asked if she could also have a ride. The concierge (being a concierge) obliged, never guessing that the woman would call back a few days later to ask to be picked up and taken back home!

When a hurricane came roaring through his city, a concierge had to deal

> *with each guest's private reality while attempting to get everyone under safe cover. One guest called from his room to have a shirt pressed. Another called to ask if he thought it would be a good day for finding shells on the beach. The concierge, a master of quick wit, calmly replied, "Wait a few minutes. You'll be able to open your door and the shells will come to you."*

In this case, it was a sense of humor that saved the day.

HEIGHTENED SECURITY

For this subject, I thought it best to interview Michael Romei from the historic – almost magical – Waldorf Towers in New York. He holds an interesting and specialized position when it comes to the issues of security, visiting dignitaries, heads of state and the Secret Service. The Waldorf Towers (literally) has the Presidential Suite, which houses former President John F. Kennedy's rocking chair.

When a president is visiting, the Secret Service now handles all matters of security. In the past, concierges helped to hold the elevators and were informed of presidential comings and goings. They even worked with the Secret Service and were able to take photos with the president (a Waldorf tradition). However, due to heightened security, this practice has ceased. At one time, concierges were even called upon to help the president in a pinch. In a situation where theater tickets were purchased for the wrong day, a concierge called the theater owners and show producers for help. (It's rare that a concierge has the honor of asking a favor on behalf of the White House.) Even then, however, it was no small matter, as it involved security, Secret-Service entrance and exit strategies, as well as rescheduling other patrons – quite a complicated last-minute task!

In today's security-conscious environment, many high-profile guests travel with their own security teams, with whom concierges work with closely. At the Waldorf Towers, there is also a special motor court, which allows these guests to enter and leave the hotel unseen.

The following story highlights just how much the need for security has changed:

> *At the Waldorf, concierges were responsible for specialized tours, which included showing guests where the bulletproof railroad car dropped President Theodore Roosevelt off, four floors below the hotel, so no one would ever see him get out of his wheelchair. After 9/11, the area was sealed off and is no longer part of the tour.*

THE WAY OF THE WIZARD

ONE OF MY COLLEAGUES summed up the challenge of communication this way:

> *"The concierge is a style wizard of information management. The goal is to provide the right information and solutions in the most meaningful and satisfying way for each and every guest, based on his or her unique personality and perceptions."*

CHAPTER THREE

3 The Joys and The Challenges

OBJECTIVE

The following chapter will equip readers to:

Become aware of the distinction between the challenges and benefits of being a concierge and the reality of what lies ahead for those starting out in the profession.

Oh, The Joys . . .

ANY DISCUSSION ABOUT THE JOYS OF THE JOB needs to be tempered by the disclaimer that the "glamorous" aspects of the job are better described as responsibilities. It's a critical part of the job responsibility to know what's playing at the theater and what to order at the city's top restaurants. This aspect of the position can extend the "on-the-job-time" by several hours a week.

The position of the concierge offers opportunities that are not available to other professions, and a bit of glamour is one of the rewards. It is a special and wonderful way of life, with invitations to restaurants, exciting places, parties, lavish treatment and opening nights – a lifestyle, normally available only to the wealthy. Some outings are so special that they become the concierge's treasured memories, such as a helicopter ride to the wine country, a spin in a luxury car, a sailing excursion, or a ride in a blimp. But again, these activities are all in a day's work and often extend the concierge's day long beyond the "nine-to-five" or "seven-to-three" as the case may be.

In businesses that are highly competitive and ones where word-of-mouth referrals substantially affect the bottom line, introducing concierges to their services is beneficial. In the case of estheticians, massage therapists, limousine companies, car-rental companies and hairdressers, the concierge is often the fortunate and grateful recipient of offers for these services. The concierge must look polished at all times and massages feel wonderful after an especially stressful day, so these complimentary services are certainly welcomed.

It is the competitive world of restaurants, however, that brings the majority of invitations because the concierge can impact a restaurant's business significantly. Restaurant referral is very big business. Most restaurateurs understand this and are only too pleased to host the concierge. (Incidentally, the life of the concierge can be very fattening and hazardous to one's waistline!)

It's important to keep in mind that these aspects of the job, though enjoyable, are not about the concierge's personal recreation. "All the glamour" is not a good reason to take the job, although it can sometimes get one through the tough days. It's important to recognize that these perks are bestowed as a result of the concierge's position and the hotel the concierge represents. Invitations are not to be "expected," and it's important not to assume that you're somehow entitled to special treatment. No matter how glamorous it all may seem, the functions attended are responsibilities of the job. It can also be humbling to learn that the invitations and events have little to do with the concierge personally. Sadly, no matter how terrific one's relationships with restaurateurs, public relations firms, tour operators and limousine owners may be, invitations will typically cease the moment employment stops.

Day to day, being a concierge involves dealing with person after person, problem after problem; organizing, planning, assessing, fixing, being front and center, wheeling and dealing, making things happen, greasing wheels and being a catalyst for action. Concierges are the eye of the hurricane – an oasis of calm in the midst of clutter and clamor – and they love every bit of it. The true value of the job comes from the satisfaction derived from the work itself.

> *I loved the adrenaline rush I got from my fast-paced hotel lobby. I was constantly affirmed by people returning to tell me they enjoyed the places that I recommended.*

When considering the job of concierge, the question to ask yourself is: *"How does serving others serve me?"* Then, the actual day-to-day experience of the job becomes the major benefit in and of itself. And to love one's work is the greatest gift of all.

A SENSE OF SELF-EMPLOYMENT

Being a team player is of the utmost importance in building a successful concierge department. Working cooperatively is imperative, and the ability to provide ultimate service is contingent on teamwork. That being said, the position of concierge also requires an independent spirit. Quick problem solving is an important requirement of the job, so working efficiently and independently is a natural requirement. The position empowers the concierge to use his or her unique talents, resources and skills to make well-advised decisions and solve problems independently. It's not the type of job that requires consulting a procedure manual or superior every time a decision needs to be made. In fact, that would be impossible.

> While there is a great deal of independence and a sense of self-employment, the concierge also needs to keep in mind that he or she is an employee of the hotel, which has certain parameters within which its employees can operate. On one occasion, a concierge, with the best of intentions actually flew to a guest's city to personally return expensive jewelry the guest had left behind. This presented liability issues for the hotel, and unfortunately, the concierge was ultimately reprimanded for his good, but not altogether prudent, deed.

I Know a Guy, Who Knows a Guy . . .

A word needs to be added here about contacts. Concierges are not only encouraged, but also expected, to have a well-managed set of contacts (people at restaurants, theaters, local businesses, etc.) that belong to them as business people. Contacts and personal relationships developed by concierges are theirs alone – not the property of their hotels. The value that management places on the concierge has a direct connection with whom the concierge knows and what the concierge can accomplish because of their contacts. Networking beyond the parameters of the lodging operation allows the concierge to experience the freedom normally associated with self-employment. It also offers a deep sense of personal accomplishment and self-reliance.

CREATIVITY AND PROBLEM SOLVING

Not only is creativity one of the necessary attributes of the concierge, it is also one of the greatest joys. Creativity goes hand in hand with the freedom to make independent decisions, develop one's own contacts and feel personally successful. Being on the frontline and reacting quickly under pressure encourages the concierge to be a creative problem solver – and take joy in it.

There are very few jobs that are as freeform as that of the concierge, and, aside from ethical constraints and hotel policy, there are few guidelines or boundaries. As mentioned above, when faced with a bizarre request or unexpected dilemma, the concierge cannot simply turn to a procedure manual to find out what to do. One must be creative and figure it out. IMAGINATION is vital. CREATIVITY at a concierge desk is not just a nice concept. It is a reality and a necessity and used so frequently that one must consider it a tool of the trade.

In fact, the entire profession was conceived in the United States by concierges, who actually designed their own jobs. In 1978, concierges all over the country actually "created" their own positions. When I started in 1976, there were no full-service concierge desks within Hyatt Hotels. I literally made up the job as I went along. Marjorie Silverman and Abigail Hart did the same thing at the Westin and the Four Seasons in Chicago, through very innovative proposals at their respective hotels.

For Marjorie, creative problem solving was one of her favorite aspects of the job. Case in point: A large group of approximately 200 guests celebrated their last night in her hotel with a formal gala in the grand ballroom. On the ceiling, balloons were held by nets, awaiting the stroke of midnight, at which time a string was pulled to release them. Unfortunately, the florist who had arranged the balloon drop had attached the string to the overhead sprinkler system. To the elegantly dressed guests' surprise, midnight brought not only a shower of balloons, but an outpouring of rusty water from the pipes overhead. Thinking quickly, the concierges suggested that the guests change their clothes and bring them their soggy garments. To make the situation right, the clothes would be professionally dry-cleaned and sent to the guests. While the guests were changing, the room was quickly "wet vac'd" and cases of champagne were ordered. The party continued into the wee small hours, with even more enthusiasm than before. Afterward, the hotel received amazing compliments, because the concierges had turned disaster into delight.

THE WORKPLACE

The working environment for concierges is usually exquisite, with impressive hotel lobbies and elegant décor. At times, however, the design or the positioning of the concierge desk is not optimal, which can make the role more challenging. I noticed in one hotel I was visiting that the desk was located in a part of the lobby where there was literally no lighting. My heart went out to the concierges who could barely see what they were doing! (There's more information on the design and location of the concierge desk in CHAPTER 11.)

In addition to the beautiful environment, the benefits of working with the public are countless. There is little boredom and workdays pass quickly. Working conditions are exciting and promote professional and personal growth. The opportunity to meet travelers from all corners of the earth and all walks of life make the work stimulating. Although many tasks are routine, it is the unpredictability of a hotel lobby that is especially appealing to concierges.

ACKNOWLEDGMENT

Being acknowledged for one's efforts is vital and often underrated. In fact, it is a major benefit. Guests returning with high praise from a place recommended by the concierge offer great positive acknowledgement, and this happens regularly. The concierge is the ultimate "Memory Maker," and it's always a wonderful feeling to know you've made someone's day!

SELF-ESTEEM AND A SENSE OF VALUE

Being a concierge involves interfacing and interacting with every aspect of the hotel and making contact with people worldwide. If the concierge is doing a good job, the benefits include respect from fellow employees, management and a host of outside business people, as well as positive guest relationships.

The life of a concierge has countless rewards, but it's important to remember that it is through years of dedication, hard work, longevity and trust that these rewards come, and one's value is earned. Self-esteem and service continually work together to reinforce each other. If one continually provides ultimate service, it will lead to higher self-esteem, which leads to still better service, resulting in an even greater sense of worth and so on, ad infinitum.

. . . OH, THE CHALLENGES

The environment of glamour can make the downside of the concierge's job seem inconsequential to the casual observer. If one is considering becoming a concierge or is presently working in that capacity however, the drawbacks are very real and deserve attention.

Although concierges are a positive group and love their work, many agree that the most difficult and frustrating aspect is the unrelenting stress. The "Double Ds" (Disrespectful and Demeaning) guests take their toll. They are part of the reality of dealing with the public.

It is true that all jobs have some degree of associated stress. Being a concierge, however, has the added pressure of being "on stage," front and center, constantly bombarded and having to do too many things in too little time. This puts a constant strain on the concierge.

> *One concierge compared this experience to what a scarecrow must feel like, after getting picked at all day long. On the other hand, I try to put requests in their proper perspective. We are not performing brain surgery and 99 percent of our requests are not life-threatening situations. Having said that, I am still a firm believer that the high level of stress the job creates cannot be dismissed or treated lightly.*

Maintaining calmness, composure and grace in the midst of madness is not only challenging, it is extremely stressful. Though appearing calm on the outside, our bodies are experiencing physical strain. There is not a concierge around who does not have some neck and shoulder pain from holding telephones, and working at a fast pace can be exhausting. It makes no difference whether the concierge is sitting or standing. The toll of being on the front line affects the body.

Stress is a very real job hazard! But there are ways to live with it, relieve it and work through it. An entire chapter (CHAPTER 13) in this book is dedicated to stress relief, because it is an extremely vital part of being able to survive as a concierge and enjoy the job's many rewards.

REPETITION

A concierge's job is not considered boring by any stretch of the imagination, but there is enough repetition to include it as a challenge. As an example, in San Francisco, telling people where to find the cable car at least 20 times a day, 100 times a week, 52 weeks a year is *a lot* of "Where is the cable car?" It is a major challenge to repeat oneself continually without sounding bored or indifferent. I imagine the concierges in New York City have the same challenge with the Empire State Building, as do the concierges in Philadelphia with the Liberty Bell, the Eiffel Tower in Paris, etc.

Innovative Thinking

One summer, the hotel celebrated its 20th anniversary by offering cut-rate room prices, which attracted many guests who had never visited San Francisco. During that time, we had an outbreak of Chinese-restaurant requests. Every weekend, the hotel would fill up with tourists – all of whom requested restaurants in Chinatown. If this doesn't sound terribly challenging, try repeating it 250 times in one evening. It was becoming a major obstacle for the staff on the Friday and Saturday evening shifts, so I had to find a way to handle this question with some flair. We generally recommended only four restaurants in Chinatown, so I called a specialty fortune cookie company and had the names of the restaurants placed inside the fortune cookies. I put the cookies in "to go" boxes and when guests asked for a Chinese restaurant in Chinatown, they got to pick their fortune. It was a great deal of fun that lightened up a very frustrating shift and got us through a wildly busy summer.

One of our responsibilities as maestros of service is to say the things we've said countless times, as if we've never uttered them before - much like an actor in a play. After years of marking an "X" on a map and saying, "you are here" or repeating "turn left at the corner," etc., enthusiasm can begin to wane. A good idea is to switch the words "you are here" with "we are here." Though subtle, it brings the concierge and guest into the present moment and helps to cement a connection.

LACK OF ACKNOWLEDGEMENT

While acknowledgement is one of the joys of being a concierge, the lack of it can be an emotional challenge. At times, guests are rude or act as if the concierge is invisible, which can be very disheartening. Also, when guests leave without saying goodbye, without a handshake or word of thanks, it can be difficult for the concierge not to feel slighted and disappointed. This is especially true after a four- or five-day stay, after the concierge has provided a great deal of help and begun to feel a kinship with them. I'm not necessarily talking about passing on an envelope with a gratuity, but at least showing a sense of respect for the people who made their stay memorable. While concierges make every effort not to take things personally, this can actually hurt their feelings. In situations such as these, it's helpful to focus on all the moments in our days that give us occasion to celebrate and congratulate ourselves on providing professional, top-notch service and for making a difference in people's lives.

THE CONCIERGE AS ALCHEMIST

AS WITH ANY CAREER CHOICE, there are pluses and minuses to the profession of hotel concierge. To best serve their guests, it is incumbent on concierges to handle both aspects with a level head and spirit of selfless service. Because concierges can either make or break a guest's overall experience and are in a position of high visibility, it is especially important that they consistently "accentuate the positive and eliminate the negative." In fact, it is all part and parcel of the artistry of the concierge – turn alchemist – to transform the challenges that come their way into joys for their guests, themselves and their team.

CHAPTER FOUR

4 What to Expect

OBJECTIVES

The following chapter will equip readers to:

Establish the demands that the role of concierge makes on one's time, personal commitments and financial wellbeing.

Recognize the high expectations that organizations have of the concierge and that the role stretches far beyond the superficial glitz and glamour.

Make an informed choice around whether the concierge role is an appropriate career alternative aligned to their vocational needs.

As discussed in the previous chapter, the benefits of a concierge include job satisfaction, interesting challenges, creativity, lovely working environments, a sense of freedom and a glimpse of glamour. And, as in all jobs, there are downsides. This chapter is devoted to the "nitty-gritty" of the profession and practical matters, such as income, hours, expectations and job requirements.

JOB REQUIREMENTS

IN ADDITION TO THE SPIRIT, CHARACTERISTICS AND VALUES discussed in CHAPTER 1, there are additional, more tangible skills required of a concierge, including:

- Excellent communications skills and impeccable grammar.
- Basic keyboarding skills.
- Basic computer skills, including proficiency in Word, Excel, Outlook and e-mail.
- Ability to write and format a business letter.
- Computer aptitude – the ability to quickly learn the hotel's property-management system and concierge-specific software.
- Good handwriting (for handwritten thank-you and welcome notes).
- Knowledge of two or more languages is not a requirement, but a beneficial skill.

SALARY

A concierge's compensation varies from city to city and from hotel to hotel. In some locations salaries are high, and in others, relatively low. The same can be said of other benefits. They can be massively different, depending on the individual situation. For instance, a concierge at a Beverly Hills hotel will have a very different job experience and a higher income than those of a concierge at a resort in Wisconsin. There are geographical factors involved, as well as management styles and philosophies.

In general, the base salary for a concierge is considerably lower than most hotel guests would imagine. People are amazed at what concierges earn, relative to the skills, knowledge and expertise required to fulfill their roles. When people see concierges with a phone to each ear, calls on hold and four people waiting at the desk, it's a reminder that very few concierges choose the position on salary alone. The starting salary ranges from $27,000 to about $55,000 per year. This will increase with years of experience. It would be great if all hotels provided their concierges with expense accounts, but only a few do. For this reason, most concierges rely on invitations from restaurants, tour groups and theaters to become familiar with the outings they will be recommending to guests. Many concierges also take it upon themselves to try local restaurants on their own, so they can recommend them from experience. In these cases, they may visit a restaurant and order a couple of hors d'oeuvres to keep the cost down.

COMMISSIONS

Commissions are fees for referrals, usually given by rental car companies, travel agencies, tour companies and limousine services. Commissions are standard throughout the travel industry and may be given to the hotel or personally to the concierge. Commissions are not considered gratuities, nor are they in any way bribes or graft. They are simply an accepted and time-honored method of doing business.

Some hotels are organized so that commissions are paid directly to the hotel and are accounted for on their corporate books. Others have a policy of including the concierge in a percentage of the commissions, some work on a 50/50 split, while others use varying percentages. In many cases, hotels turn commissions directly over to the concierge. The concierge should not confuse the standard operating procedure of the commission structure within the travel industry with other areas in which the concierge operates. Restaurants, for instance, do not adhere to this policy. In fact, any commissions from restaurants would constitute a conflict of interest, as concierges need to recommend restaurants in accordance with their guests' needs, not because they will personally benefit.

Companies that offer commissions do so without inflating costs to the consumer. They pay commissions based on volume generated by long-term relationships with consistent providers. An individual customer would be given the same price as that available through the concierge.

The concierge must be careful to avoid "commission wars." Companies seeking to generate business through concierge referrals may offer commission rates above those that are standard in the industry. In these cases, concierge must be responsible and maintain a high level of integrity. The concierge should do business based on the quality of service, not on the rate of commission.

GRATUITIES

Many cynics, as well as critics, would argue that it is not the creativity or the challenge that makes the concierge persevere – it's the money. The movie, *For Love or Money*, reinforced this misconception that it's a gratuity-intensive occupation by referring to the "$50 handshake." Yet, as unbelievable as this may seem, the concierge rarely receives gratuities from guests, and the character in the movie actually does operate more out of love than personal gain.

Gratuities also vary depending on the situation, gender of the concierge, hotel quality and so on; but for the most part, a gratuity is the exception, not the rule. The concierge may be given a gift, as opposed to a monetary tip, because people are often confused about the role of concierges and a bit uncomfortable handing them money, especially female concierges. On the other hand, flowers and perfume are quite common.

When it comes to gratuities, the job of the concierge is still not well understood by the public. There are no rules to explain what to do. While most people realize that it's appropriate to tip a waitperson, bell person, or door person, they are totally baffled by the concept when it comes to the concierge. The savvy traveler who frequents luxury properties will likely offer the concierge a gratuity but, again, there is no rule of thumb.

It is inadvisable to expect a gratuity or a tip for doing the job, particularly with routine requests, such as printing a boarding pass or making reservations at a restaurant. On the other hand, when the concierge pulls rabbits out of hats or is responsible for making a vacation or business trip successful, a tip is appreciated and appropriate. If a concierge is asked, "What do I owe you?", he or she may reply with, "It has been my pleasure to serve you, and it's entirely up to you."

Concierges should never discuss the gratuities they've received with other hotel staff. Hard feelings can result, especially if the staff at the front desk are in close proximity to the concierge desk and see gratuities changing hands. Sharing gratuities with those at the front desk or making a nice gesture, such as giving them a gift card or taking them out to coffee, is a great way to maintain good relationships within the hotel.

> *A guest asked for two rooms at the Ahwahnee Hotel in Yosemite National Park on a Saturday night. A request of this nature is virtually impossible through standard channels, as the beautiful and historic Ahwahnee sells out on weekends a year in advance. Due to a very treasured contact, I was able to secure the rooms at the last minute. When the guest returned to see if I was able to meet his request, he not only didn't thank me with a tip, he said, "I guess you really owe someone a favor now, don't you?" I felt as if I had been punched in the stomach, but there were two other guests waiting to speak to me, so all I could do was look up, say, "How may I help you?" and move on.*

I can cite case after case of concierges working on intricate itineraries, driving hundreds of miles on their days off, standing in line for their entire lunch hour to purchase a ticket – never to be compensated. It's just a reality, but there is a flip side.

A concierge in San Francisco planned a three-day itinerary for pop artist Peter Max. He was so appreciative that he made her a gift of one of his original sketches.

The most memorable "tip" I ever received came from a most unexpected source. I made it a practice to keep a jar of stickers on hand to give to children and handed out dozens every day. I didn't always manage to remember every child. However, one day, I received an elaborately prepared thank you note from a boy named Alonzo, who'd drawn a picture of me with hearts and kisses and the words, "I love you, Holly." Even the seemingly smallest gestures can make magic happen.

On another occasion, I was asked by a foreign and very wealthy guest for help with mailing a letter. A member of a privileged family, he was unaccustomed to performing routine tasks for himself and was equally unfamiliar with our postal service. After I explained the price of the stamp and literally led him to the mailbox, he showed his appreciation with a $100 tip. Bottom line: Some guests are extremely generous, while others are quite the opposite, and it all comes out in the wash.

JOB SECURITY

Job security can be part of the downside of being a concierge. The reality for most concierges is that job security is tenuous. Hotels in the United States survived for almost 200 years without concierges. In difficult times, the concierge desk may be considered an easy department to sacrifice or outsource. (Outsourcing is covered in CHAPTER 16 – "Proliferation Evolution".)

In the past, the concierge desk was seen as a non-revenue producing department; and in a strictly numbers game, the value was difficult to measure. The good news, however, is that times have changed and there are a number of actions concierges can take to make themselves too valuable to lose. Today, concierges need to wholeheartedly take advantage of the opportunity for in-house selling, by recommending the hotel's spa, restaurants, gift shops, catering/convention services, etc. It is also a good idea to create and distribute formal reports, quantifying the concierges' contributions to the hotel's bottom line. If possible, the report should include the exact dollar value of the services recommended by and booked through the concierge desk. These numbers can then be tied back to the hotel's profit-and-loss statement.

Sales and service are not mutually exclusive, In fact, it's quite the opposite. The motto: **"Sales is service, and service is sales" says it all.** (This will be covered more in depth in CHAPTER 6.)

Another way to help ensure job security is to be willing to "wear many hats." This requires a where-can-I-step-in-to-help attitude and a working knowledge of other areas of the hotel. For example, if the concierge desk is slow, the concierge can pitch in to help the receptionist at the spa, if that area of the hotel is busy. In this way, you increase your value to the hotel, as now, you are one person doing the job of two and improving service levels all at the same time.

Lastly, the concierge can always be on the lookout for efficiencies – ways to streamline hotel operations that will improve service and save money. Because the job of the concierge touches on every department in the hotel, there is great opportunity for the alert concierge to see the "big picture" and suggest areas for improvement.

NEVER NINE TO FIVE – LIFE IN CONCIERGELAND

As a concierge, one can go out to dinner and to the theater, travel well and live like the wealthy, all on a concierge's salary. Opening nights are always special, as concierges frequently receive invitations for special performances. Invitations to previews of theater, dance, opera and concerts are quite common. The concierge is a vital resource to these companies in terms of selling tickets. The concierge's life may also be filled with flowers, as grateful florists and occasionally guests will thank the concierge with special bouquets. It is a mistaken notion however, to think that all is fluff and glamour in "Conciergeland." Indeed, there are marvelous benefits, but they need to be looked at in the proper perspective.

Dwelling in "Conciergeland" is a lifestyle. It is a **total commitment** and involves all aspects of life – morning, afternoon and evening. No matter where concierges are or what they're doing, they're taking note of their surroundings. The role of the concierge never ends, and going out on a steady basis after a full day's work can become exhausting. It is vitally important to learn firsthand where hotel guests can shop, eat, sleep, be entertained and well cared for in every imaginable way. It can open a whole new world for the concierge, but it is also an enormous task and a huge responsibility.

As mentioned previously, most hotels do not supply the concierge with an expense account. The concierge relies on invitations in order to be "in the know." It would be virtually impossible to afford to live the life of a guest on the salary of a concierge. Being a concierge allows one the opportunity to experience one's city from the point of view of the guests, and without these invitations, it would be impossible to do the job well.

A party was given at the world famous Gump's, a very well-established and elegant store, long associated with San Francisco history, society and style. For two years, Gump's hosted after-store-hours events, resplendent in every way. The Gump's events not only entertained the concierges, but also informed them. On one occasion, the concierges were treated to a private tour of the store and the famous jade collection, all while learning its history. The group was shown the jewelry collection, where they got a sense of what pearls worth half a million dollars were actually like. Because Gump's is such a part of San Francisco, the concierges always suggested it as a shopping "must" to guests, but after the event, they were better informed. When the Princess of Malaysia was staying at the hotel, one concierge arranged a special visit to Gump's and had her personally escorted through the store by the manager.

Cartier hosted a very elaborate cocktail party for San Francisco concierges. The best part of the evening was wearing their jewelry for the duration of the party. This extension of goodwill toward the concierges has prompted more than one concierge to call Cartier to make private appointments for their well-heeled clientele.

Concierges have also been called upon after hours to respond to "emergencies."

A concierge in a Puerto Rican hotel was sleeping peacefully, when he received a call at 2:00 a.m. It was from the reception duty manager at the hotel, who told him there was a movie crew filming a documentary on the grounds, and they needed a goat. It seemed the crew was readying to film their closing scene, when they discovered that the star of the film (an old goat) had died. This created quite a predicament. It seemed the crew needed to finalize their filming before dawn, for a very specific lighting condition. And, they were scheduled to return to their native country (Ireland) that same day.

Not skipping a beat, the concierge arrived at the hotel an hour later, knowing that being a concierge is all about service and delivering it on time. This being said, he had no idea where he might find a goat, especially at that hour. Then, he remembered that some of the staff working at the hotel were native Puerto Ricans, who frequently keep goats at their homes. With the permission of the film's director, he assembled a group from the housekeeping, security and communications departments. He then offered a cash prize from the film company to whoever could first produce a goat – and not just any goat, but an old goat, with large horns and a beard. He got his goat. Within 30 minutes, a staff member arrived with the perfect one and the filming was successfully completed.

This same concierge in Puerto Rico was called into the hotels general manager's office for an emergency meeting. It was a little nerve-wracking, as this certainly didn't happen every day. As it turned out, a package of wedding-party favors had been mistakenly returned to the sender. This was discovered on a Friday and the wedding was scheduled on the very next day. There simply were no delivery options available to get it back to Puerto Rico on time, so he suggested the package be intercepted and brought back to Florida. He then offered to fly to Miami to collect it and return to the hotel. On Saturday morning, the concierge took the 2½ hour flight to Miami, picked up the package and secured a flight back to Puerto Rico, arriving back on the island just one hour before the wedding was to start. The wedding then proceeded seamlessly, as if nothing had happened.

FACE TO FACE WITH THE FAMOUS

Becoming acquainted with and befriending actors, actresses, politicians, musicians, artists and other VIPs is a normal part of the concierge's job. Depending on the hotel and the area, this could mean everyone from Hillary Clinton to actress, Nicole Kidman.

There are times when the concierge is responsible for serving the guest the entire day or even week, as was the case of a concierge at the Park Hyatt in San Francisco. The family of a crown prince was visiting San Francisco for one week. The concierge literally moved into the hotel and arranged for every detail, including private aerobic classes, special food preparations, shopping excursions and private movie screenings.

It's important for the concierge to be especially careful when representing famous guests. They need to be assured that their privacy will be honored, and this requires special care. Even a seemingly innocent remark can create a problem. The nature of celebrity status has changed over the years, and the voracious behavior of the paparazzi can be downright dangerous.

A concierge told me that a well-known television star was taking his dog through the lobby. He went unnoticed, with the exception of another guest, who was staring at him and obviously trying to put a name to the face. At that moment, the bellman said in an audible voice, "Good morning Mr. ____________," prompting the curious guest to jump up and ask the actor for his autograph.

Another thoughtless mistake was made when a hotel employee indicated on her Facebook page that a "certain" person was a guest at the hotel where she worked.

In some hotels, the concierges have daily interaction with the famous. If one is hopelessly star-struck and overly interested in celebrity gossip, the concierge position is probably not the best career path to pursue. Celebrities generally prefer a concierge who is professional, caring and yet nonchalant with them, rather than being doted on by someone who is dying for an autograph. Sometimes, however, a disinterest in the world of celebrity can produce embarrassing (though sometimes humorous) results.

A concierge told me that, although he knew that a documentary on the Duke and Duchess of Windsor was being filmed in the hotel, he didn't think twice when making a dinner reservation under the name of "Mr. Edward Windsor." It wasn't until the maître d' pointed out the status of the royal guest that he realized it wasn't just any dinner reservation. As it turned out, Prince Edward actually loved the non-notoriety.

A concierge I know once made a significant error when judging a guest by his appearance. A very famous singer, carrying a pizza, was entering the lobby through the front door. The concierge approached him and asked that he use the service entrance. Imagine the concierge's hurry to apologize, when he discovered that the man with the pizza was not only a guest, but a famous one at that.

Serving people in the public eye requires sensitivity and discretion. When making a reservation, for instance, it is advisable to exercise great care to ensure the establishment will respect the guest's privacy and not call in the press to see their own name in print.

When preparing for a particularly famous (and possibly temperamental) guest, it is a good idea to use a little psychology. Have more than one suite reserved and allow the guest to choose the one that he or she prefers from among three choices. Show the least elegant suite first and end with the best.

When titled guests arrive, be sure to address them properly. An archbishop, for instance, is referred to as "Your Grace" and a prince as "Your Highness." Some titles call for unexpected greetings, and it is a good idea to double check with an etiquette resource on the Internet or discretely ask someone traveling in the entourage.

Discretion and respect are due all guests, particularly those who are well known. When a famous guest is visiting your hotel, "mum's the word." Often, hotels ask their employees to sign a confidentiality agreement to ensure that well-known guests' privacy is honored.

TRAVELING

Travel is one of the most glorious aspects of the job. Through Les Clefs d'Or contacts and networking, the concierge has opportunities to attend national and international conventions at some of the world's most spectacular destinations. Knowing concierge friends in hotels worldwide is wonderful and gives the concierge entree to the finest hotels and resort accommodations.

APPEARANCE

The concierge has a high-visibility position and serves as an ambassador for his or her hotel. Concierges should dress in a professional, businesslike manner for all occasions, even those of a social nature within the profession. Attire should be dignified and in good taste. Personal style is terrific, but miniskirts or jeans, for instance, would be considered inappropriate in most instances. Good grooming is important, and the concierge should pay attention to the little things, such as having well-manicured nails. There is additional information on uniforms and grooming in CHAPTER 14.

SERVING WITH POISE AND PROFESSIONALISM

BEING A CONCIERGE IS A PRIVILEGE. It should never be taken for granted, but treated with dignity and grace. The concierge not only represents him- or herself and the hotel, but the entire profession. Being gracious, behaving professionally, exhibiting good manners and being polite are fundamentals for the concierge. This applies to all aspects of the concierge's world, from first encounters through thank-you notes. It's important, for instance, to remember that the concierge must wait to be asked. It is not appropriate for the concierge to request invitations.

In addition, it would be entirely inappropriate to accept an invitation for dinner and then ask to bring six people.

In developing relationships both inside and outside the hotel, it is important to be considerate of others. Responding to RSVPs in a timely manner, for example, is more than a rule. It would be rude to do otherwise. It is the same for thank-you notes. It would be irresponsible to behave in any other way. When in doubt, refer to Les Clefs d'Or Code of Ethics, which serves as a guiding light in the areas of personal demeanor, guest relations and vendor relations.

CHAPTER FIVE

5

Telephone Manners

OBJECTIVES

The following chapter will equip readers to:

Realize the impact and importance of a professional telephone manner.

Identify ways to add artistry and finesse to tasks that you may be required to perform on the telephone.

Classify the various "Dos" and "Don'ts" of telephone etiquette.

THE TELEPHONE IS SO IMPORTANT that the job of the concierge literally cannot be done without it. It's one of the lifelines of the profession. How one is perceived on the telephone can make the difference between a satisfied guest and one who is disappointed or put off. It can also determine whether a potential guest ultimately books a reservation or decides to stay elsewhere. It can make or break the possibility of future business or a relationship with a valuable contact.

It is imperative that the concierge develops telephone skills that never fail. No "bad days" are allowed. Consistency is essential – not just in the words used, but in the way the words are delivered. Perfecting one's technique on the telephone takes conscious concentration and consistency. It's difficult to master, but it is possible.

The first and most important technique to remember is to generate a SMILE in your voice, and the only way to do this is to put a smile on your face. Even during times of stress, a "pasted-on" smile will suffice. The voice conveys what the face has begun, and the smile shows through to the party on the other end. Who knows? It may even help you feel better yourself!

Try a quick exercise:
Say, "Thank you for calling (name of hotel)" without smiling.
Then, say it again with a smile on your face.
Can you hear the difference?

THE BIG FIVE

There are five main functions, in addition to the conversation itself, which one performs on the phone:

- Greeting
- Placing a caller on hold
- Transferring a call
- Taking a message
- Closing the call

Even though these are routine aspects of the job, there are still ways to add artistry, presenting your very best and most creative self while doing it.

The Warm Welcome

First impressions count. Research suggests that customers spend less that 15 seconds deciding whether you have the ability, attitude and information to help them. One should always answer the phone in a pleasant, self-confident and professional manner, speaking distinctly and enunciating one's words. It is also important to converse in a clear and natural tone. A monotone voice indicates indifference, which is one of the worst possible impressions a concierge could convey.

Sounding calm and organized instills trust. One should avoid being abrupt or accelerating the pace of one's speech, even when under pressure. When feeling rushed or frustrated, try this trick: In addition to smiling, *raise your eyebrows*. This tends to elevate the tone of voice to sound more pleasant. Another technique is to match the caller's pace; but for the most part, it's best to take a deep breath and speak calmly and deliberately.

Every hotel has its own protocol as to how the phone should be answered. It is my opinion that telephone greetings should begin with "Good," because the word itself has an uplifting effect and puts a lilt in the voice, i.e., "Good morning," "Good afternoon," "Good evening." When answering calls, an example of the proper response is: "Good morning, Concierge. This is (name). May I help you?" Another way to say it is "Good afternoon, Concierge (name) at your service." This was the greeting we used at the Grand Hyatt in San Francisco, and at first, we hated it. After awhile, however, we grew to love it, because it was efficient. Using this greeting saved four words per call, which really adds up when you have hundreds of calls a day. An alternative greeting is "Good evening, Concierge (name). I can help you." If the phone has the Caller ID feature, you might also incorporate the guest's name into your greeting, when appropriate. For example: "Good morning, Mrs. Evans. This is concierge (name) at your service."

Sometimes, this can be tricky or downright bothersome, depending on the type of phone system you have. I can recall a very annoying situation at a hotel, where two of us were registered to the room. Typically, the person whose last name appears first in the alphabet is the person whose name appears on the caller ID. As a result, I was constantly being called the wrong name. A blanket rule does not apply in every situation. It's better to confirm whom you are speaking to, i.e., "Is this Mr. Johnson?" as opposed to greeting the caller with the wrong name. Once you establish whom you are actually talking to, you can incorporate the guest's name throughout the conversation.

The rule of thumb is that the telephone should be answered promptly, before the fourth ring. Research has proven that answering on the second or the third ring is acceptable to callers, while frustration begins to build, if allowed to reach the fourth ring.

Placing Callers on Hold

In the absence of a back-office staff to take calls, the phones at the concierge desk can ring fast and furiously. At this point, it's impossible to serve multiple guests at the same time, and it's necessary to place guests on hold. Always ask callers' permission first, i.e., "May I place you on hold?" and wait for a response before proceeding. Notice I said, "place "and not "put" you on hold. The former is so much softer sounding than the latter. Another option when the desk is busy is to give the caller an option: "I am currently with another guest. May I take your number and call you back?" If the caller chooses to hold, always use the hold feature on the phone, rather than simply laying the receiver down.

At a large hotel, the phone can ring so many times that one can't even complete a sentence with the guests in the lobby. In desperate situations (and only in desperate situations), the phones may be put on "fast busy" for a few minutes. This allows the concierge to complete his or her business with at least one guest in person. For callers, no service at all is better than bad service.

When it rains, it pours. During busy periods, a hotel lobby can be deluged with phone calls, at the same time there is a line of guests waiting to speak to the concierge. This is one of the reasons having a back-office staff to help handle calls can improve service levels tenfold. The concept of the back office is later described in detail in CHAPTER 13.

Many desks have an automatic system, which allows the concierge to forward calls from some of the phone lines to others during very busy periods. For instance, if there are six lines and only four concierges, two of the lines can be forwarded to the remaining four, to avoid phones that are "ringing off the hook." The overflow of calls is then picked up by voicemail. The downside of this system is that after the flood of calls subsides, the concierge desk is buried under hundreds of messages. This problem, too, would be eliminated by a back office.

Ideally, a caller should be placed on hold for no longer than 30 seconds. If longer, offer to call him or her back within five minutes. Or, you can give callers the option of holding or being called back right from the start.

In the event a second phone call comes in while already on the phone, place the initial caller on hold. Ask the second caller if he or she would like to hold or receive a call back, then return promptly to the first caller. If the telephone rings while you are attending to a guest at the desk, the caller should be asked to hold briefly while you finish attending to the guest in front of you.

Never answer the phone with simply, "Please hold" – CLICK! This is both abrupt and unprofessional and certainly doesn't make a good impression.

Avoid long pauses while on the phone, as it may lead the caller to doubt your competency – or your very presence – on the line! If you need time to think a moment or investigate a situation before responding to a question or request, tell your caller you will find the answer for them and ask if you may place them on hold. If you can see that you'll be longer than a few moments, offer to call the person back. If the caller has chosen to stay on hold, check back regularly if the hold time is extended. A few moments can seem like an eternity when placed on hold – even when pleasant music is playing. Be sure to give progress reports every 30 seconds or so and show your appreciation for the caller's patience, for example: "Thank you for holding, Mr. Brown."

Background "hold" music can be replaced by a recording with recommendations about the hotel's services, menus and amenities. This is a great opportunity to share ideas with your guests. Hold music is standard these days, but helpful hints are always appreciated. Whether it's music or an informational recording, it's wise to change or rotate them every couple of weeks.

When at all possible, guests in the lobby take precedence over telephone calls. However, when in the middle of a call and being approached by a guest in the lobby at the same time, it's best to finish taking care of the caller. In this case, be sure to somehow acknowledge the guest in front of you promptly and directly. Body language can be used to convey that there will be a brief delay while the business on the phone is being concluded. Simply pointing to the phone – or headset – (with a smile) works wonders.

Transferring a Call

A concierge should rarely need to transfer a call, because in most instances, he or she should be able to help the caller. Remember, ***the buck stops at the concierge,*** so calls are transferred only when absolutely necessary. When you do need to transfer a call, there are a few important facts to remember.

- Instead of saying, "I'll have to transfer you," tell callers, "I'll be happy to transfer you to ______________."
- Transfer only once. If an attempted transfer does not go through the first time, take a message and contact the other party and request that he or she return the call as soon as possible.
- Give the name and number of the person to whom the caller is being connected, in case you get disconnected. Tell the caller that you will brief the person they are being connected to, so they won't have to repeat themselves.
- Stay on the line to introduce the parties to each other before excusing yourself.
- If the extension is busy, inform the caller: "I am sorry, Mr. Stevens, the line is busy. Would you care to hold, leave a message or use the voicemail?"

Taking a Message

When a call comes in for someone else, it is not good practice to automatically ask, "Who's calling?" This may give callers the impression that the party they want to talk to is screening his or her calls – maybe even trying to avoid them! If the person they are calling is unavailable, ask the caller if he or she would like to leave a message with you or be transferred to voicemail. It's also good practice not to ask the reason someone is calling, though *a good concierge always asks if there's a way he or she can help.*

When explaining that a colleague is unavailable, it's important to be discreet and refrain from giving out unnecessary or personal information over the phone, such as, "Ms. Stein is in the restroom" or "She is out sick today." When a person is not available to answer a call, it's best to say: "I apologize, but Ms. Stein is not available at this moment. Is there something I may help you with, or would you like to leave a message?" After taking the message, tell the caller your name so that they will feel confident the message will be relayed.

When offering to take a message, it's best to say, "May I take your name and number and have Ms. Stein return your call?" This specific question can prevent the caller from launching into a long, detailed story that might get "lost in translation." If the caller insists on giving you an actual message beyond their name and phone number, be sure that all the details are read back and confirmed.

In all cases, repeat the details of the message to ensure they are correct, especially the phone number. Also, because letters can be easily confused over the phone (is it "S" or "F" or "A" or "K"), confirm the letters by clarifying: Is that "S" as in Sam" or "A" as in apple?" When writing a message, print legibly, indicating the date and time the message was taken, and be sure to sign your name.

Closing

In closing a call, take the time for a pleasant farewell, as the last impression can be as important, and even more lingering, than the first. Let the caller hang up first and replace your handset gently, or press the "Release" button on phone. To avoid sounding abrupt, never hang up before the caller.

Remember, a smile can be felt through the phone, so smile as you close. A salutation such as "Thank you for calling" or, "Again my name is ___________ . If I can help you further, please don't hesitate to call me," is always appreciated. Or, you can make it more personal, by adding, "Have a nice trip" or "We look forward to seeing you again soon."

Many hotels ask that their staff end calls by asking, *"Is there anything else I can help you with?"* While some may think this is unnecessary, I think it's a nice way to conclude the conversation and ensure that the caller has been completely satisfied. (This question may also be used when wrapping up a conversation when face to face with a guest.)

If, for whatever reason, you were unable to completely satisfy the caller, acknowledge and be sensitive to this and add a genuine word of apology. There's nothing worse for a disappointed caller than having a bright voice sum up the conversation with a thoughtless, "Have a nice day!"

TELEPHONE DOS AND DON'TS

Do

- Smile as you speak.
- If the phone rings when you are talking to a guest in the lobby, take care of the person in front of you first.
- Project positive energy into your voice.
- Be courteous.
- Always mention your name.
- Listen attentively and take notes.
- Avoid speaking on top of the caller and interrupting a conversation

more than once to talk with others or to answer another line.

- If a telephone request requires follow-through of any kind, such as ordering flowers, the concierge should repeat his or her name and add: "My name is __________, and if you need to call me back for any reason, please don't hesitate." This gives the caller a sense of security that someone is accountable.

Don't

- Interrupt.
- Though a sense of humor is important, avoid using humor on the phone. Not all people share the same sense of humor, and a caller might misunderstand your intent or even become offended. This is especially true on the phone, since callers can't read your facial expression or body language.
- Use slang, such as, "that's a bummer" or terms of endearment, such as "honey", "sweetie" or "dear".
- Be untruthful and indicate that someone is out or attending a meeting, if, in fact, they're simply not available.
- Chew gum or eat when on the phone.
- Slouch in your chair
- Give too much information, such as "He's in the bathroom," or "She's on her break."

MAKE IT A SALES CALL

Every telephone inquiry is a potential opportunity for the concierge to remember the motto: "Sales is service, and service is sales." It's important when dealing with potential guests, for instance, to go the extra mile and speak enthusiastically about all their hotel has to offer. Remember, the job of the concierge is not only to answer questions, but also to politely delve a bit further by asking the purpose of the visit, if family will be involved, whether a special occasion will be celebrated and so on. This allows the concierge to recommend features and amenities that will appeal to the potential guests' specific needs, and subsequently, fill those needs when the potential guest becomes a regular one!

OUTGOING CALLS

While concierges are frequently deluged with incoming calls, they also initiate many outgoing calls – to various contacts, colleagues and vendors. The practice of exhibiting exemplary telephone manners and conveying warmth and sincerity is just as important with outgoing calls as it is incoming.

The concierge should begin every new contact by introducing him or herself, identifying the hotel and politely asking the name of the person speaking. To make the conversation more personal, use the person's name during the conversation, but not to excess, as it then begins to sound artificial and disingenuous. When transferred to another person, the same procedure applies, and notes should be made to keep track of the process.

As with incoming calls, a pleasant, professional and polite manner should be maintained at all times. This is especially important when a call becomes, for whatever reason, stressful. Anyone can be pleasant when the conversation goes smoothly, but the concierge must remain congenial, under even the most difficult situations. Concierges must always exercise patience and try to see the situation from the other person's point of view. Most people in service positions, however, are accustomed to being polite, so as a rule, the concierge's initial contacts are painless and often quite pleasant.

When asking for a favor, it helps to use language that tends to inspire help. "I'm in a bind and would be very appreciative if you could help me" is just one example.

It almost goes without saying that making demands is counterproductive and has no place in the concierge's repertoire. Always keep the golden rule in mind. Behave to others, as you would like them to behave to you. Show interest in the other person. If it is obvious, for instance, that the person on the other end of the line is having a bad day, empathize. Be sincere and express support. Take the time to be friendly.

Our comptroller needed two tickets for a sold-out show at the Concord Pavilion, and I didn't know anybody there. I called the office and asked the name of the public relations manager, then asked to be transferred. I addressed her by name and explained my situation. I asked very nicely if there was any way I could acquire two tickets for my comptroller, who had nearly forgotten his wife's birthday celebration. Not only did I manage to obtain the tickets, but I was also offered VIP parking passes. All my comptroller had to do was stop at the box office to pick up and pay for the tickets, which, incidentally, were for third-row, center, seats. All the while, he was treated like royalty. Not only did I send her a thank-you note, I also included an open invitation for lunch for two in the hotel dining room. My comptroller was only too happy to provide the gift certificate in exchange for my success. The public relations manager became one of my most treasured contacts, becoming quite a good "phone friend."

IN THE PHONE ZONE

BECAUSE THE CONCIERGE is obviously not visible over the phone, it's of the utmost importance that the tone of voice and pace of the conversation project a caring attitude, calm and competence – no matter what the call is regarding or what sort of mayhem might be taking place in the lobby. I have a high-energy concierge friend who prides herself on "giving good phone". "One of her tricks is to take a deep breath and slow her faster-than-a-speeding-bullet mind by saying to herself, "I don't rush. I feel like listening, I am now entering the phone zone."

CHAPTER SIX

Building & Nurturing Relationships

OBJECTIVES

The following chapter will equip readers to:

Understand the importance of building and maintaining a highly regarded reputation.

Cultivate respectful and loyal relationships with both guests and vendors.

Appreciate the importance of gratitude and managing your favor bank.

See the benefits of networking.

Recognize the value of streamlined communication with medical professionals and the press.

Establish solid relationships with internal departments.

AS A CONCIERGE, RELATIONSHIPS AND REPUTATION are among one's most valuable assets. This stands true, whether it's a relationship with a guest, vendor or colleague. Maintaining and nurturing these relationships yields greater success and job satisfaction, as well as a personal sense of accomplishment. The bridges burned today may be the ones you need to cross tomorrow, so doing what it takes to maintain an excellent reputation with every contact is vital, even in difficult situations.

RELATIONSHIPS WITH GUESTS

Although the concierge typically does not fraternize with guests, personal relationships may develop under special circumstances. Because the job of the concierge is so personal in nature, it is inevitable that some friendships do develop.

> *The Maxwell's, a delightful couple from Sydney, Australia, visited San Francisco on business three times a year. They always stayed in the penthouse of the hotel where I worked, and I always called them Mr. and Mrs. Maxwell. The relationship was warm but very professional. During one of their visits, I mentioned that my husband and I would be visiting Australia, and they insisted that we stay with them on their sheep ranch in the Snowy Mountains. The invitation was irresistible. We accepted, and their hospitality was wonderful. We stayed several days, including New Year's Eve, and the Maxwell's have remained close personal friends.*

Although there are occasional and very special exceptions, the relationship between the concierge and guests should be respectful, but not familiar. One can be friendly without necessarily being a friend. When speaking with guests, it is important to remember always to use their names, keep smiling and look at them directly. The general rule is to use guests' last names, e.g., Mr. Smith or Ms. Higgins, unless instructed differently by the guest or dictated otherwise by the hotel's standards.

At the beginning of each shift, it is vital to review the arrivals list. Many hotels have morning staff meetings, where this information is discussed. These are the only sure ways to be aware of the arrival of a VIP or returning guests, whom you will want to personally greet. When time permits, introduce returning guests to the front-desk personnel, the bell staff and lobby ambassador, if your hotel has one. This generates a warm, welcoming atmosphere where guests feel very special. When a personal greeting is not possible, be sure to leave a note of welcome.

WELCOME NOTES

Welcome notes are an excellent way to personally and warmly welcome guests and acknowledge visitors. It's best to handwrite them, as it lends a more personal touch than a form letter or computer-generated document. They can be written in advance and kept on hand for convenient use. Just make sure you're using the same pen when the time comes for you to personalize it with the recipient's name, date and additional comments.

Here is just one example:

> *Dear Mr. Smith,*
>
> *Welcome to San Francisco and the beautiful Grand Hyatt.*
>
> *I hope you have a very pleasant stay with us. Please let us know if there is anything we can do to make your stay more enjoyable.*
>
> *Sincerely,*

(If the guest is celebrating a special occasion, such as a birthday or wedding anniversary, it's a wonderful touch to acknowledge it in the welcome note.)

People are bitten by mosquitoes, not elephants. In other words, little things are important, and guests are impressed by simple gestures. It's important to be on the lookout for every opportunity to interact personally with guests and demonstrate the hotel's desire to please them and make their stay memorable.

RELATIONSHIPS WITH VENDORS

The concierge builds good relationships with vendors over a long period of time – often measured in years. Good relations with restaurateurs and maître d's, ticket brokers, travel agents, car rental companies, limousine services, florists, charter companies and the like are indispensable and must be cultivated. They should never be taken for granted, as they are painstakingly formed and must be continually nurtured. Of course, relationships within the hotel are equally important and require a commensurate amount of dedication and effort. This is discussed in depth, department by department, later in this chapter.

> ***Relationships with vendors, like all relationships, are about give and take. In one hotel, the concierges would demonstrate their appreciation for the restaurants they worked with by personally delivering homemade treats to them during the holidays. It became a holiday tradition that both the concierges and restaurants 'staff looked forward to every year.***

Some relationships with vendors are dictated by hotel policy, and relationships in this category are particularly important. There may be contractual agreements between the hotel and a rental car agency or tour company, for instance, that must be maintained on behalf of the hotel.

The old saying, "It's not what you know, it's who you know," applies especially to the concierge. One person can't possibly know everything, but the concierge must have the necessary resources to find the answers. *Today, the value of the concierge is measured in part by the knowledge they can provide, beyond the information guests can find for themselves on the Internet. This requires a network of reliable and trusted sources.*

Creating partnerships and building bridges with outside groups are actually quite similar to the kinds of daily activities that concierges engage in with guests and colleagues within the hotel. Concierges are well aware that success is simply not possible without a broad network of support, and that these relationships need to be structured for the benefit of everyone involved.

Below, I have briefly described three of the best relationships Les Clefs d'Or has developed over the years. While the dynamics of these relationships may differ, they all have one element in common: Each of these companies appreciates the value of aligning themselves with the Les Clefs d'Or brand, while Clefs d'Or members and concierges across the world benefit greatly from their support.

American Express®

This long and treasured relationship began in the 1980s and is still going strong today. In 1987, Les Clefs d'Or USA hosted an International Congress in Washington D.C. – a monumental undertaking for the young offshoot of this international organization. It was accomplished with the help and support of American Express, a company that understood the value of the visibility it would gain in front of this worldwide membership.

American Express also had the vision of aligning themselves with the concierge-brand of service excellence. Over the years, they have not only supported the concierge congresses, but have also based their service model on ours throughout their worldwide network. They even have created their own concierge service in-house in their International Division, MTSI. (Many credit-card companies outsource this function.) In fact, many American Express concierges are former members of Les Clefs d'Or. Their concierge network has easy access, through years of relationship building, to the network of hotel concierges, which American Express continues to support.

While it would be great to track credit-card usage among American Express customers when served by concierges, a system to accomplish this has not been created, as of this writing. In other instances, systems are in place to concretely quantify the value of such partnerships.

Hertz®

It is easier to demonstrate in quantitative terms the monetary value of the relationship between concierges and rental-car companies, such as Hertz, Avis® and Budget®. With Hertz, every concierge is given an IOTA number (essentially, a registered travel-agent identification number). When concierges make reservations with Hertz, they use this number, so all their transactions can be tracked.

These relationships are clearly win/win, as hotel guests receive excellent rates and preferential treatment, such as free delivery of the vehicle to the hotel, when the reservations are booked through a concierge. In addition, the individual concierge and Les Clefs d'Or receive a referral fee. (referral fees or commissions are fully explained in CHAPTER 4). This is standard operating procedure and involves no extra charge to the guest. So, when booking through these companies, the concierge is helping the guest, as well as Les Clefs d'Or, in the process. This alliance has proven beneficial to guests, rental-car companies and concierges around the world.

Morris Visitor Publications

This Augusta, Georgia-based company, founded by William Morris III, has had a very collaborative and productive relationship with Les Clefs d'Or for the past 20 years. Their publication, *WHERE*, a monthly guidebook-style magazine, is available at concierge desks and guest rooms at medium- to high-end hotels. *WHERE* is published in 47 markets throughout nine countries.

Over the years, the staff at *WHERE* magazine has worked with concierges directly, featuring different concierges every month in a column that highlights their individual areas of expertise. For many years, they created and hosted an annual awards dinner, where the Concierge of the Year received the highly prized Silver Plume Award. In recent years, Morris Visitor Publications has also published the Les Clefs d'Or annual membership directory. Every concierge is well aware that *WHERE* magazine is a big supporter and is happy to pass out their magazines and use their maps.

Every day, concierges must interact with people at limousine companies, travel agencies, florists, car-rental companies, babysitting agencies, tour companies, theater box offices, brokerages, beauty salons, massage studios, restaurants and a host of others. Every person with whom the concierge interacts represents a relationship, and every relationship should be cherished and nurtured.

CONTACTS

Contacts with valuable resources can and should be made, even when there is no immediate need. A telephone call or a brief visit, sending a card, or composing a note or e-mail are all methods of establishing initial contact. For instance, personally welcoming a new business to the area or sending congratulations on an opening can work wonders in building relationships that will be fruitful for years.

> *When an important new attraction, Pier 39, first opened in San Francisco, I and another concierge went to every restaurant and every store in the complex. We introduced ourselves, handed out our cards, shook hands, collected menus, met everybody, made notes and generally spread a lot of goodwill. When we wanted tables with a view of the water on short notice for our guests, we knew exactly whom to call and they knew exactly whom was calling. We'd built a strong base from which to provide superior service to the benefit of all concerned.*

This, by the way, is yet another example of how the job of the concierge differs from a normal nine-to-five position. Such efforts never end. It is all part of the commitment and lifestyle of the concierge: Thinking, reaching out, developing relationships and compiling more and more information that can be passed along to guests.

THE FAVOR BANK & THANK-YOU NOTES

In Tom Wolfe's book, *Bonfire of the Vanities*, he talks about a "favor bank," with regard to judges and the court system. The concierge can apply the same principles. Apart from routine referrals and day-to-day business, concierges are constantly doing special favors and just as frequently asking for them. Good concierges know exactly when to ask and when not to ask, while keeping track of the favors granted them, to avoid the possibility of abusing the privilege.

For example, a concierge may have a wonderful relationship with the maître d' at a hot restaurant and be able to call at the last minute to have someone "squeezed in." However, if too many calls are made and the maître d's kindness is abused, the opportunity will soon vanish.

Concierges must know when a favor may be asked and when to regretfully tell their guests that a request cannot be met. Sometimes, the restaurant is full and the show is completely sold out. This is not easy to master, since making these judgments is subjective and depends on a number of factors. However, the decision must be made and a balance struck.

If the concierge tried to grant a last-minute request for every guest who asked, obviously there would be no more "special" favors for people like the general manager or VIPs. The favor bank must, therefore, be managed thoughtfully and prudently.

Favors are "drawn" when the account is full, and favors are "deposited" as frequently as possible to keep the account in good order. Thank-you notes, flowers and small gifts help keep the account balanced, and constant personal nurturing of these relationships is necessary. Appreciation must be demonstrated. Favors are contingent on give-and-take relationships and must not be taken for granted.

Be creative and consider sending a gift at an unexpected time, whether an Easter basket or a gift on Valentine's Day, instead of the traditional Christmas gift.

A NOTE ON THANK-YOU NOTES

A note of thanks is an important aspect of nurturing relationships. Thank-you notes are not only polite and the appropriate way to respond to invitations and favors, they are also a way to cement contacts and ensure that the concierge is remembered positively. There is NO excuse for not writing a thank-you note. If there is any question, the answer is ***write it. Write it right away.***

Whenever the concierge has accepted an invitation or receives a favor or a gift (even a generous tip), a note is appropriate. A good concierge will write quite a few every week. Following are a few of the situations, which warrant thank-you notes:

- Gratuities
- Gifts
- An overnight stay at a hotel
- Dinner at a restaurant never before tried
- Dinner at a restaurant not seen in a long time
- Dinner at a restaurant not especially favored
- Opening events
- Theater tickets
- Other entertainment
- Favors granted by colleagues, either within or outside the hotel

THE CONCIERGE IS THE CONCIERGE'S BEST FRIEND

In addition to the rare guest relationships and the many business connections, relationships with one's concierge colleagues often go well beyond "a strictly-business" category, becoming deep and lifelong bonds.

A colleague in New York, where the perfect apartment at the right price is a rare commodity, is forever grateful to his former hotel colleague – now an apartment manager – who called to inform him of an available unit. She had remembered him over the years and appreciated the way he had always helped her when she worked with him at the hotel. When the vacancy became available, he was the first person to come to mind.

A concierge in New York City sums up the networking potential available to concierges in the simple statement, "The concierge is the concierge's best friend." One of the many benefits of knowing other concierges is the secure feeling that you are not alone, that you are among co-survivors of an often demanding and unpredictable job. It's a great relief to speak with others, who have had the same experiences. There's just no substitute for the support, wealth of talent and knowledge from which to draw on when these relationships are strong.

Concierges are fiercely loyal to each other and this enables them to maintain networks around the world. A good concierge can make hotel, dinner, or theater reservations anywhere on earth with a simple phone call or e-mail to a colleague. Part of the mystique of the profession is that concierges will do anything to help another concierge. If tickets are needed and cannot be secured with one's own contacts, a call or e-mail to a colleague will almost certainly produce magical results. One would not expect to be let in on their source, but the tickets would be found.

In addition to calling on colleagues in other cities for assistance, it is also an excellent idea to keep their cards on hand. When a guest travels from your hotel to another where you know the concierge, presenting the guest with the concierge's card – and a personal note of introduction – will make his or her arrival quite special.

Technology has made friendship and cooperation between concierges even easier. Through social-networking sites, such as Facebook, LinkedIn and Twitter, information can be shared and introductions made between many colleagues at any time, anywhere in the world.

This worldwide network doesn't diminish the importance of cooperation between concierges working in the same hotel. *Within a hotel, the term "concierge" refers not only to a person, but to a team.* At its best, the team is multi-dimensional. Preferably, the team members will have different personalities, skills, knowledge and interests, so they can help each other by sharing expert information that they "specialize" in.

The loyalty that concierges are known for is especially important behind the concierge desk, where guests should find a strong and cohesive team. As one concierge put it, "We truly love and respect each other." Problems may arise now and then, but one should never discuss them with other departments or make disparaging remarks about other team members. The goal of the concierge department is to provide "seamless" service, which can be accomplished with communication, cooperation and thoughtfulness. For instance, concierges should always be sure the colleague who comes in after their shift is provided with all the information needed to take care of guests without interruption. Behind the concierge desk, it is "all for one and one for all," and decisions are based on what is best for everyone, not necessarily on seniority. The better the team works together, the easier the job looks (and, in fact, is!) Working as a cohesive team and providing the outstanding service that results is one of the greatest joys of being a concierge.

LOCAL CONCIERGE ASSOCIATIONS

Initially, through local concierge associations and later through Les Clefs d'Or, the concierge builds a comprehensive base of contacts – and friends – that is invaluable.

Most major cities have established concierge associations that meet on a monthly basis. At these meetings, which often include visits from vendors, interesting and valuable information is exchanged. A typical venue might include speakers with novel tour concepts, boat charters, or specialty services. Vendors such as car-rental companies are seldom in attendance, since their services are similar and routine.

Some local associations meet as infrequently as twice a month – once for a regular meeting and again for a special event, which might include dinner, a party or an opening. Many others meet more often. Through such meetings and social events, the concierge is able to foster friendships with colleagues and come to know first-hand the concept on which Les Clefs d'Or is based: Service through Friendship.

Through friendship, the concierge discovers the security in having a network of support. When a problem arises, help is as near as the closest telephone, e-mail, text message or social-networking site. Although it is not good form to plague colleagues with questions that could be solved personally, creative "brainstorming" between concierges is encouraged. Most concierges are especially knowledgeable about a particular area of expertise, and it is a good practice to contact them when a related situation arises.

In most large cities, concierges constantly call on each other. One is conversant with opera, another knows sports and yet another is an Olympic-class shopper. Requests from fellow concierges should always be given top priority, and each detail should be handled personally. Concierges are the best contacts possible, which is why participation in a local association is so important and highly recommended.

Local and regional concierge associations may offer educational seminars, trade shows, speakers and so on. These associations also come together to give back to their community, with fundraisers and other philanthropic activities. Some associations host an appreciation event for general managers and vendors. For countless reasons, these associations are truly an invaluable resource to the concierge.

I was once asked by a hotel executive, "What is it that you get out of the concierge association?" My response, "Exactly what you put into it." This, of course, is true of any endeavor in life.

RELATIONSHIPS THROUGH LES CLEFS d'OR

As the concierge's career matures and eligibility is earned for joining Les Clefs d'Or, the available network of expertise expands and becomes global. A wealth of opportunities then exists through attendance at conventions, on both a national and an international level. (Membership qualifications for Les Clefs d'Or are outlined in CHAPTER 17.)

It was very satisfying to have regular guests call on me in San Francisco to secure tickets on the Orient Express or to book a special room at a hotel in Venice. Because of the relationships I had developed by attending concierge meetings worldwide, I was able to accomplish many tasks far removed from my own city.

THE DESK THAT WORKS TOGETHER . . .

Nothing short of an entire team effort can build a successful concierge department. It is not simply the chief concierge! I like to think of the word team as representing the acronym:

T ogether
E veryone
A chieves
M ore

It is of ultimate importance that every concierge accepts the responsibility of acting as an integral part of a team effort. As with all relationships, cooperation, communication and commitment are required within the concierge team to best serve its guests and make the desk a harmonious and rewarding place to work.

That being said, it is also important to share the more tangible rewards (such as commissions and tips) with other team members. If a guest specifically tells you a tip is for you, it can be kept in good conscience. However, it is unfair to keep all tips, when it's nothing more than blind luck that one person receives a gratuity instead of another. In Europe, the concierge team shares everything and divides gratuities in accordance with established percentages. Typically, the chief concierge receives 25 percent, and the remainder is divided according to seniority.

MEDICAL RESOURCES

Periodically, the concierge must deal with medical emergencies or problems requiring medical attention, which lie beyond the scope of the "house doctor." In such cases, it is important that there be a contact within the medical profession on whom the concierge may call. This might be a doctor or a trusted friend who is a nurse. When health-related problems or questions arise, it is then possible to consult with a knowledgeable specialist for guidance and assistance.

I recall a very pleasant guest who stopped at my desk and requested a "private" chat. I took her aside, and she informed me that she was alone in the country and had just discovered a serious medical problem. She was very frightened, as there was no one to turn to. I called a friend who was head nurse at a local hospital, who put me in touch with a doctor who was able to see the guest immediately. I accompanied her on the visit and learned she needed immediate surgery, which was performed the same day. Afterward, I visited her at the hospital and helped during her convalescence at the hotel. We became quite close, and I continued to hear from her regularly for years. Without my contact, I would never have been able to feel confident about recommending the doctor, and the guest might have had to resort to an emergency room. Thanks to my friend, I was able not only to help someone through a difficult period, but I also made the hotel I represented look quite special.

In another instance, a guest from outside the U.S. came to me for help in determining the level of treatment his ailing brother was receiving at a hospital in San Francisco. I called my friend, who was a consulting nurse at the University of California Medical Center, to ask if she knew the head nurse connected with the case. She was able to arrange for her to speak with the family and provide detailed information. The family was reassured that the patient was receiving the highest level of care, and my guest was comforted to know that he had every reason to feel confident and enjoy his stay.

DEALING WITH THE PRESS

When receiving a call from the press, it is standard procedure to make an appointment to call the journalist back and advise the public relations department immediately. Depending on the topic, the public-relations manager or general manager may want to handle the interview.

If the concierge is chosen to participate in the interview, which is becoming more and more common as the public becomes more interested in the world of the concierge, the concierge should always be discreet and never reveal "secrets." The privacy of guests, especially famous ones, must be respected. While interesting anecdotes can be told, they must be related in terms that protect guests' anonymity and privacy. In fact, many companies require their staff to sign confidentiality agreements, strictly forbidding them to reveal personal details about guests. This agreement typically extends beyond the term the concierge is employed, thus preventing the possibility of writing a tell-all memoir, even after employment has ceased.

It's helpful to determine the "spin" of the article before having the conversation with the reporter. If possible, ask for a list of questions in advance, as this makes it much easier to prepare. Be aware, however, this may not be possible, and even if the questions are available beforehand, there's a good chance they might change in the actual interview. The most important rule of thumb is to be prepared.

Expect the unexpected, but do prepare your responses beforehand, so you remain in control. Stories about the most interesting, the most outrageous, or the most difficult requests should be clear in the concierge's mind and related clearly. Journalists often take facts out of context or misinterpret them. One concierge told me he was so nervous in an interview that he used someone else's story and claimed it happened to him. It was a very embarrassing situation and might have been avoided if he had prepared himself ahead of time.

Stories fall into two general categories: Soft news and hard news. The former is more of a "fluff" piece that advises or entertains the reader or viewer. In the hotel industry, they typically take the form of funny and interesting tales that often appear in travel magazines. Hard news is more about the facts: who, what, where, when and why. These generally appear in more serious media, such as *The Wall Street Journal*, city newspapers or business magazines. These stories are more likely to take a negative spin, especially when the questions involve labor disputes, compensation, kickbacks and the seamy aspects of the city, such as prostitution or drugs. If not handled carefully, these types of stories can reflect badly on hotel concierges as a profession, the hotel itself., or perhaps even your city. In such cases, it's especially important to consult the public-relations department and never, ever, let one's guard down. ***Remember, no matter what the reporter says, there is no such thing as "off the record."***

Here are a few additional tips to help make interviews with the press flow smoothly:

- Speak in sound bites, as the press appreciates short, pithy answers that get to the point.
- When you need to buy some time, repeat the question the reporter has asked or request that he or she return to the question later in the interview.
- Tell the truth. Honesty is always the best policy and reporters will often check for accuracy. In reality, there's no need to embellish

stories, as what actually happens at the concierge desk is usually much more interesting than anything one can fabricate.

- Keep a log of outrageous requests, as this is the topic reporters are most interested in.
- Keep your stories fresh. Internet articles can have long shelf lives, so if concierges are interviewed often, they should "Google" themselves periodically, to review the stories and images they've used in the past.
- Don't take your "adventures" for granted. What a concierge may brush off as business as usual may seem extraordinary to the press.

A concierge I spoke with admitted he was simply at a loss when attempting to call to mind an outrageous request to relate to a reporter. Winging it, he responded, "Of course, we prepare for the unexpected, but as a rule, we primarily handle the everyday requests – yacht charters, private jets, lavish parties at the last minute – it's ordinary stuff for us." The reporter loved his response and printed it verbatim.

Most importantly, remember the story is not about you. While you might be the spokesperson, the story is really about the hotel, the profession and the exceptional, creative and interesting services concierges provide. It's always good form to say something positive about the profession, one's local association and Les Clefs d'Or. Each professional concierge is an ambassador for us all.

I interviewed a well-known concierge from a storied hotel in New York City. His hotel has been featured in a wide variety of broadcast media, from VH1 to CNN and an even wider variety of publications from The New York Times *to* Travel + Leisure *and* Conde Nast Traveler *magazines. Unlike advertising, this type of positive press is free, credible and quite literally priceless, because its value cannot be fully measured.*

A ROMANCE WITH YOUR CITY

While this might sound odd to those not in the profession, it is highly recommended that concierges maintain a love affair with their cities. Taking care of a crowd of clamoring guests, all wanting dinner reservations at the same time, is much like speed dating. We read guests quickly and match them with dinner reservations that will delight them. The opposite is true of the relationship with one's city, which is long-term. It is a cherished, enduring and dynamic relationship that concierges just can't wait to share with their guests.

Most good, long-term relationships are based on intimate knowledge, and such is the connection the concierge has with his or her city. Concierges should know their city and surrounding areas inside and out and speak of them with pride and enthusiasm. This kind of knowledge is gained by exploring the city, not only in response to invitations, but whenever one is out and about – in other words, 24/7. Such is the lifestyle of the concierge. It's also advisable to periodically "take a walk around the block" to keep abreast of any changes in the neighborhood that might affect hotel guests. No one wants to send a guest to "the pharmacy around the corner" that just went out of business.

INTERFACING WITH OTHER DEPARTMENTS IN THE HOTEL

At one point or another, the concierge interfaces with every department in the hotel. Some departments are affected profoundly by the presence of the concierge staff, such as the bell department and the front desk, while others, such as banquets or stewarding, have limited encounters. Regardless, the concierge must interact and have a relationship with every department in the hotel, in addition to all his or her outside contacts and responsibilities. Without good relationships within the hotel, the resources and value of the concierge are extremely limited. As expressed in the film *For Love or Money*, "The hotel is more than facilities and amenities. It's a family."

General managers, food and beverage directors, rooms executives, catering directors, chief engineers and directors of housekeeping all need to understand the concept of the concierge department, because the concierge is often the end of the line for guest requests. Beyond management support, it is part and parcel of the concierge's position to create good working relationships with every employee of every department of the hotel. Since concierges are viewed as ambassadors of goodwill, both inside and outside the hotel, it is their job to foster kindness and cooperation throughout their working environment.

Concierges need to think of themselves as team players, not simply as members of the team behind the concierge desk, but also in respect to every department in the hotel. The good concierges are always thinking, "Where can I step in to help?" They should be willing to actively step in, wherever needed. For instance, if the spa needs a receptionist to fill in, instead of thinking, "I am not a spa receptionist," think "I can enhance the spa experience by offering concierge-caliber service. Perhaps I can even offer to book a dinner reservation after the spa appointment."

By the same token, all staff members are expected to respond to concierges' requests on the behalf of hotel guests. Because the responsiveness of fellow employees is so important, it behooves the concierge to have good relationships with everyone in the hotel. For instance, if an engineer or housekeeper is needed to help with a guest request, the concierge who has good relationships with these departments just might take priority. This, in turn, translates into good service for the guest, which not only reflects positively on the service of the concierge department, but also on that of the hotel.

The time period allowed for other departments to complete a task should be respectful and reasonable – for both the guest and the service provider. Requests for housekeeping, for instance, should be given about 15 minutes before the concierge calls to verify completion of the task. The same basic timeframe and follow-up procedure applies to most tasks completed by other departments of the hotel. When calling another department to follow up, it's important to always maintain a polite and pleasant manner – even with the most urgent requests.

If your hotel doesn't already have a system that allows for instant intra-hotel communications, you might suggest it to management. Equipping staff with cell phones and walkie-talkies or enhancing the computer system with remote devices can make follow-up requests and "Mission Accomplished!" reports much easier to convey.

Finally, every interaction with another department needs to be tempered by the awareness that it is the concierge who sets the style of service, giving the hotel as much personality as its architecture does. Many departments look to their concierges to set the standard for service levels throughout the hotel, so the concierge should present him- or herself as knowledgeable, respectable, available and always – in all ways – helpful.

Effective ways to foster relationships with other departments:

- Be available to help fellow employees with their travel plans.
- Share complimentary coupons with employees who have done favors or given exceptional service.
- Ask, but never demand.
- Be the area of the hotel that is a point of light – one that reflects positive energy and a polished image.
- Treat fellow staff members as you would a valued guest.
- Let your colleagues in on the exciting new developments you've come across when exploring your city.
- Avoid gossip, "back biting" and blaming at all costs.

When a concierge I know was chosen as employee of the year in her hotel, the cheering in the room and the feeling after the ceremony was electric. This kind of energy results when a concierge makes a supreme effort to have excellent relationships with all of the other departments in the hotel.

CREATING POSITIVE RELATIONSHIPS DEPARTMENT BY DEPARTMENT

Accounting

Depending on the individual hotel and its internal systems, the accounting department will work with the concierge in different ways. Generally, the concierge works with the accounting area when charging guest accounts for the variety of services the concierge department has provided. These include tours, theater tickets, limousines, flowers and airport transportation. In addition, there are many instances when the concierge needs cash to purchase various items, most notably, theater tickets. The need for a variety of miscellaneous items can arise, such as shoe or luggage repair and dry cleaning. It is important that a system of front desk "paid-outs" be worked out between the concierge and the accounting department to enable the concierges to perform these duties.

Receipts must be included with the front desk paid-out and, in some instances, a messenger fee is attached which is not reflected on the receipt. This is standard operating procedure at the concierge desk, but it needs to be clearly explained to the accounting department. The concierge also works with accounting, as does every other department, in respect to payroll.

The concierge also posts billings directly to guest rooms. In such cases, the vendor will bill the hotel directly for their services, such as a tour or a limousine charge. When the concierge bills charges to the guest's hotel room, it's a good idea to have receipts for these services as well. In these situations the concierge has not received cash, as he or she would in a paid out, but simply posted the charge. So, when the bill from the vendor arrives, the accounting department can automatically pay the vendor, as the hotel has already been reimbursed for the charges at the time of check-out.

Lastly, accounting helps with post billings. This need arises when guests have already checked out, the room charges have been paid, but the extra charges were not posted before check-out, leaving one or more of the vendors unpaid. In this case, the concierge needs to review past records and obtain credit card information, phone numbers and addresses, so the guest may be charged.

For all the above transactions to go smoothly, communications between the concierge and the accounting department must flow clearly and regularly. For many reasons, a friend in accounting is a good ally to have.

Petty Cash Bank

While many concierges maintain their own banks in the interest of simplicity, the accounting department may establish and maintain the petty-cash bank. In this case, all reconciliations must be directed back to accounting for reimbursement. Therefore, it's necessary to have ongoing communication, so any adjustments needed when balancing the books can be corrected accurately and smoothly.

The Business Center

The concierge needs to fully understand what the business center has to offer and be available to handle the "lighter" business services for their guests at the concierge desk. These might include receiving an e-mail or printing a few pages.

A guest told a concierge that the hotel's business center wanted to charge him $15 to receive a one-page fax. This sounded outrageous, so the concierge, in the spirit of always being helpful, offered to have the fax sent directly to his desk. (After all, concierges are always happy to help with "light" business-type services.) As it turned out, the "one-page" fax was actually 15 pages! The moral of the story: If something doesn't sound right, it probably isn't. Always double-check.

Catering and Convention Services

The catering and conventions department works closely with the concierge team, since the concierge can be a great asset to a catering manager. The catering department books functions and coordinates group activities, and the concierge can assist with incidentals, such as arranging for coffee breaks, easels, audio/visual equipment, pens, water and room-temperature control. It's important that concierges attend any preconvention meetings, to reassure clients that they will be happy to serve them throughout their stay.

If a client has not hired an outside ground operator, the catering manager can count on the concierge to coordinate all the transportation to and from airports. Concierge desks can also plan private bus charters, excursions outside the city and sports-oriented activities, such as fishing or golf. All the catering director needs to do is give the concierge the name and number of the client, and the concierge department can do the rest.

VIP tour buses are commonly requested for small board meetings. These types of busses are usually equipped with a bar and have luxurious swivel seats, televisions and elaborate sound systems. The concierge can help the catering and convention department, by taking care of all the bus, van and limousine requests that the clients require.

When a group has a shuttle bus planned or has arranged for an organized tour, the concierge and the catering department need to be in communication at all times.

Other areas in which the concierge works closely with this department can require creating packets of information to give out at check-in. Concierges might also act as speakers for programs designed for the spouses. The concierge can give a talk on the city, pass out maps, offer ideas and speak about public transportation, shopping and dining opportunities. Groups can be billed for this type of service, and it makes the catering department and the hotel shine.

While the catering and concierge departments want to promote the hotel's services to clients and guests, there are times when groups want to try other places in town. Again, all the catering director needs to do is consult with the concierge, who will be aware of restaurants appropriate for group bookings. In the case of "free nights" during a convention, the concierge can supply a list of recommended restaurants and nightclubs. Of course, the concierge is a focal point for directions and information of all kinds. For this reason, a separate concierge desk is sometimes set up for the exclusive use of meeting attendees, to assist them with their needs.

I had an interesting group from New Zealand which was instructed to send home 120 postcards per person. Since each person needed to purchase 120 stamps and there were 150 people in the group, I was a bit concerned about the logistics, especially in light of the everyday postal traffic generated by other guests. We worked it out by taking down the names and numbers of cards sent for each of the group members and running them through a postal meter. The charges were sent to their respective rooms on the last day of their stay. Figuring this out required good communication with the staff in charge of this group, since people brought us ten cards at a time. If we hadn't devised this system, selling stamps individually would have taken the entire week.

The Front Desk

The front-desk staff and the concierge are so interrelated that they are often located in close proximity to one another. While concierges are not usually responsible for checking guests in and out, they are happy to do so, should it become necessary. The front desk should be able to count on the concierge for help, but they should also be capable of handling simple directions and information, without referring each and every question to the concierge.

When I first started, I created a monster. I wanted to "prove" that I was valuable and so asked the bellman and front desk to direct all inquiries and requests to the concierge. It got to the point where even the most mundane questions such as, "Where's United Airlines," was referred to my desk. I quickly learned my lesson.

Concierges also help the front desk a great deal, by relieving them of coordinating outside activities. The concierge should be helpful to the staff at the front desk, but not to the point where they stop supplying simple information that should be common knowledge.

> *Realizing that I'd created a situation that became a disservice to guests, I created books for the front desk and the bell desk. They supplied answers to simple requests, such as the location of banks, ATM machines, currency exchanges, churches, airport-direction cards and so on. It took awhile to catch on, because I'd made it too easy to say, "See the concierge," which can be an occupational hazard.*

Often, when the front desk is slow, the concierge is extremely busy and vice-versa. The front desk sees the guests on arrival and departure, while the concierge takes care of them in between. With the presence of a strong concierge department, the front desk is able to function as a front office, which is vitally important to the overall operation. This frees the front desk to give more efficient service and allows the concierge to help guests with more involved situations.

The front-desk staff is constantly calling the concierge to help answer guest requests, and the concierge is constantly calling the front office for assistance with guest concerns. There is a very close relationship between the two departments. When possible, it is an excellent idea to escort arriving guests personally to the front desk and introduce them to your front-desk colleagues. This not only makes the guest feel especially welcome, but it also adds a personal touch to interactions with colleagues within the hotel.

It is important to remember that although the concierge department's commitment is to "handle everything," it does not automatically mean that other departments don't perform their duties. In a new hotel, this should not be a big issue, but in a hotel that has been operating without a concierge for many years, there is a tendency to dump every irritating and unwanted request onto the concierges.

Front desk paid-outs

While every hotel handles paid-outs differently, this is the way it is typically done: Room charges are handled through the front-office cashier, so several times each day the front desk and the concierge have transactions through paid-outs and miscellaneous charges. Paid-outs are forms for cash charges applied to the guest's bill that have been paid by the front desk cashier to the concierge. Miscellaneous charges are forms for items charged to the guests' bills that will be paid for by the hotel's accounting department.

Bell Staff/Luggage Attendants

There are various ways of managing a concierge department, and styles and responsibilities may vary according to the size of the hotel and location. Basically, there are two major configurations. In one case, the concierge department is responsible for uniformed personnel, including the bell staff, doorpersons, valet-parking attendants and limousine drivers. In other cases, the concierge department deals exclusively with guest requests. While the former makes the job of the concierge more complex, there is an advantage to managing uniformed personnel – the assurance that the level of service in the lobby is consistent – and superior across the board.

In either case, it's a good idea for the concierge to provide the bell staff, valet parking staff and transportation department with helpful information they can pass along to guests. These might include directions and maps to common destinations, a list of fun activities for rainy days and other itineraries the concierge has developed. It's a great way to gain rapport with these departments and provide hotel guests with a "Wow!" experience.

Where the concierge department deals exclusively with guest requests, the bell staff and the concierge have the most important "marriage" of any of the departments in the hotel. Guest requests that are typical to the bell department, such as "fronts" (taking the guests and their luggage to their rooms) and checkouts, often go through the concierge department, as do requests for valet parking and package delivery.

The area where the bell staff helps the concierge most is often a rather delicate issue in hotels, which is commonly referred to as "dead work." Concierges often rely on the bell staff to deliver packages, flowers, luggage for repair and a myriad of odd requests that require delivery or pickup. These errands normally are not attached to a gratuity, and for concierges to receive priority treatment on behalf of their guests, the interactions with the bell staff need to be extremely smooth. It is important for the concierge to be good to the bell staff – to always be respectful and speak to them pleasantly. The concierge should ask, not demand.

Among other tasks, the bell department is responsible for storing and retrieving luggage. In the event that a bell person is unavailable, the concierge could act in their stead by taking a guest's luggage and issuing a standard claim form. By the same token, guests should not be kept waiting to retrieve their luggage, and the concierge can be helpful in that way also. As with all guest requests, "the buck stops at the concierge."

The following is an example where a team effort by the concierge and bell staff collaborated to save the day.

> ***A family vacationing at a hotel in Berlin, Germany realized they had left their four-year-old daughter's stuffed bunny at home. They came to the concierge for advice, since the child couldn't sleep without it. When it***

became clear that no substitute would do, the concierge arranged for a member of the bell staff to drive the five hours roundtrip to retrieve the beloved bunny from the family residence.

Communications

Communications agents (formerly called operators) can be very helpful to the concierge, because they handle routine questions and directions, making it unnecessary to put every call through to the concierge department. In some hotels, faxes are handled in the communications department, and telephone messages, as well. The relationship with this department is very important, since the concierge often arranges for wake-up calls and do-not-disturb instructions, which must be relayed to communications. It would be a rare day, indeed, if the concierge did not interact with the communications department.

The IT (Information Technology) Department

The concierge needs to have a good relationship with this department, as so much of their work now involves the computer. Concierges need total Internet availability, including e-mail, GoConceirge, social networking sites such as Facebook, etc., which other departments may not have access to. The IT department is also called upon to help with any technical difficulties that may arise.

Engineering/Maintenance

It is often said that the most important people to befriend are the maintenance employees. Good relationships with engineering ensure quick responses, and this is vital when the concierge is faced with a leaky sink or broken lock.

Once, when doing a consulting job at a Hawaiian hotel, I heard a guest request a piece of sandpaper from the concierge. The engineering department refused to comply, claiming that they were not authorized to do so. I was upset by this blatant lack of concern for the guest's needs and by the obvious lack of communication between the two departments. In my opinion, the concierge department was at fault, failing to have established a working relationship.

The Executive Offices

Concierges agree that the quality of the concierge department depends a great deal on management. If the general manager (GM) is understanding and cooperative, the concierge department can thrive. If not, concierge services might be sacrificed, and guest satisfaction will suffer. A general manager needs to understand the complexity and workload concierges face day in and day out, so the department can be properly staffed. When this is not the case, the understaffed concierge's desk becomes "service under siege." In an ideal world, the general manager would understand the importance of the concierge and appreciate the efforts needed to serve guests' needs. Unfortunately however, a common complaint is, "My manager doesn't understand!" This can prove to be a very upsetting situation for the concierge, who wants to be understood, respected and appreciated.

> *A general manager at my hotel had a ceramic fish hanging on his wall, with the caption: "The fish stinks from the head." This graphic wall hanging was to remind him that if managerial expertise and support doesn't flow from the top down, all departments in the organization are compromised – including the concierge desk.*

The general manager should always be awarded VIP status by the concierge, and there should never be an occasion where the GM is given short shrift. The general manager should be treated as well as a guest and offered the services of the concierge. This allows the GM to gain experience firsthand of the level of service concierges deliver and makes it possible for him or her to gain an appreciation for and understanding of the complexities they deal with on a daily basis.

> *A concierge in San Francisco made golf reservations for his general manager on a regular basis and each time wrote out a confirmation card with directions included. When asked by the general manager why he goes to such pains, the concierge smiled and replied, "I want you to experience our service completely and as often as possible."*

The concierge should reach out to the hotel executives. If the concierge department has been responsible for increasing business in the hotel restaurant, spa or gift shop, every "sale" should be quantified and reported to the GM. Each encounter is an opportunity for the concierge to shine. Even if some execs go a bit overboard with requests, fulfilling those requests is time well spent. It is an excellent idea to have the general manager spend time at the concierge desk to familiarize him/herself with the realities of the job.

> *A general manager once chose the concierge department for one of his series of "In Touch Days," enabling him to work side by side with the hotel staff. Although he thought he was knowledgeable about what concierges do, he anticipated he'd be asked mostly for directions to the cable cars and to the bathroom. To his surprise, he was required to find a special type of exotic woman's shoe, which turned out to be available only in southern California. Next, he found himself faced with a city that was out of cars to rent, and a hotel full of guests demanding them (convertibles, no less). The straw that*

broke the camel's back was a guest who called three times in ten minutes to see if he'd managed to obtain her theater tickets (to a sold-out show). Running low on patience, he lost his cool, snapped at the guest and immediately regretted it. The last thing he wanted was for the hotel to receive a "negative comment card" about the general manager! After only one hour on the job, he had to sit down – not because his feet hurt, but because the stress had become overwhelming!

On a positive note, a concierge who worked in a major metropolitan city experienced a great deal of support by management and appreciated it greatly. The procedure at his desk involved receiving "paid outs" from the front desk in order to "front" certain expenditures for their sophisticated guests. At one point, the concierge desk "owed" the hotel $4,000. At the time, a new management company had purchased the hotel and examined each paid out with a fine-toothed comb. The general manager was called on the carpet and asked how such a situation could happen. Having worked with this particular concierge staff for 11 years, he knew they lived by the motto: "Our word is our bond." He told the new management company there was no need to change their policies, as he had complete faith in his staff. He remained true to the concierges and the level of service they provided to their upscale clientele.

Rooms Executive

The rooms executive normally handles the supervision of the concierge, front desk, reservations, communications, housekeeping, maintenance/engineering and security. It is advisable to treat him or her as a VIP and encourage as much personal interaction as possible.

Food and Beverage Director

The concierge should support the food and beverage director and promote the hotel restaurants, both through the desk and also through other concierges in town. Special promotions and holiday events present excellent opportunities for the concierge to steer guests toward the hotel's restaurants and bars. It is also a good idea for the concierge to be the "eyes and ears" of the hotel and share the wealth of his or her experience. Getting out and about and visiting many restaurants is fundamental for the concierge, and the many good ideas that result may be shared with the food and beverage department.

The food and beverage director and the restaurant managers should ideally view their own hotel concierges with the same respect shown the concierges by outside restaurants. The primary reason for this is that concierges represent significant potential business for the hotel restaurants and bars. Unfortunately, this is not always the case, so concierges may need to "go the extra step" in making other departments aware of the revenue resulting from their recommendations. The concierges may also suggest that they be invited occasionally to sample the fare at their own restaurants, so they will be knowledgeable about recommending the hotel services. Many times, it is the concierge who makes the reservations for the hotel restaurants, so the relationship between the concierge and the food and beverage department needs to be very close.

Housekeeping

There is constant interaction between the concierge and the housekeepers, because a wide variety of guest requests involve that department. For instance, "lost and found" is a housekeeping task that the concierge taps regularly. Guest requests for pillows, blankets, hangers, irons, bed boards, vases and extra amenities are all handled by the housekeeper, but generally the requests originate at the concierge desk. Sometimes, guests' preferences are stored in the computer; for instance, their choice of a feather or foam pillow. These notes should be passed along to housekeeping. It is important that the concierge have confidence in the level of service delivered by housekeeping, and this is possible only when a good relationship has been developed.

Assistant Managers

The concierge relies on the assistant managers to take care of problems that would normally disrupt the smooth operation of the concierge department. While the concierge takes pride in not "passing the buck," certain situations require the intervention of an assistant manager. In the event, for instance, that a guest is extremely irate, the assistant manager is vital in moving the disturbance away from the focal point of the lobby.

Human Resources

Because most professional concierge departments consist of excellent and long term employees, the Human Resource Department is not a department with which the concierge frequently interacts. Human Resources is helpful when an addition is being made to the concierge staff. They handle the initial interviews and explain all hotel policies and procedures. During the orientation for all new hotel employees, which is handled by human resources, it is also advisable to encourage a visit to the concierge desk, so that the concierge function is understood by all hotel staff.

Public Relations

The public relations department and the concierge should have a strong and close relationship. The concierge may be the contact for travel writers, for instance, and occasionally may be interviewed, thus representing the hotel to the press. Should the phone call be routed directly to the concierge desk, the concierge should always apprise the public relations department before granting an interview to a writer or reporter.

The concierge also presents opportunities for publicity through concierge functions. Hosting visiting dignitaries, for example, usually falls to the concierge, and it is important that the public relations department be aware of who is in the hotel. Because of the concierge's multitude of contacts, he or she can be valuable to the public relations department in generating "think-tank" groups as well. For example, if a public relations person is new on the job, the concierge is able to put them in touch with contacts with local public relations firms, reporters, convention bureaus and so on. Lastly, because of the growing interest in concierge service as a whole, the public relations department should also be provided with information about the hotel's chief concierge, including background and credentials. Articles featuring the concierge are an excellent source of positive public relations for the hotel and the concierge profession as a whole. For many reasons, the relationship between the concierge and public relations department should be close and favorable.

On one occasion, a concierge in New York City helped his Les Clefs d'Or colleagues negotiate a rate for their Pan American meeting at a sister property. He happily stepped in and contacted the corporate public relations director, who contacted the president of the entire chain of properties. The president then called the general manager of the sister hotel directly to settle the matter. While the concierge would never use his contacts and relationships lightly, he was willing to leverage his ability to create priceless positive press by helping a colleague and Les Clefs d'Or. Needless to say, one would need to withdraw such favors from the "favor bank" sparingly.

In San Francisco, the Northern California Concierge Association conducted a major fundraiser for an AIDS hospice and raised $30,000. This was a marvelous opportunity for positive public relations.

Room Service

The concierge interfaces with room service many times every day. Special amenities such as a basket of fruit, champagne and other goodies are generated within the concierge department, but carried out by room service. When a complaint is received, the concierge relies on room service to deliver a token of apology. Flowers coordinated with champagne and other special food items are also delivered by room service.

Incidentally, room service often keeps a pot of chicken soup hot and ready to send to guests who are not feeling well. When the concierge encounters a guest with the sniffles or in need of calling a doctor, room service may be able to add a bowl of steaming soup.

To be prepared, the concierge should keep a copy of the room-service menu at the desk and also be able to access it quickly on the computer, so it may be easily printed out.

Sales and Marketing

Sales is service; service is sales. This should be the motto of every concierge. It's imperative that concierges understand their role as salespeople. In no way does sales undermine service; in fact, it enhances it. Good concierges naturally provide more than what's asked of them and offer helpful suggestions to make a guest's stay a memorable one. Is it service or is it sales? It is both, and they are two sides of the same coin. One complements the other. The better the service, the higher the sales; the higher the sales, the better the service.

The concierge is a huge asset to the sales department. Sales should think of concierges as "honorary members" of their department, as concierges are perfectly situated to promote the hotel's restaurants, spa, business center, catering and convention services and entertainment. The responsibility of concierges as salespeople is double faceted. First, they serve both guests and the hotel by recommending the many services their property has to offer. Secondly, through the ultimate service they deliver, they inspire guests to come back again and refer the hotel to their friends and family.

It is good practice for sales departments to feature the concierge as a major attraction of the hotel, and may take advantage of the concierge's reputation and connections to create a good impression with potential guests. On their part, concierges should help with booking transportation and planning itineraries for incoming groups. They play a very active role in sales with catering and conventions. It is a very clever idea to include the concierge on sales trips and at conventions. Who better to sell the hotel service, than the person actually providing it!

Concierges are often asked to write a hotel newsletter for guests, which can be an outstanding marketing tool. For instance, an article can announce the upcoming events and festivities throughout the year. It's a great way to encourage repeat business.

They may assist sales in designing personal itineraries and are often able to pass along leads for group business. They are also aware of what the competition is doing and are able to develop leads from contacts with the convention bureaus.

Concierges should have their fingers on the pulse of the marketing department's activities, to ensure that they know about special packages before the guests do. If the guest is the first to know, it can be very embarrassing for the concierge.

> ***I can remember an occasion when the marketing department came out with a special package that involved the concierges, who were to provide special services for the guests. Unfortunately, the first time we heard about***

it was through a guest! This kind of thing is not uncommon, so it behooves the concierge, as well as the marketing department, to take a proactive and collaborative approach to offering special packages and promotions.

The concierge should regularly attend meetings with the sales and marketing departments, not only to obtain information from them, but to provide it. For instance, concierges can report, firsthand, what guests are saying, suggesting and requesting. These departments can also benefit greatly from the skills and experience of the concierges, by soliciting their input for the hotel website and asking them to participate on panels for social media sites.

Shipping and Receiving

In smaller hotels, the concierge may be responsible for receiving packages and working with shippers. In larger properties, both incoming and outgoing mail is generally handled by the shipping and receiving department. In these cases, this department is constantly called upon by the concierge. Shipping and receiving is responsible for tracking all packages through UPS, Federal Express and other companies. They also provide boxes in response to guests' requests and take care of wrapping all guests' packages. As with every relationship within the hotel, help from the shipping and receiving department should never be taken for granted. It is a simple matter to remember to be especially polite and appreciative, occasionally rewarding the staff with special favors or a small gift to say, "Thank you."

Reservations

The concierge works with the reservations department in a variety of ways. This department constantly refers guests to the concierge for limousines, flowers, theater tickets, directions and a host of other matters. In turn, the concierge should be able to rely on the reservation department to help secure guest rooms, research information for incoming guests and obtain occupancy forecasts or group prospectuses. Reservations is also the first department to be aware of the arrival of VIP guests.

It is important to cultivate a good working relationship and maintain close communication with reservations. In the event that guests cancel their hotel reservations, this department needs to inform the concierge immediately, so that any other reservations (limousine service, dinner or theater reservations, etc.) may be canceled as well. In fact, it is helpful for the concierge to make a note of these arrangements on the reservation itself, so the reservations department will be sure to advise them, should the guest cancel his or her stay.

It is also a good idea to educate the reservations department to interact creatively with the concierge for special occasions such as New Year's Eve. When guests are making reservations, for instance, it is a simple thing to have the reservation agent ask if they have made plans and, if not, offer to have them transferred to the concierge. The concierge is then able to plan something special and personal that the guest may not even have thought possible. Booking in advance also prevents the disappointment caused by sold-out shows and booked restaurants, when guests try to make plans at the last minute.

The Fitness Center

If there is a fitness center onsite, the concierge needs to know what equipment is available and have a listing of the classes, if any. In addition, should a guest report a broken or inoperable machine to the concierge, it is his or her responsibility to report it to maintenance.

If there isn't a fitness center in the hotel, or if the guest has requested information on a more extensive one, the concierge should be knowledgeable about the health clubs nearby.

The Spa

Like any other hotel amenity, the concierge should be very familiar with the services offered by the spa. For example, familiarity with the difference between a Swedish and sports massage and knowing how the various facials differ will help the concierge recommend just the right service. Hopefully, one will be able to make firsthand recommendations, as receiving invitations to experience spa services for oneself is a delightful way to recover from a busy day, while gaining valuable information to pass along to guests.

> *Every year, a concierge in New York was given a special gift of expensive face cream made from caviar. Once, while being interviewed by the press, he mentioned that he used this special cream, which later appeared in an article. Ten years later, a guest casually asked him what type of facial cream he used, and he excitedly told her about the caviar cream. She was so impressed that he was still using it, that she went directly to the spa and purchased some. This story illustrates the power of the relationships formed between other departments in the hotel and the press. It also showcases the role of the concierge as a salesperson and revenue source.*

The Gift Shop and Boutique

In a few hotels, the concierge oversees the hotel's gift shop. Even when this is not the case, the concierge needs to know the inventory in these shops very well. More and more, hotel gift shops are expanding their offerings to literally bring their brand name home. For instance, some are selling items found in the hotel rooms, such as pillows, mattresses and robes. This is an excellent opportunity for the guests to enjoy a useful souvenir that will serve as a daily reminder of their stay – and the hotel brand.

Risk Management

Concierges work closely with the risk-management department to protect their hotels against legal action. Because concierges are responsible for referring so many third-party vendors, it is very important that they work closely with the risk-management area to ensure there is ample insurance coverage and that the corresponding paperwork is on file and up-to-date. This is especially important when recommending transportation options, such as helicopter tours, boat and plane charters, bus tours and limousine services.

There are also other potentially high-risk situations the concierge needs to be aware of. One hotel was held liable, for instance, when a guest was mugged on a jogging trail that the concierge had suggested. The safety of guests is paramount and keeping them out of harms way is a top priority. Risk management can help by informing the concierge of potential pitfalls.

Security

Among the best friends a concierge can develop are the security director and everyone on the security staff. The concierge calls on security to respond to emergencies, injuries and suspicious behavior and works with security in emergency situations. In the post 9/11 world, it has become especially important for concierges to remain alert and report any questionable behavior immediately.

Less dramatic, is the need to gain access to areas that are otherwise locked. If, for instance, the flower shop is closed and the concierge needs access to flowers, security can help. This is also true of areas such as the high-value lost-and-found room.

THE BALL AND THE BUCK

A final word on relationships with other departments in the hotel:

PEOPLE ARE HUMAN and mistakes are occasionally made. If another department should drop the ball, remember, *the buck stops at the concierge.* As one of my concierge friends put it: If a ball is dropped, concierges don't simply stop to pick it up. They pick it up and run with it.

CHAPTER SEVEN

7 Routine Requests

OBJECTIVES

The following chapter will equip readers to:

Turn recurring, ordinary requests into extraordinary guest experiences.

Identify routine tasks and the standard procedures associated with each

Become aware of their surroundings and the value of nuanced general knowledge.

Understand the relevance of legal compliance.

"The concierge asks, tries, denies, replies, demands, insists, begs, borrows, borrows some more, searches, finds, explores, tests, calls, answers, looks for, looks up, looks at, looks in, reads, writes, adds up, subtracts out, tastes, lights, extinguishes, walks, runs, fixes, mends, uses, advises, consults, warns, advocates, advertises, admonishes, provides: airline schedules, airline seating, airport exits, aircraft, trains, cars, limos, limos with phones, limos with bars, limos with a bottle of champagne, limos with a bottle of champagne and a pitcher of Bloody Marys, limos with a bottle of champagne and plenty of beer, opera tickets, opera seats close to the stage, opera seats far enough away from the stage, opera seats not near the brass section, opera seats close to the bar, theater tickets for shows on Broadway, off Broadway, off-off Broadway, shows in Los Angeles, hit shows, shows that closed out of town, shows with great acting, shows with very little talking, restaurants with great wine lists, restaurants close to the hotel, French restaurants, California grill restaurants, restaurants without purple in them . . . for doctors, lawyers, used-car salesmen, presidents of large companies, presidents of large countries, ex-presidents, movie stars, ex-movie stars, has beens, wanna-bes, actually ares, judges, ex-cons, future cons, politicians, senators, congressmen, voters, people with not enough money, people with too much money, people with more money than anybody knew really existed, Indians, Japanese, Magyars, Czechs, sheiks, shamans, honeymooners, second honeymooners, divorce lawyers . . ."

—John Neary, *Hotel Concierge*

WHILE THE ROLE OF THE CONCIERGE encompasses a wide variety of challenging and often uncommon requests, there are fundamental tasks that are handled consistently, day after day. Though routine, each of these tasks carries with it its own set of challenges, requires problem-solving skills and offers opportunities to add artistry to even the most mundane tasks.

The most important thing to remember is that each request be approached from the point of view of the guest. The guest's needs are first and foremost. It's up to the concierge to fulfill those needs in a pleasant and efficient manner that creates a positive experience for the guest.

HOTELS

Booking hotel reservations is a standard procedure. There are, however, a few tricky areas, as price, room type, availability and cancellation policies can create problematic situations. For instance, let's say a guest requests a room with a king-size bed with an ocean view on the Island of Maui at a specific hotel for a particular date. This sounds simple enough, yet the concierge can't simply assume that all will proceed without a hitch. Maui could easily be booked up for a convention, leaving perhaps only one double room with a mountain view. Adding to these difficulties is the fact that most requests for hotels that reach the concierge's desk come at the last minute.

The concierge always needs to be able to react quickly and decisively on behalf of the guest. Therefore, at the point of the initial contact, it's imperative that the concierge establishes alternatives and obtains the guest's permission to act on an alternative plan, if necessary. *Always ask for alternatives,* and have a backup plan. A good way to ask the question might be; "I'll do my very best to book your first choice, but if that isn't available, what would be the next best alternative?"

As for requests to cancel hotel reservations, it's important to keep in mind that there are often strict cancellation policies. It's a common practice for hotels to require a client's credit card number as a guarantee of the first night's stay, with a nonrefundable one-night's charge for last-minute cancellations. (Hotels typically require from 24 hours to one week's notice.)

When working with hotel reservations, the concierge always needs to obtain as many details as possible. When appropriate, ask questions such as: "Are you and your wife celebrating a special occasion?" or "May I make a reservation for a spa service while I have you on the line?" When booking hotels, always obtain the following basic information:

- Full name of the party (credit cardholder)
- Number of people sharing the room
- Room type and bed type
- Choice of smoking or non-smoking
- Name and location of hotel, keeping in mind that hotels in metropolitan areas often have multiple locations
- Date of arrival and departure
- Credit-card information (see below)
- Special needs, such as baby cribs, access for those with disabilities, etc.

How to Book Hotels

- When possible, use the Internet to determine availability and make the reservation.

- If needed, call the hotel, preferably the concierge, to ask any questions beyond the scope of their website, provide specific information about guests' needs and to make the reservation.
- When getting a "no-vacancy" response through the hotel's 800 number or website, always call the hotel reservation desk directly. Hotels cut off room availability to those calling 800 numbers and using their websites, before actually selling out completely. So, it's always worth a try to call the concierge or reservations desk for the "final answer."
- You can also book hotels through a travel agent.
- When guests specifically ask that you book their reservations through travel sites, such as Hotel.com, honor their request. Otherwise, booking through the hotel directly is the preferred method.
- When calling the hotel, identify yourself to the concierge or reservationist and ask for his or her name.
- Print out a confirmation number for the guest from the Internet or write it down on a confirmation card, if the reservation is taken by phone.
- Make sure to be clear about cancellation policies and print them out or write them down.
- Get the exact address and directions.

A "tool of the trade," *The Hotel and Travel Index*, can be invaluable to the concierge. It is an excellent reference that supplies information on hotels around the world. When I started as a concierge, it was a huge book and weighed a ton. Today, the same information can be accessed paper-free on:

www.hotelandtravelindex.travelweekly.com

OBTAINING CREDIT CARD INFORMATION

Fulfilling guests' requests usually requires credit-card information, which includes not only the credit card number, but also the expiration date, telephone number, home address and, in some cases, the name of the bank on which the card is drawn. Concierge software programs, such as Gold Key Solutions, can store this information securely, with encryption codes and password requirements.

Note: The CVV (Card Verification Value Code) number is a three- or four-digit code, printed on the back of the credit card. It's a security feature that provides a cryptographic verification of the information embossed on the card and helps prevent fraud. The CVV code is often required for "card-not-present" transactions (e.g., via the Internet and telephone), and now appears on most (but not all) major credit and debit cards. (VISA® refers to the code as CVV2, MasterCard® calls it CVC2, and American Express® denotes it as CID and is usually printed on the front of the card.) The concierge should always ask for this number, as it typically cannot be stored on the computer.

CREDIT CARD TIPS

AMERICAN EXPRESS always begins with the numbers 37, with the following sequence:

37__ ______ _____

VISA always begins with the number 4. The sequence may be one of two formats:

4___ ___ ___ ___ or 4___ ____ ____ ____

MASTERCARD always begins with the number 5. The sequence may either:

5___ ___ ___ ___ or 5___ ____ ____ ____

DINERS CLUB always begins with the numbers 36, with the following sequence:

36__ ______ ____

When booking hotels, always obtain alternatives and a way to guarantee reservations.

AIRLINE TICKETS

Helping guests with airline tickets is not always straightforward. It can be a complicated process and, because it is so complex, it is always best to have the guest available (in person or by telephone) as the task is performed. There may be questions regarding the class of the ticket, seating choices, meal preferences, the number of bags that will be checked, as well as possible extra charges for those bags. Every airline has different requirements, so it behooves the concierge to be well versed as to what they are. Thanks to the Internet, most arrangements can be made online, saving the concierge the extended telephone hold times of the past.

There may be times, however, when the concierge must call the airlines on behalf of the guest. Again, it is always preferable to have him or her present. In the interest of privacy and confidentiality, some airlines may not want to speak to the concierge and will ask to speak to the guest only. If this is the case, and the guest is not present, having the guest's cell phone number on hand can really save the day.

When discussing tickets already purchased, have a copy of the e-ticket in hand or on the screen when calling the airline to assure that you have complete and accurate information. Very often, airlines request information that may appear obscure to the layperson. They offer a wide variety of flight and fare options and often code their classifications. In the event that a reservation has become lost, having the e-ticket allows the concierge to pursue the task by speaking with a supervisor and supplying him/her with the ticket number, origin of purchase and any other information that may be helpful in resolving the issue. Another good reason for obtaining the actual e-ticket is to have the exact spelling of the passenger's name. The airline may have recorded the information differently from the guest's actual spelling.

To be truly efficient, one should obtain the name of the person at the airline, the person's sign-in code, the city the person is in and the "record-locator" number. This makes it easier to follow up, if necessary, and confirms to the guest that the task has, indeed, been accomplished. In the event of confusion at the airport or at the gate, it acts as notification to the airline that the flight had been confirmed.

Guard e-tickets carefully and return them to guests personally. Do not leave them in hotel rooms because sometimes guests change rooms!

Printing the Boarding Pass

One of the most frequent guest requests that involve the Internet and the airlines is checking in online, which involves the printing of boarding passes. In addition, many airlines now offer a feature when checking in online that allows you to pay the checked-baggage fees. This generally costs less than paying for checked baggage at the airport. There is a great deal of information needed to print out a boarding pass, especially if it is for an international flight or involves checked-baggage fees. As with other procedures involving the airlines, it is definitely easier to check a guest in if they are with you at the time. All the airlines require different information, and check-in is more complicated for international flights, as you generally need the guest's passport to generate their boarding passes.

Southwest Airlines is particularly unusual when it comes to online check-in, as they don't offer prearranged seat assignments. Unless you pay extra for preferred seating, the order of boarding is determined by the zone and number printed on the boarding pass. Most of their regular customers know this, so it has become desirable to check in for Southwest flights at the first moment online check-in becomes available: 24 hours prior to flight time. That way, you have a greater chance of getting in the first boarding zone and sitting in the section you prefer.

As with e-tickets, boarding passes should be guarded carefully and returned to guests personally.

Many hotels have installed a printer for boarding passes that guests can access themselves.

Purchasing Tickets

There are times when the concierge initiates an itinerary, and the airline ticket is actually purchased for the guest. In purchasing tickets, there are four methods of ticketing:

- Internet
- Phone
- Travel agent
- In rare emergencies, a visit to the airport

Questions to ask the guest:

- What is the point of origin?
- What is the destination and desired airport? What airline is preferred?
- Is there a frequent flyer (FF) status? If so, ask for the FF number.
- Date of flight(s)?
- Preferred time of day?
- What class of service?
- What is the seat preference? Aisle or window? Front or back of cabin?

If not in the computer, you will also need to obtain the guest's complete credit-card information, as outlined under the "Hotels" section of this chapter, along with the full names of all passengers, as they are printed on government-issued photo IDs, such as passports or driver's licenses. (Note: The name on the passenger's credit card may differ from that on his or her government-issued ID, and you will need to have both.)

After booking, an e-mail is sent to the concierge to confirm the flight. This confirmation is saved in the system and forwarded electronically or given in hard copy to the guest. It should not only include the details of the flight, but also any rules and restrictions associated with the fare.

When making airline reservations, it's important to make sure that the exact destination is clear. There are, for instance, many major cities that have more than one airport, such as LaGuardia, Kennedy and Newark for New York City, Reagan and Dulles for Washington, D.C. and Chicago's O'Hare and Midway.

An invaluable tool of the trade in working with airlines is the *Official Airline Guide* (OAG®). The OAG is best known for its airline-schedule database, which holds future and historical flight details for 900 airlines and more than 3,500 airports. Using these vast databases, OAG provides a range of multi-lingual products for the travel industry, which are available on the Internet, for PDAs and mobile phones, and last but not least, in good, old-fashioned print. This online subscription-based resource, which is continually updated, is an absolute essential for the professional concierge.

Changing a Flight

Attempting to change a flight can get complicated, and it is mandatory to have the e-ticket in hand or the information visible on the computer screen. If possible, also have the guest available or in touch by telephone, as decisions may need to be made that will require his or her permission and/or a statement of personal preferences.

Guests may insist that they are holding changeable tickets, when, in fact, they are not. Never argue with the guest, but simply record the information and get in touch with the airline to confirm. One may be faced with any of the following situations:

Situation 1 The guest wants another flight, but has a restricted or non-refundable ticket. In this case, when the guest purchased the original ticket, he or she made a binding contract with the airline, and the existing ticket simply can't be changed. In such situations, the concierge can only empathize with the guest and offer to book a new ticket.

Situation 2 The guest wants a different flight and has a changeable, but somewhat restricted ticket that allows for change with a penalty. In these cases:

- Make it clear to the guest that there will be a penalty for making a change.
- Access the website or call the airline and obtain the exact charges.
- Obtain the guest's permission to add the charges before actually making any changes.

- When permission has been secured, make the change on the website or by phone and log all the information.
- Obtain a record locator-number and write it on the guest's confirmation card or print it out from the Internet.

Situation 3 The guest has a nonrefundable, restricted ticket, but wants another flight and is willing to go on standby.

- Standby status does not require a reservation. Call the airline to determine if standby is allowed on that ticket.
- Determine availability on the desired flight.
- Inform the guest.

Situation 4 The guest requests a change in the itinerary, but the flight desired is not available.

- Check to determine if seating is available in another class.
- Search online or call the airline for options and write them down carefully.
- Contact the guest and obtain their preference(s).
- Call the airline to make the appropriate change.
- Get a record-locator number and write it down on the guest's confirmation card.

Situation 5 The guest requests a specific flight, which is available, and changes are allowed on the ticket. However, the desired flight does not go to the final destination, but rather an interim destination.

In such cases, always call the airline, rather than relying on the Internet and:

- Obtain the guest's *entire* itinerary in order to coordinate connecting flights.
- Call the airline for flight availability and write down the information.
- Inform the airline of any subsequent connecting flights.
- Confirm the reservation.
- Obtain a record locator number and write it on the guest's confirmation card.

Situation 6 A guest requests an upgrade without changing the flight (e.g., from coach to business class or from business to first class).

- Consult the Internet or call the airline to determine availability and the price difference.

- If the guest wants to use Frequent Flyer miles to pay for the upgrade, get the FF number.
- Inform the guest and obtain permission to proceed.
- Make the change online or over the phone with the airline and print the confirmation of the change.

A guest asked me to purchase a ticket for a specific flight from San Francisco to Los Angeles. I did as asked and bought a nonrefundable ticket for him, only to learn later that he was connecting with an international flight at LAX and didn't have enough time between flights to make it. This is what is known in the airline business as an "illegal connection." Had I known his entire itinerary, I would have been able to anticipate the problem, catch the mistake, and save the guest time and aggravation.

Lost Luggage

Most airlines now offer online tracing for lost luggage. Guests whose luggage has been lost en route receive a report from the airline's baggage office, which has a ten-digit code. The first three letters indicate the arrival airport. The next two digits are the airline code, and the last five are unique to that particular request. The 10-digit code can be entered into the airline's website to track the status of the lost baggage.

RAILWAY TICKETS AND LOCAL MASS TRANSIT

AMTRAK reservations can be easily made online (www.AMTRAK.com) or by calling 1-800-USA-RAIL (1-800-872-7245). They may also be booked through a travel agent. When purchasing tickets for AMTRAK passengers, always obtain the following information:

- Guest's name and hotel room number
- Date and time
- Number and names (as shown on a government-issued ID) of persons in the party
- Destination(s) and itinerary
- Class of service requested
- Choice of seating and sleeping accommodations
- Choice of meal options
- Complete credit card information

They will give you the train number and reservation number, together with the departure time. Make sure that the guest is given the information so that he/she may pick up the tickets.

AMTRAK tickets cannot be changed online, rather you must call their reservations office. Sometimes, especially if the reservations telephone lines are busy, it can be easier to book a new reservation according to the guest's wishes, then cancel their existing reservation.

The Internet is the best way to obtain schedules for most local transportation options, such as BART in the San Francisco Bay Area, Metra in Chicago or New Jersey Transit on the East Coast. The concierge should also keep current schedules of local transportation options readily available to hand to guests.

FLORAL REQUESTS

Floral requests are simple procedures, provided that a good working relationship has been established with the florist(s). Dependable florists respond quickly, are willing to create mixed bouquets on short notice, have long hours, reasonable prices, and, of course, beautiful fresh flowers. The concierge should know a florist who has evening, as well as Sunday and holiday hours.

Flowers may be ordered over the Internet or by phone. Either way, the information needed is typically entered into the computer, using the hotel's concierge software. Below is an example of a form from GoConcierge.net, used at the St. Regis, Punta Mita, which includes all the information a concierge needs to ensure a floral request is handled properly.

The concierge should make sure to include the message for the card that will accompany the flowers and ask if there are any special instructions (for example, "no daisies or carnations"). The great concierge takes special pains to gain extensive knowledge about flowers and floral arrangements. For example, it's helpful to know when certain flowers, such as peonies, are in season, or which fragrances might trigger an allergy. Asking the individual ordering the flowers educated questions about their preferences shows caring and demonstrates knowledge.

When flowers are delivered to a residence, it's important to obtain the phone number of the recipient. If the recipient is not at home at the time of delivery, and proof of delivery is required, the recipient may be contacted to arrange for an alternate delivery time.

ST REGIS
PUNTA MITA

FLOWER ORDER WORK SHEET/FORMA PARA ORDEN DE FLORES

Name of recipient/Nombre a quien envía: Mr. Adam Isrow
Address/room#/Direccion/hab.#:
Telephone/Teléfono: 818-263-8993

Name of sender/Nombre de quien envía: Adam Isrow
Address/room #/Dirección/cuarto#:
Telephone/Teléfono: 818-263-8993

Date needed/Dia en que las necesita: Monday, June 21, 2010
Time needed/Hora en que las necesita: 5:00 PM

Florist/Floreria: Las Rosas de Aurelia
Order (type of flowers)Orden (tipo de flores): 1 Dozen red roses

Price/Precio: $125-150
Contact at florist/Contacto de floreria: JT

Card Message/Mensaje en la tarjeta: Happy Anniversary!

Method of payment/Método de pago:
Room number/Numero de hab:
Credit card/Tarjeta de crédito:
Expiration/Expiración:
Code number/Código (amex):
Delivered to room by bellman/Enviado a la hab. por bellboy: BP

Computer-generated floral order form

If flowers are to be delivered to a guest room before arrival, the room of that guest needs to be specifically blocked. Be sure to make a note in the computer as well, indicating that flowers are to be delivered to that room. This way, should the guest change rooms at check-in, the flowers can be transferred accordingly. In addition, make sure the room has been cleaned before the flowers are delivered. If the flowers are delivered to the room before it is cleaned, housekeeping may assume they belonged to the previous occupant and remove them.

AUTO RENTALS

It would be wonderful if rental companies always provided perfect customer service: door-to-door pickup and delivery, no waiting time, and confirmation of car type, including make, model and color. Unfortunately, this is not the reality. During busy periods, clients may be subjected to a wait, even with a confirmed reservation. Furthermore, auto-rental companies can rarely confirm the exact car the client will receive, guaranteeing only certain categories, such as compact, midsize, or luxury. While high-end luxury rental-car companies can guarantee the exact car a client will receive and have it delivered, most car companies don't and require the client to appear at the rental office in person to collect the car. This, of course, varies from city to city and from hotel to hotel.

In making arrangements, it's necessary to confirm that the driver is over the age of 21. Some rental companies even require drivers to be over 25. It is also mandatory to make certain that the driver has (in his or her possession) a valid driver's license. This is a requirement that is not negotiable.

Most rental companies also require a credit card, which must be in the same name as that on the driver's license. In some circumstances, a car company might accept a cash deposit in lieu of a credit card.

There are times when a rental company will require an extra fee for dropping a car off in another city, and some stipulate that convertibles must be returned to the place where the rental originated. Each company is different, and it pays to know the requirements of them all.

Some people will ask for the "best deal," so it is necessary to keep an updated list of price variances on the computer database. The creation of this database can be assigned to a team member as a project during down time. There are several smaller companies that provide lower rates than the major companies offer. In general, rental prices differ dramatically, depending on supply and demand, so rates should not be quoted to the guest without confirming them.

Traditional car rental companies rent cars for a 24-hour period, with a grace period of 59 minutes before charging for an additional day. Cars are now rentable by the hour, as well, through companies such as Zipcar®, which is currently the predominate player in the short-term rental market. As of this writing, hourly car rentals through Zipcar are available in more than 50 cities throughout North America and the UK. They are also available at many universities and colleges.

How to Book a Car Rental

The following are questions to ask the guest:

- Guest's full name.
- Any preference as to the rental company.

- Date, location and time of rental.
- Date and location of return.
- Type of car preferred.
- Credit card information.
- Special requests, such as GPS or child seats.
- Any possible discounts the guest may have through such organizations, such as AARP, AAA, etc.

Situation 1 The concierge makes the reservation with the rental-car company. The guest picks up the car and fills out paperwork at the rental agency.

- In this instance, the initial information obtained (as indicated above) is sufficient.
- Contact the auto-rental company either by phone or Internet to make the request.
- Obtain the exact rate.
- Inform the guest and supply directions to the rental company.

Ask the company when their busy times are, so it will be possible to recommend an optimum time for the guest to pick up the car without waiting.

Situation 2 The concierge makes the reservation with the rental company and arranges for the car to be delivered to the guest at the hotel. This service is usually contingent on the concierge establishing a working relationship with the rental company. Budget Rent-a-Car in San Francisco has developed a system whereby the guest may fill out the company form, which can then be faxed to Budget. For an additional fee, the car may be delivered. In San Francisco, Hertz and National will deliver cars as well, but check with the car-rental companies in your city to determine if this service is offered. Guests in most luxury hotels will not wait in line at rental companies and expect cars to be driven to them. It falls to the concierge, therefore, to develop relationships with rental companies to supply such a service routinely.

Situation 3 The hotel has a rental company on the premises and the concierge handles all the paperwork directly. In this instance, the concierge acts as the agent for the rental car company, dealing with the actual rental agreement.

LIMOUSINES

Limousines are still considered a luxury by limousine companies and their clients, and both are very particular in terms of their requirements for this service. As with all bookings, limousine requests require detailed information, and the concierge must be able to quote prices precisely. It is important to explain to the client that there are cancellation fees and a minimum number of hours of service required. The charges may be based on time and mileage, or there may simply be an hourly charge. In some cities, universal rates and commission regulations are set. Either way, the concierge needs to know all the details.

There are several different kinds of limousines available. It is necessary for the concierge to be familiar with all of them and be able to explain the differences, especially since the meaning of the term "limousine" may vary from location to location and may also vary in the guests' perceptions. Clear communication will, as with any situation, avoid problems and misunderstandings.

Fortunately, both concierge software programs, GoldKey Solutions and GoConcierge have automated logs for limousine services, so accurate data can easily be kept. This makes it easy to keep a computerized record and forward the information to the limousine company via e-mail. Since one can also bill limousine charges to the guest's room, an e-mail should also be sent to the hotel's accounting department.

When sending short e-mails of this nature, it's helpful to include all the information the recipient needs in the subject line, enabling him or her to see the information in a glance.

LIMOUSINE TYPES

Sedan A luxury car such as a Cadillac Seville, Lincoln Town Car, or Mercedes.

Limousine A standard, formal black limousine with a back seat and two jump seats.

Stretch Limousine An elongated limousine holding six passengers with special amenities such as a television set, video player, bar, phone and moon roof.

Super Stretch	An elongated limousine holding eight to ten passengers, with full amenities.
Wide Body	This limo is widened as well as stretched and built to hold more passengers.
Luxury Mini Busses	Some guests prefer vans or SUVs. Cargo space is sometimes needed in situations such as transporting college students (and their belongings) to school.

LIMOUSINE AIRPORT PICKUPS

Airport pickups have their own peculiarities and a unique set of rules. Limousine prices will be different if the driver has to wait for a passenger to clear customs, so the concierge must determine if the flight is arriving from a domestic or international location. For instance, the standard limousine price for a domestic pickup could be doubled for an international arrival.

The concierge should confirm with the passenger the place the driver will be meeting them, such as just beyond customs or at the baggage-claim area. A common and very upsetting problem on all sides occurs when the driver is waiting at the airport and cannot locate the passenger. As with all tasks facing the concierge, paying *attention to details* can usually avoid this problem.

Details, Details . . .

- Have the exact information about airline, flight number, origin of flight, date and time of arrival. Repeat the information to the caller.
- Make sure that everyone involved is clear about the exact meeting place.
- Obtain the cell phone number of the passenger and the limo driver and pass them on to each other.
- Check the Internet or call the airline to confirm the exact arrival time one hour before the flight is scheduled to land. This is usually done by the limousine company, but it is a good idea to double check. If the flight has been delayed, the limousine company should be made aware of it. The front desk needs to be advised, as well, that the guest will be arriving late. This is especially important if the hotel is sold out or there are special suite reservations.
- When secretaries, relatives or friends order a limousine for another party, the concierge should get their name and number, as well as the passenger's name and number.

- On the day of the job, always reconfirm with the limousine company.
- When arranging for a limousine to meet a private plane, the concierge must get the tail number and FBO (Fixed Base Operator) of the airplane.

An all-too-common problem arises when guests indicate they didn't know a car was waiting and instead, take alternative transportation from the airport. A great way to avoid this is to send a text message to the guest after the plane arrives, such as: "Welcome! Your car is waiting." Add a phone number to contact the limousine driver.

REQUESTS FOR LIMOUSINE SERVICE

When guests request a limousine in person at the concierge desk, the following information is needed:

- Date and time of pickup
- Cell phone number of the limo driver and the guest
- Duration and specific type of service (tour, wedding, shopping, airport drop off, etc.)
- Drop-off destination
- Type of car
- Guest's name and room number
- Method of payment: Room charge, cash or credit card. (Credit-card payment must be accompanied by appropriate information, as outlined under "Hotels" earlier in this chapter.)

The following need to be asked of the limousine driver to ensure the guest receives all the necessary information:

- Are tolls included or additional?
- Is the gratuity included with the charges?
- What are the cancellation policies?

If the person making the reservation is an administrative assistant, travel agent or friend of the guest, the same information is needed, *along with the name and telephone number of the individual actually making the reservation*. Again, be sure to quote exact prices, including tolls and gratuities and cite the limousine company's cancellation policies.

The House Car

Some hotels operate their own in-house limousine service, which is normally coordinated through the concierge. The primary function of the service is transportation to and from airports for VIP guests, but its secondary function is to transport guests to various destinations within the city. The service is operated on a first-come, first-served basis and at the discretion of the concierge and driver(s). Most house-car services operate only within a relatively short distance from the hotel.

To avoid confusion, the most effective way to provide house-car service is to direct all inquiries to the concierge desk first, so the concierge can make the arrangements and enter the information into the computer. Coordination of the house car necessitates good communication between the concierge and the doorman to avoid overbooking. It is also important to maintain a tight system with the sales department, catering and with the office of the general manager. Following each booking, the concierge should key in the name of the guest, person confirming the limousine and the hours and destination for the day of the reservation. With this information entered into the computer, it is possible to reconfirm it on the appropriate day and avoid the loss of reservations.

Establish a policy whereby the department ordering the house car makes the request to the concierge directly and follows up with an e-mail or written order. Request sheets left in the concierge's mailbox without personal contact are insufficient. They can all too easily go astray.

In Europe and Asia, fine hotels hire an employee who's dedicated exclusively for greeting guests at the airport and escorting them to the hotel limousine. It's standard procedure. This position typically falls within the responsibilities of the concierge department.

When the house limousine is equipped with a telephone, give arriving guests (especially VIPs) a call to welcome them and provide the same service for departing guests, as a bon voyage. As an added personal touch, ask the limousine driver to alert you when guests will be arriving at the hotel, so you may personally greet them.

GIVING DIRECTIONS

Giving directions is one of the most frequent and routine tasks performed by the concierge. Though some may dismiss this aspect of the job with an offhanded "Ho-hum," I propose that its status be elevated to that of an art form. Because these requests are so common, they present the concierge with countless opportunities to make a great impression and forge positive relationships with guests.

Aside from a way to dazzle one's guests, providing directions can also take on a great deal of importance. Guests absolutely depend on the concierge to provide accurate directions. While Mapquest and GPS (Global Positioning Systems) have been known to make mistakes, guests count on the concierge to be 100 percent accurate. Incorrect directions can result in missing the beginning of a much anticipated game or show, or worse yet, missing an important meeting or flight. Given one wrong turn, a guest might also stumble into a dangerous neighborhood. All these situations put the guest, hotel and concierge at risk.

THE ART OF GIVING DIRECTIONS

When giving a talk to members of an International Clefs d'Or Congress, I suggested that, instead of handing guests a map and pointing out, "You are here," I suggested changing the verbiage to "We are here." I felt this would help keep concierges in the present moment and create a bond with the guest. It might also remind them that, though it might be the ten-thousandth time they have given the exact same directions, it's the first time the guest is hearing them.

It's important to remain present when giving directions – or conveying any information, for that matter – no matter how automatic it has become. I once figured out that I had instructed guests how to take the cable cars to Fisherman's Wharf approximately 47,000 times! When a guest would say, "Wow, it sounds as if you've said that before," I realized I'd slipped into "robot mode." I immediately shifted gears to make the next Fisherman's Wharf direction discussion sound exciting, personal and fresh.

Even when providing simple directions to locations within the hotel, such as a meeting room, it's important to show guests personal, caring attention. Rather than simply pointing a finger or nodding your head in the right direction, carefully explain how guests can find their way – or better yet, walk them to the destination, or at least partially there.

I got pretty good at giving directions to guest after guest as if it was my first time, but began to lose patience when I had to repeat the same information to the same guest again and again. I learned to overcome my frustration by simply pretending I was speaking to a different guest. Remember, it's as if the concierge is on stage, and the theme is: "Lights, Camera, Action!" Performance actors are no strangers to repetition and seem to always recite their lines with the same enthusiasm. The concierge should strive for no less than this.

DRIVING DIRECTIONS – Golden Gate Bridge

GRAND HYATT SAN FRANCISCO ON UNION SQUARE

1. Head WEST on **Sutter St** toward **Powell St** 0.8 mi
2. Turn RIGHT at **Van Ness Ave** 1.0 mi
3. Turn LEFT at **Lombard St** 1.1 mi
4. Continue onto **Richardson Ave** 0.2 mi
5. Continue onto **US-101 North/Doyle Dr**

Parking South end of bridge: Take a right at the last San Francisco exit off US-101 just before the Toll Plaza. The exit ramp sign reads, "Golden Gate National Recreation Area View Area." Proceed to stop sign, turn LEFT into the southeast side visitor parking lot.

Parking North end of bridge: Follow US-101 north across the Golden Gate Bridge. Take the first exit called "Vista Point" and turn RIGHT into the parking lot.

Pre-printed direction card

DIRECTION CARDS

One of the smartest things I did as a concierge was to create preprinted direction cards to help guide guests from our hotel to the most frequently requested sites. When I first designed them, I made a multitude of mistakes: I made the print too small, neglected to print the address of the hotel on the cards and used unwieldy paragraphs, instead of bullet points.

Today, direction cards can be produced with the various hotel-software systems. In fact, most systems are interfaced with Google Maps. However they are generated, accuracy and ease of use are always paramount. Directions that can be faxed and e-mailed to guests should also always be at the ready. Hotel websites should include directions to the hotel from various points, as well, and the concierge should make sure they are accurate, thorough and consistent with the directions provided at the concierge desk.

Creating preprinted direction cards saves an enormous amount of time, reduces stress and provides guests better service. It's well worth the effort to brainstorm the most frequently asked directions and go through the process of preprinting them. The following are helpful suggestions to keep in mind when designing direction information:

- Make sure the print is large and legible.
- Indicate directions (N), (S), (E) and (W), alongside specifications of (LEFT) and (RIGHT).
- Create a new line for each change of direction.
- Include the hotel's address and phone number.

- Identify the distance from the hotel and the estimated time it will take to walk and/or drive to the destination.
- Include directions for the return trip from the destination back to the hotel.
- In directions to the airport, include gas stations along the route.
- Check and double check. Test drive the routes and be on the lookout for one-way streets, tollbooths, road construction and dangerous parts of town. (When helping tourists find their way, sometimes it's better to provide a slightly longer route, rather than directing them through dicey neighborhoods or confusing interchanges.)
- When printing directions for a museum, salon, or place of worship, it's helpful to include the hours of operation or the times of services.
- Have walking directions preprinted for popular places near the hotel, including information regarding areas where walking is not advisable.

Direction cards from the airport(s) and railroad terminals may be sent out with hotel reservations and confirmations.

Preprinted direction cards are only a tool, designed to enhance service levels. They are not meant to replace the human touch of carefully walking the guest through the directions. To simply hand a guest the card, saying, "Here ya go" just doesn't cut it!

When giving directions, you will need three items: a map, highlighter and direction card. Read the directions to the guest while marking off the route on the map with a highlighter. After providing the directions, check with your guests to ensure they understand fully. It helps to look them in the eye and to be attentive to any body language that indicates they are confused. Even though they may have heard every word you said, there's no guarantee they completely understood what you meant. Sometimes, the instructions need to be broken down into bite-size pieces.

After going over directions with a couple from South America for nearly 20 minutes, a concierge I know was still not convinced they understood. When he stopped to ask them if they were clear on what he had just said, they looked confused and asked, "Are left and right the same here?"

REQUESTS FOR DIRECTIONS TO THE HOTEL

Telephone requests for directions to the hotel don't necessarily require the service of the concierge personally. To assist others in the hotel to provide this information, the concierge should prepare directions to the hotel from all frequently requested sources, such as the airport(s), railroad terminals and major arteries. This information can then be passed on to other departments, such as communications, security, the front desk and bell and door staff. These departments can easily supply directions to the hotel, provided that they have clear, reliable information.

When the call is directed to the concierge, he or she should handle the request, providing clear directions from the guest's point of origin.

Check to ensure the caller has paper and pencil available before beginning to provide the information, to avoid the need to repeat yourself.

Directions to the hotel from various points of origin should also be available in a version that can be easily e-mailed, if the caller prefers. Be prepared for the guests on the way to the hotel, who call from their cars and ask to be lead to the hotel turn by turn. The concierge should remain patient and calm under these circumstances and aware of any unusual construction or weather conditions that may alter normal routes.

BABY-SITTING AND CHILDCARE

Guests request babysitting services regularly, though most parents experience at least some anxiety about leaving their children in a strange place with people they don't know. I don't think I ever booked a babysitter without the parents expressing some degree of concern. They were afraid to leave their child in the company of a stranger and wanted assurance that I had used the sitter in the past and found him or her reliable. For this reason, childcare requests require extra sensitivity. It is vital for the concierge to project comfort, compassion and confidence when assuring guests their children will be in the care of a reliable and responsible sitter.

The concierge should be well prepared with a list of available sitters who are trustworthy, reliable and who genuinely enjoy being with children. After all, children are guests too, and they should be as well cared for as their parents, by a loving and competent professional. Reliability is equally important. One unfortunate possibility that can arise if the babysitter doesn't arrive on time – or at all – is that the concierge finds him or herself in the position of babysitter! When using a sitter often, his or her documentation should be kept on file. Children of different ages can necessitate sitters with different skill sets, so a well-prepared concierge has a computer file divided into qualified providers who are appropriate for the care of infants, toddlers and school-aged children.

Most cities have bonded agencies specializing in babysitting and childcare services. Provided that good relationships have been developed with these agencies, the concierge is able to make one telephone call to the proper agency, which will take it from there. A bonded company has secured funds, which are controlled by the state and available for consumers' claims against the company. This money is directly available for complainants for various reasons, as controlled by a state agency. Essentially, this creates an additional guarantee that the services will be provided exactly as stated in the contract.

Information Needed When Booking a Babysitter:

- Name of guest
- Room number
- Date and time of request
- Duration
- Number of children
- Age and gender of children

The concierge needs to inform the guest of the cost involved in booking a babysitter, as well as any special requirements, which may include a minimum number of hours, parking or transportation charges and extra charges for a group of children or for a group from more than one family. Each city and each agency has its own regulations, and it is important for the concierge to become familiar with those that apply in their city. Guests are typically responsible for paying babysitters directly. However, in some luxury hotels, the guest simply signs for the sitter, and the cost is added to their room bill.

For liability reasons, many hotels don't allow concierges to book babysitters. Instead, they are equipped to provide a list of two or more licensed and bonded services to choose from. The guest then books the sitter directly. This information needs to be kept up-to-date and readily available on the computer to print out for guests.

EXTENDED CHILDCARE

There are cases when children travel with working parents, and the need for childcare is not as simple as supplying a sitter for a few hours in the evening. I have been asked to arrange for entertaining and taking care of a seven-year-old boy for four days, while his father coordinated a symposium at the hotel. Options exist for such requests and need to be researched by the concierge in his or her city.

For an additional fee, some resort hotels are equipped with in-house childcare facilities. Although such services don't usually fall under the umbrella of the concierge, one must be aware of such programs and be able to enlighten interested guests.

PET CARE

Some hotels are pet friendly, allowing canine and feline guests to stay with their human companions. Four Seasons Resorts and Hotels, for instance, are known for their pet-friendly policies. The amenities provided in a room where a pet is staying include a pet pillow, food and water bowls, squeaky toys and a list of local veterinarians. Feline guests are provided litter and a litter box. These properties even offer a room-service menu for pets!

Of course, not all hotels cater to pets to such an extent. There may also be maximum weight limits, e.g., allowing only pets weighing less than 15 pounds, as well as regulations, such as requiring pets to be supervised in the room at all times. The concierge may be called upon to arrange for pet sitters or ask a co-worker, such as a member of the bell staff, to walk a guest's dog. Concierges even occasionally find themselves on the other end of a leash! If the hotel does not allow pets on the premises, the concierge should be able to provide a list of reliable pet-care options and veterinarians in his or her city.

ITINERARIES

The concierge is often called upon to create itineraries for honeymoons, engagements, anniversaries, reunions, birthdays and so on.

A nervous guest once approached me, explaining that he had been estranged from his wife for three months. They were scheduled to meet to determine if it was possible to reconcile their differences, and he wanted a romantic itinerary that suited the occasion. I planned an entire weekend full of idyllic events, including a picnic at a secluded spot and even brought in my own picnic basket for him to use. The next year, on the anniversary of their reconciliation, they sent me a note of thanks for helping them save their marriage.

A concierge friend in San Francisco helped plan an engagement and arranged for the gentleman to propose on videotape. She scheduled a limousine to pick up his girlfriend and take her to a restaurant in Sausalito, just over the Golden Gate Bridge. In the middle of the bridge, the driver started the tape. On the other side, the limo stopped at the overlook to pick up the waiting and expectant prospective fiancé. She said yes.

An example of a guest itinerary. Since it is stored in the computer, it is accessible to the entire staff.

Vivi's Hideaway

Itinerary for Mrs. Isrow

The following Itinerary has been created for your convenience. If you have any questions please contact the Concierge at (818) 263-8993. Thank you. Adam Isrow

Date:	**Thursday, November 04, 2010**
Time:	**10:00 AM**
Task:	Massage
Type of Service:	Swedish
Preference:	Female
Comments:	We will have extra towels prepared as you requested.

Date:	**Thursday, November 04, 2010**
Time:	**8:15 PM**
Task:	Restaurant Reservation
Vendor:	Crustacean
Vendor Address:	9646 S Santa Monica Blvd,Beverly Hills, CA 90210
Vendor Phone:	310-205-8990
# People:	2
Comments:	Have a wonderful anniversary celebration!

Date:	**Friday, November 05, 2010**
Time:	**7:30 PM**
Task:	Restaurant Reservation
Vendor:	Il Cielo Italian Gardens
Vendor Address:	9018 Burton Way,Beverly Hills, CA 90211-1618
Cross Streets:	Burton Way and Almont Dr
Vendor Phone:	310-276-9990
# People:	4

Prepared: 11/9/2010 2:17 PM Page 1 of 1

15433 Ventura Blvd., Sherman Oaks, CA 91403
Telephone: 818.263.8993 Facsimile: 818.263.8998
www.miamiworldcenter.com

Creating itineraries requires great attention to details and, at times, help from fellow concierges. The following is an e-mail from an American concierge to a concierge in Paris, regarding a special itinerary for a honeymooning couple:

> *The couple will arrive at 7:00 a.m., and, after resting, they would like to book a late lunch at Jules Verne, nonsmoking, at about 2:30 p.m. Could you verify that there is a prix-fixe luncheon available?*
>
> *On the following day, for dinner and dancing, they would like to dine on the Bateau Mouche. Is black tie appropriate?*
>
> *Next day, can they just attend a show, or do you recommend dinner and a show? How is the food?*

On their last day, they are open to your suggestions for a memorable and romantic dinner. They asked about Laserre. Do you think it's too stuffy? Do you recommend it for lunch?

The couple want a wonderful and memorable honeymoon, but they don't want to go overboard with money. Please let me know your thoughts ASAP.

Thanks!

The return e-mail verified every detail and included even more exhaustive information and suggestions. The entire process took less than 12 hours.

TOURS

Depending on the city, recommending and organizing tours for guests can be a significant part of the work of the concierge. The concierge should be familiar with the variety of tours available, the points of interest surrounding the city and the companies that service those areas. When available, brochures should be kept handy at the concierge desk. As explained in previous chapters, it is helpful if the concierge has had personal experiences with the tours, so that the information provided the guests is correct and clear, as well as enthusiastically delivered.

People interested in taking tours are usually on vacation, and they appreciate a full explanation from a person who is obviously interested in and familiar with the area. While enthusiastic and brimming with ideas, the concierge should not give too many options. It is best to present two or three of the most popular attractions and the best companies handling those sites. If possible, guests should be given time to digest the possibilities before they arrive at a decision. Concierge departments are superior to city tourism centers, as they make a special effort to "read" their guests and make specific recommendations based on their personalities and interests. Information centers can feel impersonal and present a dizzying array of possibilities, from highbrow tours to activities for pre-school children. In short: Information overload!

To cater to every taste, concierges need to be aware of customizable and offbeat tours, as well as the more traditional fare. For example, in New York City and Chicago, there are various "Mafia tours," which guide tourists through areas where mobster history was made. Many cities also offer ghost-spotting jaunts, such as Washington D.C.'s Capital Hauntings.

A concierge in Chicago remembers preparing a detailed itinerary for a television personality and his girlfriend. The gentleman wanted to be met by a limo and driven to the hotel. He approved the charges for a violinist to play Italian music and requested an Italian meal, preferably lasagna with salad, bread and dessert. He asked that the chef prepare a sweet potato pie

and wanted a bottle of red wine and apple juice. The meal was to be waiting for the couple in their suite with candles lit and the lights dimmed.

Obtaining information regarding the availability of tours and confirming them is generally done online. Methods of payment can vary, and some companies require that deposits be made prior to the tour.

Some excursions may involve various requirements. It is incumbent on the concierge to be aware of them and clearly convey them to the guests. For instance, if a guest wants to take a helicopter tour, he or she will need a government-issued ID.

More common, however, are requests for visitors to see local well-known landmarks and points of interest. It is advisable, therefore, for the concierge to prepare several well-constructed itineraries in advance. It's also helpful to group itineraries into general categories, such as those suitable for large groups, senior citizens, newlyweds, activities for children, art lovers, antique lovers, shoppers, etc. This being said, the concierge should also always be prepared to create very personal itineraries for special guests. (More about prepared itineraries in CHAPTER 11)

TICKETS

Obtaining tickets for guests can be an involved or an easy process, depending on the request and the popularity of the event requested. The sale of theater and event tickets is subject to local and state laws and varies from area to area. In some states, for instance, ticket brokers are completely illegal, so it's important to know the legitimate options in your city. Following are the various ways tickets may be secured.

THE BOX OFFICE

Obtaining tickets at the box office is time consuming and requires the concierge or a reliable messenger to go in person to the box office, wait in line and purchase the desired tickets. It's important to note that there is often a difference between the theater box office and the theater company itself. As an example, a theater organization such as Schuberts may have control over tickets. A production company, such as Cameron Macintosh Productions in New York, may also be a source. In some cities, there are companies with special concierge hotlines, while tag systems may also be established to facilitate the process.

Regardless of the method used, relationships between concierges and theaters are delicate and must be dealt with respectfully.

Creating a Tag System (Voucher System)

A tag system is an excellent method of purchasing tickets, which requires a good working relationship between the concierge and the theater box office. To initiate the process, the concierge calls the box-office manager and requests that a tag system be established. This means that the concierge is able to call the box office directly at any time and order tickets by telephone.

When this system is used, the guest is given a tag receipt (voucher), which they, in turn, present to the box office prior to the performance. They are then given the tickets. The theater bills the concierge department on a weekly basis for all tickets purchased via the tag system. It is then the concierge's responsibility to exert gentle influence on the accounting department to make sure that these bills are paid on time. Promptly paid bills go a long way to cementing good relations.

All tags must have a number, which is the only way for the theater to know they are talking to the correct guest. It also facilitates accounting. Tags must also explain clearly that tickets are nonrefundable and that there is a service charge. The only way in which guests may avoid service charges is by purchasing tickets themselves through the box office.

Once a tag system has been established, the concierge needs to:

- Obtain the guest request and alternatives to his or her first choice.
- Call the theater.
- Give the guest's name and tag number, number of tickets needed, date of performance and seating preference.
- Record the name of the person contacted at the theater and/or get a ticket-confirmation number.
- Collect payment (room charge, cash or credit card).
- Give the appropriate portion of the tag to the guest.
- Keep the concierge's portion of the tag for the bookkeeping needed for verification of charges.

Using a tag system is easy and less expensive than using a ticket broker. One telephone call does the trick. However, not all box-office managers are willing to establish tag systems. Some feel that it requires too much effort on their part, too much paperwork and an undue load on their small staff. Others may require that the hotel put up a bond (guarantee) before allowing sales through a tag system.

ONLINE TICKET OUTLETS

Another method is to purchase the tickets through a sales and distribution company such as Ticketmaster®, which sells many of its tickets online, some by phone and some at its many ticket outlets. Ticketmaster and similar outlets, such as Telecharge.com and StubHub, are large, computerized companies that act as agents for a wide variety of venues. These online outlets charge a modest fee, often offering a real-time, live view of the seat maps, so one can actually see the seat before selecting it. Some hotels have their own Ticketmaster account, allowing for easier access.

While it may seem as if purchasing tickets on line would be the hassle-free way, this is not always the case, as the process has become quite complicated. For instance, many sites require extensive credit-card information, which the non-cardholder (such as the concierge) may not have at his or her fingertips. Understandably, these services are taking measures to prevent fraud, but it makes for a cumbersome process. In addition, at least one of the online services "times out," if one is not quick enough in entering the information, taking the user back to square one. A concierge I know became so frustrated that he uses online services only when the guests are standing in front of him to field any questions that might arise.

To be on the safe side, call the box office to confirm the information given online is accurate.

TICKET BROKERS

In locations where such services are legal, ticket brokers purchase tickets in advance through subscription arrangements or via individual sales. In so doing, they have access to tickets on an as-needed basis for last-minute requests or for obscure shows. They charge brokerage fees for their services, which can be substantially higher than the face value of the ticket purchase price. When using brokers, it's especially important to pass exact price information along to the guests.

Brokers' prices are justifiably higher, because they provide an invaluable service, especially since many requests to the concierge come at the last minute when box offices are sold out. Brokers tend to supply the best seats, since they have carefully cultivated long-term relationships. This is a marvelous service, but pricey for the guest.

It's important to use only established and reliable ticket brokers, avoiding classified ads (print or online) and people selling tickets on the street.

A concierge at an elegant hotel in a big city purchased two tickets from a man who strolled into the lobby, said he couldn't use the tickets, and wanted to sell them. The concierge bought the tickets (to the opera) and, in turn, sold them to a guest. When the guest arrived at the opera and were taken to their seats, they were met by a policeman and escorted out. The tickets they purchased had belonged to a season-ticket subscriber from whom they'd been stolen. That concierge, by the way, is no longer employed as a concierge.

To find ticket brokers, concierges generally check the Internet, classified yellow pages, fellow concierges or their box-office contacts. It's important to always check brokers' references and their longevity in the business. It's tempting to overestimate the profitability of ticket brokers, but keep in mind that they take expensive risks in buying tickets in advance. They predicate their purchasing policy on the premise that the venue will be popular and the tickets in demand, which may or may not ultimately be the case. Different brokers specialize in different types of tickets. One may be well connected for sporting events, while another has excellent opera or symphony availabilities.

HALF-PRICE TICKET BOOTHS

Some cities have half-price ticket booths, which make tickets available on the day of the performance. Many of these services deal with cash only and offer limited seating choices. The concierge may direct guests to this type of service if asked, but since they frequently involve long waits, the concierge normally does not handle such a service personally.

WHEN GUESTS REQUEST TICKETS

In general, obtaining tickets can be challenging, since it requires attending to detail, establishing exact parameters and being clear on prices and refund policies. When securing tickets for guests, the concierge should first get the guest's preference for the date and seating, while always obtaining alternatives, in the event the first choice is not available. In addition, the concierge should clarify the method for payment: room charge, credit or cash. ***It is also imperative that the concierge inform the guest of the policies concerning the purchase of tickets, particularly that tickets are not refundable under any circumstances.***

Because ticket purchases are not refundable, it's necessary to obtain permission from the guest to purchase seats within an established price range. A guest may ask for the best seats in the house, but at the time the tickets are purchased, only the balcony may be available. The concierge needs to be clear about what will be acceptable to the guest. Some people insist on one of the first ten rows-center, whereas others are more flexible with seating.

Always obtain the guest's signature in establishing permission to act on their behalf. This may be done on a room charge slip for guests who have already checked in to the hotel. When the guest inquires as to ticket availability only, the concierge should explain that the information may change from hour to hour when providing the information.

Before handing tickets over to guests, the concierge should open the envelope and look at the contents or download the e-mail confirmation. The tickets should be checked to make certain they are for the correct performance on the correct date and that the seating is acceptable.

When booking theater and event tickets, ask guests about their dinner and transportation plans. This is an excellent opportunity to demonstrate caring and enhance their experience with special recommendations for exciting dining or limousine service.

"EATING" TICKETS

"Eating" tickets is a term used in the entertainment industry for absorbing the costs of tickets that are not used. It can happen to a concierge who is careless or too busy to pay attention to details, but it usually happens only once, as "eating" tickets always leaves a bad taste in your mouth!

I once bought six tickets to a performance of Liza Minelli for a Saturday night. When the guests looked at the tickets, they were furious because they claimed they'd only wanted to see a Friday performance. An old friend advised me to put a generous dab of mustard on the tickets, add some lettuce and a little salt and pepper to make "eating" them more palatable. It was a hard lesson, but one I never needed to repeat. Paying attention, repeating the request and securing total agreement from the guest as to date and seating preferences prevents having to eat tickets.

It's not unusual for future guests holding upcoming reservations at the hotel to call or e-mail requesting information for ticket availability and/or purchase prior to their arrival. However, in this instance, it's necessary to exercise caution. The expectation may be that the concierge will go ahead and purchase the tickets, which would be charged to the room upon arrival, yet this presents a raft of logistical challenges. Most ticket purchases require immediate action and tickets must be paid for at the point of purchase, requiring cash or a personal credit card. Since the guest is not actually staying at the hotel at that moment, the concierge must assume the responsibility of payment, which may take place in several ways:

- Ideally, the concierge would use the guest's credit card number, though this may not be possible. In this case, the concierge needs to obtain all of the necessary credit-card information.
- If time permits, the concierge may ask the guest to send a check.
- The hotel may be willing to "front" the amount to purchase the tickets, but this necessitates an inordinate amount of bookkeeping and check writing.
- The concierge may use his or her own credit card or cash and be reimbursed by the guest when the person arrives. Obviously, this is advisable only if the guest is well known and has a prior record of reliability.

Because tickets are not refundable, a change in plans can cause big dilemmas. One way to avoid problems is to get the guest's request and approval in writing. With the convenience of faxing and e-mail, it's simple for the concierge to obtain everything needed to assure clarity. It's necessary to have the exact date for which the tickets are requested, along with seating preference, complete credit card information, and a written disclaimer that the guest is aware and in agreement with the policy that the tickets are nonrefundable. The following is an example, which may be faxed or e-mailed:

Dear Concierge,

I am requesting four tickets to see "Les Miserables" on Saturday, August 16, 2011. The ticket price should not exceed $325 per ticket. I understand that the tickets are nonrefundable.

My credit card number is Mastercard 000-0000-0000-0000, expiring on 8/2012, CVC code 000. This may be used in the event that my plans change. If my plans do not change, I understand that the charge for the tickets will be applied to my guest room.

In the event you require any additional information or clarification, my cell phone number is (000) 000-0000.

Thank you.

Sincerely,
(signature of guest)
(Typed name and address)

While this may seem like "overkill," it's better to be safe than sorry. It's best that everyone has a clear understanding, because when dealing with items as expensive as tickets, clarity is essential.

FACIALS, MANICURES, PEDICURES, HAIRDRESSING AND MASSAGE

If the hotel does not offer spa and salon services, the concierge should be aware of several reputable establishments that provide them and have information on hand to give to guests. As with all recommendations, referrals for these services should be researched in advance and good relationships established. Concierges are continuously judged by the value of their recommendations, and a positive guest experience is the ultimate priority.

In many hotels, however, the spa is an integral part of the hotel experience. In such cases, the concierge needs to work closely with the spa staff to ensure that all guests who use the spa receive a memorable experience that meets their individual needs. This means the concierge should be familiar with all spa and salon services in order to explain the offerings fully and recommend them for each specific guest. Hopefully, the salon and spa manager sees the benefit of inviting concierges to sample their services, benefiting both the guest and the concierge, after a long day's work.

Having a spa and salon service in the hotel makes life simple and creates an excellent opportunity for generating business. However, a guest may request a specialty service, such as hair weaving, that the hotel's salon cannot accommodate. In these cases, it's necessary to look outside the hotel.

When booking appointments, the concierge should:

- Contact the salon or spa.
- Reserve the service(s) requested.
- Print out the confirmation, including the name of the establishment (if outside the hotel), the date and time, the therapist's, stylist's or technician's name and if needed, a map and directions.

MASSAGES

For massages, the concierge needs to be aware of both in-room and spa or massage-studio options. In-room massages are more expensive, so it's important that the concierge explain the exact cost and whether or not the tip is included. Though massage therapists usually provide their own tables, the housekeeping department may also need to be notified if sheets or towels are needed – especially when booking massage therapists apart from those directly associated with the hotel's spa.

There are times when the concierge is asked to book an in-room "massage," when the guest is actually requesting an erotic experience. (This presents another opportunity for concierges to "read" their guests!) In such cases, it's the responsibility of the concierge to make sure the guest is looking for a legitimate relaxation- or health-related massage. If it becomes clear that the guest is inclined otherwise, the concierge needs to explain that the hotel does not sanction or recommend such services. In most cities, the Internet or telephone classified pages will offer this information and the concierge can direct the guest to contact them directly.

Often, guests don't think about having a massage until the last minute, so the concierge needs to be aware of practitioners who cater to spur-of-the-moment calls and are able to provide in-room service at odd hours. The concierge can work with the spa in the hotel to obtain a list of these therapists. When using services outside of the hotel, the chief concierge should determine which licensed and insured professionals to use. Copies of their licenses and proof of insurance should be kept on file, along with additional information, including the gender of the therapists, their areas of expertise (Swedish massage, deep tissue, etc.).

SHIPPING

Shipping is not necessarily a difficult task, but problems do arise, and it can be an extremely detailed and time-consuming operation. Most guests underestimate the process and want to simply drop the package at the concierge desk as they fly out the door. This presents difficulties, since it makes it necessary for concierges to think on their feet, while quickly gathering the necessary information from their hurried guests to expedite the shipping arrangements without delay.

Guests often assume their responsibilities are over once the package is handed off, however, making shipping arrangements does involve some participation on their part. As for concierges, they need to understand the options available when shipping packages and be informed about the specific requirements particular to each option.

Handling shipping tasks requires that the concierge department work closely with the hotel's shipping and receiving department. Although it may seem as though this department should handle everything in this arena, it is the concierge's responsibility to interact with guests and subsequently deal with the shipping and receiving department on their behalf. (Remember, the buck stops at the concierge desk.) The influx of packages to be shipped varies from day to day. There are times when several days may pass without one request for shipping and others when the concierge desk resembles a loading dock. When it rains it pours.

SHIPPING INTERNATIONALLY

When shipping a package overseas, the concierge should anticipate a variety of possible situations. For instance, the concierge must know the contents of the package(s) and its value in order to complete the appropriate custom forms and insure the shipment for the proper amount. Concierges should never simply guess about the contents of a package. If the parcel is opened at customs and the information is incorrect, the package may be confiscated and never reach its destination.

It's also important to keep in mind that language barriers can result in miscommunications, so concierges need to verify the information several times with the guest, if they are at all unclear.

> *I know of one incident when a foreign guest dashed out the door, calling out the value of the contents of her package (an antique mirror) over her shoulder. The concierge mistook $3,000 for $30,000, which presented a serious problem with customs at the other end.*

Checking the contents of packages can sometimes resemble the opening of Pandora's box, even before the shipment leaves the hotel.

> *A concierge received a box from a guest marked "Souvenirs." When checking the contents for more detailed information, he discovered that the box contained towels, robes, ashtrays and other "souvenirs" that the guest had taken from his hotel room. The concierge removed the hotel's property and shipped the box, now containing two T-shirts and a polite note explaining hotel policy regarding room amenities.*

As with all packages, information pertaining to international shipments is logged into the computer, including the method of payment – whether by cash, check or room charge. The cost of shipment might include surcharges, customs duty, etc. If the accounting department needs to be involved, as would be the case in a paid out, they also need to be provided with the information.

International Forms

When shipping packages internationally, a form known as a commercial invoice is required. It must be filled out completely and signed by the person shipping the package – not by the concierge. Once the form has been completed (minus the signature), as many as five copies must be made. Depending on the shipping company, the guest may need to sign each copy individually, as original signatures may be required on every copy.

These regulations must be adhered to strictly. Such attention to detail may seem like an unnecessary hassle and even ruffle a guest's feather or two. However, it is nonetheless a necessity and should be politely, though firmly, explained to the guest.

> *A guest handed me a box filled with glass bottles of salsa sauce and told me to ship them to Australia. I politely explained that I would need to call the airfreight company to be clear about the rules for shipping food overseas. The guest was infuriated. She insisted that other hotels handled such requests all the time. She argued with her husband about the sauce, about the shipping, about me, about the hotel, about almost everything. They wouldn't wait for a proper answer and it was uncomfortable, but I knew I couldn't just ship the package without knowing the rules.*

Airfreight Companies

Many private companies (such as Federal Express, UPS and DHL) ship international packages, and they all have similar weight/measurement restrictions to those of the U.S. Postal Service. They require special international labels and are subject to the same customs and insurance procedures.

The concierge should keep forms from each of the companies commonly used, along with packing material that meets their specifications. It is also advisable to double check that the destination requested is, in fact, served by the carrier chosen.

DOMESTIC PACKAGES

Depending on guests' preferences and time constraints, packages may be shipped through a variety of carriers, of which the U.S. Postal Service, UPS, Federal Express and DHL are examples. It is the responsibility of the concierge to check the necessary shipping forms for accuracy, as guests will often forget to record information, such as the date or the recipient's telephone number. As with many of the other tasks performed by the concierge, it's all about details, details, details . . .

> Some companies, Federal Express for example, will not deliver packages to Post Office Boxes™. If the concierge accepts a package without checking and later discovers it's addressed to a PO box, it becomes necessary to contact the guest to obtain a street address, which often results in a delayed shipment.

As with international shipments, all domestic mailings should be logged into the computer, with the method of payment fully established. This makes tracking easier for accounting purposes and also makes it simpler to locate a lost package. It's a good idea to develop a regular pickup schedule with the most frequently used shipping services. This avoids having to call for each package.

There is a specific form to use when a guest wishes to use UPS. It is important to include a label with the form, so that both may be filled out correctly by the guest and checked by the concierge. It's especially important to obtain correct credit-card information, even if the guest has requested that the charges be added to the room account. In some instances, charges may not be posted until the guest has checked out, in which case, his or her credit card must be charged.

As a customer service, fine hotels provide package wrapping along with shipping services. In the case of fragile items or expensive paintings, it is recommended that a professional shipping service be used. Each city has specialists that deal in shipping delicate items, such as fine art and wine, and may be found on the Internet.

EMERGENCY PACKAGES

When something absolutely, positively has to get there "yesterday," shipping services are available that specialize in urgent situations – on a 24-hour basis. These services are not used often, but when they are needed, they're a lifesaver. One such method is UPS Express Critical®, which handles virtually everything and anything and does it reliably and consistently. In these situations, it is especially important to ensure that all the information is accurate, complete and logged into the computer. The concierge should also verify exactly when the guest needs the package to arrive, e.g., "I understand you want the box to arrive on Tuesday, March 23, before noon Pacific Time."

MESSENGER SERVICES

Some concierge requests involve goods that must be obtained locally, from outside the hotel and delivered to the guest. European concierge departments are staffed with pageboys, whose job it is to "run around" for hotel guests. In the United States, however, very few concierge desks are equipped with "legs," and getting the job done may be challenging. In many cases, concierges perform the errands on their lunch hours or after their normally scheduled shifts. In other cases, an outside messenger service is engaged. In such situations, a messenger fee is usually added to the price of the item. Waiting in line for 25 minutes to purchase theater tickets or waiting in a crowded post office to insure an international package definitely warrants a few dollars' service charge.

When using a messenger service, the following information should be entered into the computer.

- Complete and accurate information, as to the pick-up destination, including suite number, if needed.
- The exact charges.
- Arrangement for payment by the guest by cash, a room charge, or credit card.

- The estimated time the pickup and delivery will take.

For seven years, pageboy chores were no problem, because a wonderful elderly gentleman on a fixed income stopped by the desk every morning at 10:00 to see if we needed anything. He then checked with us throughout the day to determine when we had a job for him. Edward earned a $5 runner's fee each time he performed a task. He enjoyed getting out and about, and it saved us an enormous amount of aggravation.

FAXING

Depending on the size of the hotel and the business facilities available, the concierge may be called upon to send faxes. This is as simple as making a telephone call, once the concierge has learned how to operate the hotel fax machine or the faxing function of the all-in-one printer. Because the content of the faxed material may be confidential, it's important to ask guests if they would like the material returned to them or destroyed after it has been faxed.

The concierge may also be responsible for receiving faxes and ensuring they are promptly delivered to hotel guests. In this case, too, the material may be sensitive or confidential, so the fax should be delivered directly to its intended recipient. While concierges were once inundated with faxes, it has become much less common, with the advent of scanning and e-mail.

POSTAGE STAMPS

The concierge is often called upon to supply postage stamps for hotel guests. One of the best ways to ensure stamps are available at the concierge desk is to purchase them from the head cashier, who typically buys them in bulk. The concierge can then requisition $100 to $200 worth of stamps from the cashier to keep on hand and provide to guests, as needed. On the other hand, some concierge desks have postage-metering machines, which generate the postage needed, the amount of which is then charged to the guest's room account. At some hotels, the concierges are responsible for purchasing stamps directly from the U.S. Postal Service. Fortunately, this no longer requires waiting in line at the post office, as stamps can now be easily purchased online.

Stamps may be conveniently stored in a small, sturdy logbook. The first page should contain a chart, listing the current pricing of stamps, so the concierge doesn't need to memorize the denominations. Each denomination is then filed in its own section with a tab to indicate the amount.

The concierge also needs access to an accurate scale, to weigh letters and packages and apply the correct postage. Most office-product companies offer an excellent selection of these scales, with updated charts when postage rates change.

The U.S. Postal Service currently has regulations that require special handling of stamped envelopes and packages weighing in excess of 13 ounces. The concierge should always be up-to-date on such regulations and when in doubt, consult their website (USPS.com) for information.

MAKING CHANGE

As indicated in CHAPTER 5, concierges need to have a petty-cash bank for making change and making inexpensive purchases. Sometimes, this is arranged through the accounting department, while other concierges maintain their own to simplify the process. When making change for guests, the amount should be counted carefully and then counted back aloud to the guest.

You might want to have a counterfeit-banknote-detection pen at the desk to ensure that bills in large denominations are legitimate. These pens contain special iodine-based ink that can detect counterfeit bills. They are available at most office-product stores or on the Internet.

THE CONCIERGE: NEIGHBORHOOD EXPERT AND AMBASSADOR

The requests outlined in this chapter are by no means an exclusive list, as guest needs run the gamut from photo printing to notary services to doctor appointments. Since most guests prefer to walk, rather than negotiate strange areas by car or public transportation, it pays to know the neighborhood surrounding the hotel inside and out.

Concierges continually respond to questions that relate to the immediate area surrounding their hotels. Because businesses come and go, it's imperative that concierges are "in the know" about all the activities taking place within a three- to four-block radius. Nothing accomplishes this quite as well as taking a walk once or twice a month, as a little reconnaissance mission. It's also a great opportunity to leave your business cards with new establishments in the neighborhood and stay in touch with long-established contacts and resources. Take notes on anything you find new and interesting. You might even consider taking along a small camera or video recorder to share the up-to-the-minute local scene with your fellow concierges.

NEGOTIATING THE LEGALITIES OF "ROUTINE" REQUESTS

The topic of hotel law is sufficiently involved to comprise a separate book entirely. It also varies from hotel to hotel and locality to locality. One universal law, however, is that every company with whom the concierge works should be fully licensed and insured.

The concierge also needs to be aware of union regulations that dictate the parameters within which the concierge may act to accommodate a guest. In some cases, for instance, even the most basic electronic requests must be met by a member of the local electricians' union. When in doubt about such matters, the concierge should contact the human resources or legal department for direction.

Last but not least, concierges need to maintain open lines of communications with the risk-management department, legal counsel and executive staff to be absolutely clear as to what they may safely offer to their guests. This is imperative to ensure the wellbeing of their guests and protect their hotels from litigation.

Even seemingly innocent situations can result in serious problems. It has been determined, for instance, that concierges should not *specifically* recommend a jogging or walking trail. Because of a precedent-setting suit involving personal injury, concierges are now limited to offering general information only.

MUNDANE CAN BE MAGIC

IN THIS CHAPTER, I have tried to include the most important information regarding the most common guest requests. As illustrated in previous chapters, there are bound to be requests that fall outside – sometimes "waaaay" outside – the routine and ordinary. In the latter case, the concierge is called upon to quickly don his or her "wizard cap" and make magic happen. By the same token, the concierge's magic wand can easily sweep over even the most routine of situations and create magical experiences. All in all, every situation encountered by the concierge can be approached with both the artfulness and technical knowledge that create a wonderful experience their guest will never forget.

CHAPTER EIGHT

8

Working With Restaurants

OBJECTIVES

The following chapter will equip readers to:

Build rapport and foster influential relationships with restaurant staff.

Appreciate the importance of their role in generating income for their in-house restaurants.

Recognize the value that technology adds to the convenience of reservations and information management

Utilize criteria for evaluating restaurant suitability

Understand the intricate care and detail involved in recommending appropriate restaurants.

Experiment with a few role-play examples.

RELATIONSHIPS

RELATIONSHIPS CONCIERGES DEVELOP with restaurant owners, maîtres d', managers and reservationists are very personal and fundamental to the success of a concierge department. It is actually one of the most important and enduring business relationships that exists in the field. If maintained with skill, they are solid, two-way relationships, based on mutual respect, goodwill and the desire to be of help to each other.

As with many other aspects of the job of concierge, there can be challenges. Restaurants that don't take reservations, for instance, can be frustrating and a concierge may find it difficult to cultivate relationships with them. It's not easy to explain to eager guests that their chance of being served at a reasonable time cannot be predicted. Furthermore, concierges feel powerless when unable to persuade their contact at the restaurant to relinquish a table without a wait. On the other hand, it's sometimes possible to break through the barrier and develop a rapport that invites compromise and fosters better service to guests.

> *A San Francisco restaurant has a policy of not taking reservations, yet they've been farsighted enough to appreciate the value in cultivating goodwill and cooperation among hotel concierges. In this spirit, they have devised a way to offer preferential treatment without the formality of taking a reservation. Concierges give the guests their business card to present to the restaurant's host or hostess, and in this way they are alerted to put that guest at the top of the waiting list. Simple solution. Good relationship. Everyone wins.*

The restaurant business is extremely competitive. A restaurant's success is based not only on a good reputation and good food. Restaurants also depend on continuing goodwill, which results in repeat business. It's in the best interest of restaurateurs to get the attention of concierges and encourage them to experience dining in their establishments. This way, concierges will be able to make enthusiastic recommendations firsthand.

Concierges can affect a restaurant's business significantly. In a large hotel, a concierge may send 300 people out to dine in one evening alone. This is significant on any scale. Since this is so obvious, it always amazes concierges that some restaurants seem uninterested in potential business. Fortunately, these situations are not the norm, and most restaurateurs do appreciate the benefit of having good relationships with concierges and cooperate with them fully.

Sometimes, however, the more trendy restaurants that are overwhelmed with business can find a call from the concierge more of a nuisance than a valued source of continuing business. The concierge may know a dozen restaurants that are more charming, more hospitable, with infinitely better food than the currently "hot" one. However, when guests insist on being accommodated at the city's most popular dining spot, it's best not to try to dissuade them, apart from pointing out any drawbacks, such as noisiness or extended wait times.

Restaurants also count on feedback from concierges. If there is a negative reaction from a guest, it's important to convey that information to the restaurant. In fact, it's the concierge's responsibility to follow up and share guests' opinions, both positive and negative. Honest, but gently delivered, feedback is an integral part of building the relationship.

THE HOTEL RESTAURANT

A close relationship between concierges and the staff at their own hotel's restaurant(s) is essential, as concierges have a great opportunity to generate business in this area. In fact, the concierge has a responsibility to recommend his or her hotel's restaurants to their guests. At the same time, it's incumbent on the concierge to recommend the best possible dining options for each individual guest. Fortunately, these two imperatives are no longer at odds. Today's hotel restaurants are among the most excellent dining choices in many cities, featuring celebrity chefs and five-star fare. For most concierges, it's a pleasure to recommend his or her hotel restaurant and they do so with confidence.

Steering guests toward the hotel's restaurants falls into the category of *"sales is service and service is sales."* Guests enjoy a highly rated and well-located dining experience, while the concierge serves as an ambassador of the hotel in all its aspects and helps contribute to the hotel's bottom line.

Of course, many guests come to the concierge for information and advice about dining outside the hotel, to experience something of the life of the city. The top priority is always to delight the guest by helping manifest the guest's "vision" of a wonderful afternoon or evening. When it is appropriate, however, the concierge should recommend the hotel restaurant as a matter of course. A natural way to open the conversation is: "Have you tried the restaurant here in the hotel? We have a fabulous chef who specializes in . . . " Of course, be sure to have a copy of the menu readily accessible to hand to the guest.

Another effective way to promote the hotel restaurant or bar is to attach a small flyer to theater tickets and confirmation cards for outside restaurants. It might say, for example, "After your evening out, stop at Club 36 for a nightcap and live jazz." The public relations and sales departments can be of great help in producing these materials.

When booking a reservation with a restaurant within the hotel, the concierge should **record it** – either on an electronic spreadsheet or manually – including an estimate of the total bill. These reports can then be presented to management as substantiated evidence that the concierge desk is an invaluable revenue-generating hub.

If a guest has already enjoyed the hotel restaurant(s) and wants a change of pace, a wonderful win/win way to work with your concierge network is to recommend a colleague's hotel restaurant. This will typically result in reciprocity, whereby one's colleagues send their guests to enjoy the restaurant at your hotel.

ENTER TECHNOLOGY

Online tools, such as OpenTable® Concierge (OT Concierge), have considerably changed the way concierges interact with restaurants. This useful site was created by and for concierges, allowing them to:

- Make reservations instantly, and around the clock, at top restaurants.
- Search multiple restaurants by neighborhood, cuisine or price.
- Notify restaurants that you are the referring concierge.
- View, cancel or change reservations in one click.
- Talk to your guests and make reservations simultaneously.
- Print hotel-branded confirmation pages.
- Make reservations, even when the restaurant is closed.

OT Concierge is an extremely useful site on which concierges can efficiently research options and make restaurant reservations at many venues around the world, anytime day or night. It's especially useful when dealing with the guest who calls on a Sunday, asking for a restaurant reservation for a Monday lunch, for a restaurant that's closed on Sundays. You can make the reservation for her critical business luncheon before the restaurant opens, and she can convey the details to her colleagues in the click of a button.

As an incentive to book reservations through their website, OpenTable offers concierges one point for every reservation they book through the site. The points can then be redeemed toward any restaurant in the OpenTable system. At one point, there were questions regarding the ethics of using this system, as concierges were concerned it might be considered a "kickback," which would violate the Les Clefs d'Or Code of Ethics. However, the fact that it is a reward for using the system and is expressed as points to be used at any restaurant has quelled these concerns. It is when a concierge accepts a reward for recommending one restaurant over another that ethical boundaries are crossed.

Amid all the benefits of using the system, however, there is one potentially serious drawback: OT Concierge can reduce the amount of direct contact between the concierge and restaurant staff and possibly undermine these important relationships. The truth of the matter is, however, that no website in the world can take the place of the relationship between concierges and restaurant owners, maître d's and reservationists, which are among the most sacred relationships in our business. Concierges can spend years building these connections at various restaurants! To mitigate this potential downside, all concierges need to continue picking up the phone on a regular basis and connecting with their contacts – whether it's to confirm reservations, request additional services for special occasions or provide valuable feedback. Concierges confirm that OT Concierge never needs to eclipse these friendships. In fact, they report that it allows them even more time to chat with the restaurant staff when making uncomplicated calls, such as the simple business of confirming a reservation.

The points earned through OT Concierge make an excellent gift for doormen, bellmen and the staff at the front desk, as a way to express your appreciation.

Not all restaurants are listed on OT Concierge. If a guest's request is nowhere to be found on their website, search the Internet and pick up the phone.

Staying in direct touch with one's colleagues at restaurants is the most powerful way to remain confident that their establishment is a good recommendation. The reception the concierge receives from the restaurant, whether indifferent or eager to please, will be the same as that experienced by the guest. Therefore, it's important, especially for the new concierge, to make direct contact with the restaurant, to ensure he or she is putting hotel guests in the best of hands.

PERSONAL CONTACT

As just mentioned, while booking reservations online offers convenience, it is vital for the concierge to also stay in touch by phone. Every day, the concierge interacts with a number of "phone friends," who contribute greatly to the value of the services offered by the concierge.

Strong opinions are often formed solely on the basis of effective verbal contact, and this works both ways. Concierges assess establishments based on the reception they receive over the phone. Similarly, opinions of concierges are being formed on the other end of the line, which then become opinions of their hotels and the concierge profession as a whole. For this reason, I've devoted CHAPTER 5 of this book to perfecting one's telephone manner.

This two-way responsibility is so important that many years ago, the Northern California Concierge Association created an award, honoring excellence in this area. They called it "The Golden Phone Award." To demonstrate their appreciation, this honor was given to the maître d' whom concierges felt had the best phone manner. The criteria for winning was not based on the availability of tables at their restaurants, but on politeness, attitude toward concierges and willingness to accommodate them and their guests. Again, this works both ways, and concierges are expected to extend the same level of courtesy.

> *One recipient of the award was William Bridi of the Donatello Restaurant, who was maître d' during a period when the Donatello was consistently full. The restaurant was small and extremely popular. Quite frankly, they didn't need tourist business. Yet, every time a concierge called requesting a table for a guest, William said, "Hold on a minute. Let me try to get them in." Usually, it was impossible, but he never failed to try and always thanked us for calling and for thinking of his restaurant. He would also put our guests' names on a waiting list in the event that a table became available. Wow. That's good service! Even though William couldn't always accommodate us, he said "no" with such style that our association awarded him the Golden Phone Award. Rightly so. It sure beats the blunt response we received from some restaurants that actually did have open tables: "5:30 or 10:30. Which do you want?"*

As strongly evidenced by the above example, *it's not so much what you say, but how you say it that counts.*

PHONE ETIQUETTE

Though I've devoted an entire chapter in the book to this topic, some specific tips are helpful when working with restaurants. When calling a restaurant on behalf of a guest, the concierge should "schmooze" a little. A concierge should always begin with his or her name and the name of the hotel, then ask for the name of the person to whom he or she is speaking.

A pleasant manner should be maintained at all times, and yes, it is important to "schmooze." In other words, be aggressively, but genuinely, pleasant. A genuine, "How are you today?" is just one example of a pleasant opening. Since the concierge will most likely be working with popular restaurants, they're also likely to be quite busy. It's important for the concierge to be understanding of and respectful toward the people at the other end of the line. Be pleasant, but don't consume their time with idle chatter. It's also important to always ask, rather than demand, and remain flexible. The need for flexibility should also be gently conveyed to guests, by explaining that their first choices for time, table preference, etc., may require some adjustment.

If the concierge is reserving a table for a VIP or for a special occasion, such as a honeymoon, it's important to make the details clear to the maître d or reservationist and to reconfirm the details with a follow-up call.

COMPLIMENTARY MEALS

Invitations for complimentary meals are the way in which most concierges learn the necessary in-depth information about restaurants in their cities. Unless hotels give their concierges substantial expense accounts for such "research," (which is rare), accepting complimentary dinners is the only way to become personally knowledgeable. Technology will certainly never take the place of complimentary meals, as concierges need to experience the sights, sounds, tastes, aromas, and "feel" of a restaurant before they can confidently recommend it. Looking at a webpage simply isn't enough. It's just not a good idea to recommend restaurants that are untried personally, unless they have been "investigated" and given a thumbs-up by a trusted colleague.

It's important to note that the concierge is under no obligation to recommend a restaurant in exchange for a complimentary dinner. It's up to the restaurateur to make sure the dining experience is thoroughly enjoyable, since the result is sure to be increased referrals. If the experience proves inadequate, the concierge should not feel obligated to recommend the restaurant. The potential for conflict of interest in this regard is significant. It would be a disaster if guests felt that the concierge was steering them to a restaurant because of what amounts to a "bribe." *A complimentary meal is not a payoff, but a way of staying informed.* This important distinction should be clearly understood by the concierge, the guest and the restaurant management.

PROTOCOL FOR COMPLIMENTARY MEALS

When invited for complimentary meals, concierges always put their best foot forward. It's imperative that they conduct themselves in a manner that reflects positively on themselves, on the hotels they represent and the concierge profession as a whole. To keep it simple, there are basic guidelines. Remember, complimentary meals are not personal gifts. Concierges are invited because they represent a hotel that represents potential business to the restaurant. One must not confuse the pleasure of dining out with the professional nature of the occasion. When invited for a complimentary meal, it's necessary to:

- Always remain professional – in dress and manner.
- Bring your business cards.
- Refrain from ordering expensive wine, rather choosing wines on the lower end of the price list. Better yet, ask the wine steward to make a recommendation.
- Try a variety of items on the menu, as the object of the invitation is to sample. A great way to accomplish this is by ordering small plates and hors d'oeuvres.
- Leave a tip of at least 20 percent of what the bill would have been and be especially gracious to those who serve you.
- Always write a thank-you note.

The concierge must not only sample places once, but somewhat regularly. Chefs come and go. Menus change. Places are bought and sold. Trends disappear and evolve. It's all about staying current. Some restaurants offer concierges standing invitations for complimentary meals. While regular visits are encouraged, the concierge should also take special care not to abuse this privilege and frequent any given restaurant no more than once or twice a year. Additionally, it's dangerous to automatically assume the meal will be complimentary, unless you have been given a certificate or note to that effect. An offhanded remark, such as, "You should stop by for dinner sometime," is not necessarily an invitation for a complimentary meal. You should always be prepared to pay in such cases, if presented with a bill.

The adage, "There's no such thing as a free lunch" can certainly apply to complimentary meals. If the concierge doesn't have an expense account, he or she is responsible for the tip (based on the actual value of the meal), gas, parking, tolls, etc. Just be aware that all this can add up. In addition, it's likely that this aspect of the job will be done on one's own time.

CRITERIA FOR EVALUATING RESTAURANTS

IN GENERAL

Everybody is a critic, as evidenced by the proliferation of restaurant guides such as Zagat®. Being a professional critic, however, requires in-depth knowledge and the ability to make educated judgments. Before making any evaluation, one must gather information systematically and without a preconceived bias. Every aspect of a restaurant should be observed and weighed in the light of personally developed expertise. The methods outlined in this chapter furnish an almost foolproof way to critique objectively.

There is no need to feel pressured to evaluate *every* restaurant in the city, but it is important to sample a variety, especially those within walking distance of the hotel. This process could take years. Start with about three restaurants in each major category.

- Seafood: elegant and casual
- Italian: northern, southern, elegant, trattoria
- French: elegant, classic, country, nouvelle, bistro
- Japanese: sushi, elegant, casual, teppanyaki
- Chinese: Schezwan, Cantonese, elegant, casual, dim sum
- Steakhouse: elegant and casual
- American: new American cuisine, diners, sandwich shops, pizza, delis, the best burger, elegant, barbeque, southern
- Asian: Thai, Korean, Indian, Vietnamese
- Mexican: elegant and casual
- Greek: elegant and casual
- Middle Eastern: elegant and casual
- "Kiddy Cuisine," (e.g., where to find the best hotdog and PB & J)
- Vegetarian, Vegan and Raw

In addition to variations in cuisine, the concierge needs to be aware of other features, such as:

- Views
- Romance and intimacy
- Business atmosphere
- Group business
- Private rooms
- Solo dining
- Historical significance

The concierge is constantly asked for restaurants in areas surrounding major cities, such as the wine country in Northern California, Cape Cod in Boston and the Hamptons in New York. In small cities with fewer choices, the emphasis is on the quality of the dining experience, rather than a great variety of possibilities. It becomes important, therefore, for concierges to concentrate more on making the experience memorable with special touches, such as tables by the window or complimentary wine.

For a richer comprehension of all the options, it's advisable to subscribe to magazines. For instance, *Bon Appétit* is an excellent publication to round out a basic knowledge of food and restaurants. There is also a great deal of information online, on sites such as Zagat.com and Chowhound.com. It's also a good practice to talk with chefs, beginning with the ones in your own hotel. Ask questions about their specialties and their methods. Find out what makes them unique. Share notes with other concierges, too. Gathering information is an ongoing project and a full-time job.

FIRST IMPRESSIONS

How does the restaurant "feel?" Is it uplifting? Is excitement in the air, or is it subdued and subtle. Notice the ambiance, the décor, the linens, china and silverware. Always pay attention to the distance between tables. This is important, especially when recommending a restaurant for a business dinner or romantic evening, where guests may want to converse privately. Check the attention to detail: Are the flowers fresh and uniforms crisp? Are the menus dog-eared and spotted? Is the place spotlessly clean?

How were you greeted? Were you made to feel especially welcome, or were you dealt with as though you were a number? Were you kept waiting without explanation? Were your reservations honored, or did you spend time languishing at the bar?

How were you seated? Was the chair held for you? Were you noticed immediately by your server, or did you have to wait? Was the prevailing tone of the service polite? Aloof? Dignified? Friendly?

BECOMING FULLY INFORMED ABOUT THE RESTAURANT

Observe

Study the menu. Is it simple or complicated? How are the prices? If it is a specialty restaurant, do the dishes represent the best in its category? For example, a seafood restaurant with three varieties of seafood plus chicken, veal and steaks could not be really considered a serious seafood restaurant, even though it may be excellent otherwise. Remember why you are there. Be objectively aware that you will be recommending restaurants to a wide variety of guests. Pay attention. Does the menu entice? Does it stay on one theme, or is it adventurous or eclectic?

Time to Order

Order responsibly. Bear in mind that you are there to critique, so everyone at the table should order different dishes. Choose a variety of foods and sample as broadly as possible.

Notice whether or not the server is accommodating. When selecting dishes, does the server offer assistance? Advice? Are the servers and restaurant flexible in making substitutions? Can they deal with changes? Observe people at other tables and notice how they are being treated. Do other diners appear pleased? Remember that it is unlikely that guests will be treated as well as you are. Restaurants normally go to great pains to impress concierges.

What About Service

How does the food arrive? Is the hot food hot and cold food cold? Is the presentation Impressive? Casual? Homespun? How was the service timed? Did the courses arrive at a comfortable pace? Did you feel rushed? Were you kept waiting too long?

. . . And the Food?

Last but not least, how was the food? Remarkable or just so-so? Admittedly, this is subjective, but it helps to put your personal preferences aside and sample more than one item from the menu. Take notes, especially of those dishes you find particularly memorable. Would this be a place you would want to send an adventurous diner? What about a meat-and-potatoes guest?

How did the overall feeling upon leaving differ from your impressions when entering? Were you pleasantly surprised or gravely disappointed? Will you feel confident when recommending the restaurant? What type(s) of guests might be best suited for this dining experience? Are there any caveats to mention when making the recommendation?

Thanks for Sharing

When returning to the hotel, always share your newfound knowledge with the concierge team, which is typically accomplished by entering your findings in the notes section of your computer program. Share your experience with concierges outside the hotel as well, whether at networking gatherings, over the phone or Internet social-networking groups. You'll be able to learn a great deal that way, too! You might want to copy this page and fill it out to share with colleagues.

MAKING RESTAURANT RECOMMENDATIONS

While the job of recommending where to go and what to do isn't brain surgery or a life-and-death situation, it's still an important responsibility. *Spending people's money and time is a critical responsibitity.* For some guests, a night on the town is a big deal. All experienced concierges can recount stories about people who have deliberated on a dinner reservation for hours and changed their plans several times before settling on a restaurant. In these cases, the concierge probably wants to scream, "It's only a dinner!" but of course, they bite their tongues, smile politely and do their best to accommodate the guest.

Guests will sometimes ask you to book reservations at more than one restaurant in the same timeslot, allowing them to pick one at the last minute. This practice is unethical and unfair to the restaurants and other diners. In such cases, the concierge should politely tell the guest that he or she is unable to do so, but will be happy to make a reservation at one of the restaurants, once the guest's choice has been finalized.

Concierges realize that the choices made about how guests spend their time outside the hotel are a significant part of how people form their opinions about the hotel and its services. It's a little unfair that the hotel and concierges are judged by guests' opinions about outside services. However, this is the reality and the reason concierges must be well informed and confident about their recommendations. When making a reservation in this light, one begins to understand the scope of responsibility.

Not only do concierges spend their guests' time and money, they are also instrumental in creating lifelong memories of honeymoons, anniversaries, birthdays, or even important business events. People put their vacations, special occasions and memorable moments in the concierge's hands. Because concierges are entrusted with guests' very personal experiences and are responsible for very important memories, it becomes vitally important that each request is treated individually, with personal care. Only the human touch will do, which is just another reason concierges can never be replaced by an electronic device!

The notion of merely delivering customer service has evolved into the broader promise of creating the customer experience – and of course, making it a wonderful one. The job of the concierge involves quickly "sizing up" each guest and finding the perfect restaurant match. Customizing each restaurant reservation is not a task for the faint of heart, as the concierge desk can be deluged with 50 to 70 hungry guests – all within a 2 to 2½ hour "prime-time" window. Concierges call this the "dinner triage," where they're called upon to read the guest and situation, prioritize and quickly make decisions based on the information they're able to absorb. "I just breathe, make my assessment and keep people moving along," explains one concierge.

This same concierge compares the situation to speed dating, a process where singles are given a very short amount of time to determine if the person sitting before them is compatible. Then, they move on to the next candidate, and on it goes. Like the speed-dater, the concierge has limited time to assess the guest and his or her needs to find the perfect restaurant match.

YOU ARE NOT GOING

Recommendations are so subjective and people are so hungry for personal treatment, that the question, "Where would *you* go?" is often directed at concierges. I've stressed this fact in earlier chapters, but I want to emphasize the importance of it again when recommending restaurants. "Where would *you* go?" is a loaded question and usually not what the guest really wants to know. In short, you need to remember: *You're* not going.

Always recommend for the *guest.* Resist the temptation to tell the guest where you would go. What they really mean to say is: "Recommend something special for *me.*" Just because the concierge has a preference for some out-of-the-way café with sublime paella doesn't mean that it's right for everyone. Of course, it's important to steer guests to places the concierge has personally experienced and awarded high marks, but the concierge needs to remain objectively subjective – considering first what's best for the guest, then choosing from a list of possibilities that have met the above criteria. Remember, though they might not know how to ask the question, guests always want what you think is best *for them.*

A great way to preface your suggestion is: "I have just the perfect place for you." This lends an added personal touch. Even better, finesse the situation by lowering your voice when providing the information, as if you're sharing a secret. It will make the outing all the more special for the guest.

People often want to steer clear of "tourist traps." On the other hand, many cities do have attractions that guests want very much to see and experience, such as the Eiffel Tower in Paris or San Francisco's Fisherman's Wharf. Though not necessarily on the concierge's top-ten list, it's counterproductive to dampen the guest's obvious enthusiasm. For this reason, concierges should always have a list of tested, tourist-oriented restaurants on hand that can be recommended with confidence.

As a new concierge, I tended to steer guests away from restaurants that based their entire business on tourist clientele. But as I became more experienced, I realized that people want to see these places. My responsibility, therefore, was to develop relationships with restaurants in this category that would please my guests.

I began by recommending a place at Fisherman's Wharf that was popular and did, in fact, have good food. The restaurant didn't take reservations and tended to make people wait, but at the time, I thought it was still the best choice. I later learned that my guests weren't treated well, which was unacceptable. I knew I needed to find an alternative. Eventually, I found a restaurant that fit the bill, whose staff appreciated our recommendations and treated our guests (and concierges) with respect. They did their best to seat guests on busy nights and even offered a window table, when possible. Furthermore, they were pleasant, hospitable and gracious on the phone, as well as accommodating. Needless to say, I didn't think twice when asked for recommendations for a spot on the wharf, (and no longer did I immediately discount a restaurant because it was too "touristy.")

THE ART OF THE RECOMMENDATION

Recommending the right restaurant for the right guest is a skill that sets the great concierges apart. Food is typically of prime interest to the traveler and going to restaurants an event unto itself. When a guest doesn't particularly enjoy a play or tour, they tend to be less disappointed than when they don't enjoy a meal. Knowing the right place for each person, couple or group, thinking of it at the right moment, and making all the necessary arrangements are part and parcel of the fundamental job standards for the concierge. The ability to accomplish this while juggling other tasks takes talent and dedication.

I was once accused of ruining a guest's anniversary and her entire trip, because she had an unhappy experience at a restaurant I recommended.

Recommending restaurants seems like a "fluff "job to those who haven't seen a busy concierge in action. Far from fluffy, suggesting restaurants for guests requires a great deal of knowledge and responsibility. Again, concierges are entrusted with people's time, money, memories, vacations, business deals and impressions of their cities. To make it more complicated, reviews of restaurants are highly subjective. In fact, it's entirely possible that two parties at the same restaurant on the same day may return to the hotel with entirely different feedback.

> *I once sent two parties to a seafood restaurant. The first returned with the worst possible review: It was terrible! The second reported that it was the best dining experience they'd ever had. It was fabulous! Go figure.*

UP CLOSE AND PERSONAL

If at all possible, try not to recommend restaurants over the phone. To do the job properly, concierges need to share the guest's vision, which always works better in person. Nothing substitutes for face-to-face dialogue. When a concierge gets a call for a recommendation for a restaurant, he or she might say, "I'd really like to meet you, if at all possible. I feel better recommending on a personal level and would appreciate your stopping by the concierge desk." This is especially important if dancing is part of the evening's plan. One would not want to suggest a lively disco for people from the Big Band era. Most guests will oblige in making contact. Some won't. The concierge could then remind them that sample menus are available at the concierge desk. This usually sparks interest.

> *I once made a telephone recommendation for a guest who simply asked for a "nice restaurant." I suggested a beautiful, elegant little place all done in pastels, with romantic flowers and elegant, formal decor. When he showed up at the desk, I saw that the voice belonged to a 6-foot, 7-inch Texan in a ten-gallon hat. Mercifully, I was able to make a second choice and steered him to a restaurant I knew he'd find more enjoyable.*

ESTABLISHING THE VISION – Getting Beyond Good and Nice

When guests aren't sure what they want, they often resort to requesting "good food." If asked about the atmosphere they're looking for, their response typically is "nice." Responses such as these leave the concierge at square one. Sometimes, it's best to ask "What type of an outing are you looking for?" – or their "vision" of the perfect evening. Ask, "Can you give me vision of the evening you would like to have?" It's only possible to suggest "the perfect place," when the guest offers at least a basic concept. The concierge can offer leading descriptors, such as elegant, romantic, business oriented, candle-lit, homey, upscale, trendy, good for people watching, etc. Of course, the culinary categories can be explored, such as French, Thai, Chinese, Vegetarian,

Continental and so on, along with pricing considerations and distance from the hotel. Once the basic "vision" has been established, the right choice can be made.

This technique requires knowledge of the restaurants in the city, the types of food, the best table, the maître d', hours and price ranges. Good or bad suggestions can cause the guest to value or discount the suggestions of the entire concierge department and the hotel itself, so it's definitely better to be safe than sorry. When in doubt, it's helpful to sum up the guest's request in your own words and ask: "Does this sound like what you're looking for?"

Guests might tell the concierge, "Money is no object." This should never be taken literally. The concierge should discretely inform the guest of the price range of restaurant options, to ensure they are, in fact, within an acceptable price range.

When booking restaurants, the concierge may not always be able to offer the guest's first choice of time, so again, it's important to remain flexible and explain the need for flexibility to the guest. There are also occasions when the first choice of restaurant isn't available. In both cases, it's good to have a backup plan that has been agreed to by the guest(s).

WHAT THE CONCIERGE ASKS

Getting a clear vision from guests requires a series of specific questions, as they sometimes forget to include valuable information. Though you don't want to overwhelm them with a barrage of questions, you do want to have enough information to make recommendations with confidence. Here are a few suggestions:

- What type of food do you feel like?
- What type of atmosphere do you prefer, e.g., casual or formal?
- What price range would you prefer?
- Is this social or business?
- Are you celebrating a special occasion?
- Is it important that the restaurant is within walking distance? (Over half the requests are in this category.)
- Will children be included? Are you looking for a family-friendly restaurant?
- What is your preferred time, and if this is not available, what might be an acceptable alternatives?

The more the concierge knows about the guests' wishes, the better able he or she will be to make an appropriate recommendation. This list of suggested questions will lead to an understanding that will still only point in a general direction. It may then be necessary to get more detailed. For instance, if the guests indicate a preference for French food, the concierge will need to determine if they are interested in classic, country or bistro. All are French, but there is a world of differences and the concierge should be aware of them. Some guests "play games" to determine the level of sophistication of the person behind the concierge desk, as both the concierge and the hotel may be judged according to the guest's perceptions of their capability.

> *I once served a guest who asked for French food and I sent her to a classic French restaurant. She came back unhappy. She wanted, "French as in gumbo." Another guest went to an Italian restaurant I'd recommended and came back to say it wasn't Italian – it was Venetian.*

On the other hand, getting all the details can sometimes backfire.

> *A woman once asked me for a seafood restaurant on the water that was casual, yet elegant, where her husband wouldn't need a jacket and tie. She wanted a panoramic view of San Francisco Bay and to be assured that no tourists would be there. Whoops! I appreciated the fact that she was so specific, but I had to confess that restaurants on the water with panoramic views could not be hidden from our tourists.*

If, after all good efforts, the guest remains vague about what he or she is looking for, it's best to play it safe and recommend an establishment that's not controversial or exotic and offers a diversified menu. When in doubt, stick with the basics. When suggesting restaurants in general, keep it simple. If asked for ideas, *it's best not to overwhelm the guest with too many choices. Offer them no more than three options that meet their criteria and let them chose from them.*

THE ART OF DIPLOMACY

There are times when a concierge is asked not to recommend a restaurant, but simply to make a reservation. In such cases, respect the guest's wishes and do as asked. It's generally not a good idea to dissuade them.

> *A guest asked for a reservation at a very popular restaurant, and without being asked, the concierge volunteered that it wasn't very good. The guest turned out to be the owner of the restaurant. Very red face. Very wrong move.*

Sometimes, a guest has specific choices with which the concierge strongly disagrees. In these situations, a proper response might be: "That's fine, but it wouldn't be my choice for you." It is appropriate, however, to mention whatever drawbacks are obvious, such as a recent change in menu or chef or the fact that the place is noisy. Or, you might ask targeted questions, such as, "How do you feel about an 11-course meal?" or "They only serve pig knuckles on Thursday. Is that OK with you?"

Here is a graceful approach offered by a concierge friend of mine who has a way with words: "That restaurant is quite good. (Pause) After hearing your needs, may I suggest a restaurant I think you will really enjoy and may even be a better fit than the one you have read about?"

BOOK 'EM

Once the decision has been made (with an alternate, as recommended earlier), the next step is making the reservation. This may be done either online or by phone. Booking online is usually the most expedient method. However, the concierge should call the restaurant if it's been awhile since direct contact was made or there are special instructions. If the concierge desk has been computerized, a confirmation form will print out automatically, which is then given to the guest. Printed or written confirmations give guests a sense of security and also something concrete to hand to the host or hostess. The record of the reservation is stored in the computer. If the hotel doesn't have a computerized system, a confirmation card needs to be

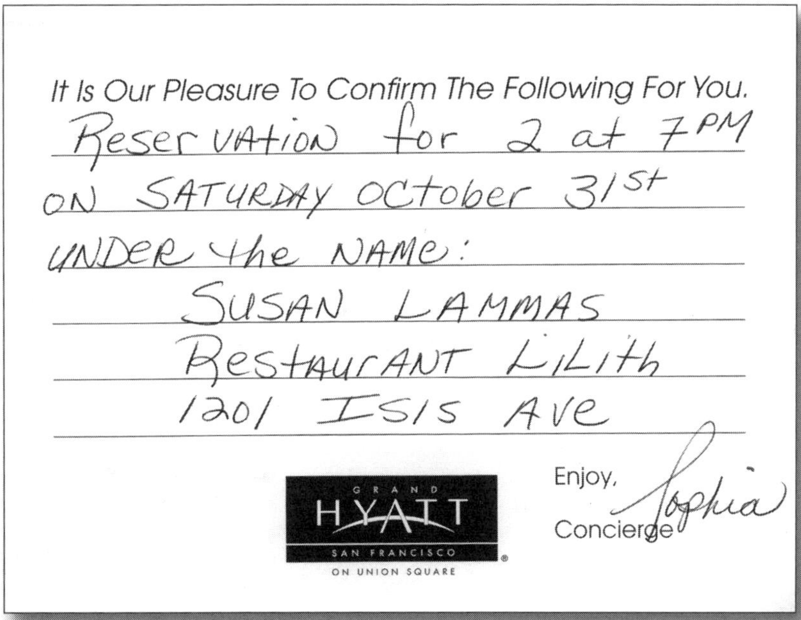
It Is Our Pleasure To Confirm The Following For You.
Reservation for 2 at 7PM
ON SATURDAY October 31st
UNDER the NAME:
SUSAN LAMMAS
Restaurant Lilith
1201 ISIS AVE
Enjoy,
Concierge Sophia
GRAND HYATT SAN FRANCISCO ON UNION SQUARE

An example of a hand-written restaurant confirmation

manually written in duplicate – with one copy for the guest and the other for the concierge to file under the guest's name. The card should include the guest's name, the name of the restaurant, the date of the reservation, the address and cross streets, how many in the party and the time of the reservation. The document might also include driving and walking directions and the estimated time to get there. It is a good idea to include the name of the person who took the reservation. Some concierges choose to handwrite confirmation cards, even though they have entered the information into the concierge-software program. They simply prefer the style, look and touch of a handwritten note.

FOLLOW UP

Make no assumptions. It's always a good idea to confirm the guest's reservation with the restaurant by phone – especially if there are special instructions or "extras" involved. With all the information conveniently stored on the computer, it's easy to verify all the details. Calling to confirm also provides a great opportunity to touch bases with your contacts at the restaurant.

MENUS

Before the computerization of the concierge desk, keeping updated menus on file was the norm. Showing guests menus gives them the opportunity to know what they can anticipate. No surprises, at least in terms of bill of fare and prices. It prevents the concierge from hearing, for instance, that the Italian restaurant chosen was not "the real deal," because it did not serve veal parmigianino.

Today, many restaurants make their menus available online, which the concierge can easily print for their guests. However, I personally prefer handing guests the real thing – like in the "olden days." Menus speak volumes about a restaurant, and there's just something about seeing and holding the menu itself that provides a more authentic "feel" for the place. Another good reason for keeping menus is that when the concierge is busy with several guests at once, menus make an excellent diversion. One guest can page through the menu, while the concierge finishes with another guest. Finally, restaurants in small resort communities often do not post their menus online, so having the menu itself on file can be an absolute necessity.

There are several tried-and-true ways to store menus for easy access. One way is to keep them in a simple A to Z file and organize them by restaurant name. Another method is to first create categories, such as type of cuisine, then file alphabetically within each category. When filing menus, indicate the date on each one and keep them updated, as prices and dishes change over time. Include photos of the restaurants, too, when available. Organizing menus may be tedious in the beginning, but it's well worth the effort.

INFORMATION ORGANIZATION

Computerizing the concierge desk has revolutionized information management. Not only can data be better organized, it can also be easily categorized and updated. Basic, as well as detailed, information, can now be stored on a database. Here are some suggestions:

- Name of restaurant
- Address
- Telephone
- Website
- Whether or not reservations are accepted/necessary
- Hours of operation
- Days restaurants are closed
- Name of maître d'
- Owner(s)
- Dress
- Atmosphere
- Alfresco dining available
- Price range
- Signature dishes and specialties
- Bar on the premises
- Cross streets
- Comments
- Credit cards accepted

The concierge can amend the database, as needed, adding both sub-categories and additional details. For instance, concierges have compiled lists of gluten-free dining, late-night options and alfresco dining. Others have categorized bars, e.g., cigar bars, speakeasy-style bars, bars that offer music and dancing and so on. The more specific the sub-categories, the better.

Concierges may also add public and private notes to the database. Public notes are available to all who are privy to the database and offer helpful information, such as: "This restaurant has a great sommelier." Private notes are for one concierge's eyes only and typically include one's individual contacts, cell phone numbers of restaurant contacts, etc.

Information is only as good as it is accurate. Always make sure that all information is entered accurately and clearly. Be sure, too, to back up all files in the event of a computer "crash."

Many concierges have lists they have developed for frequently-asked questions, such as nearby restaurants. The following is a great example of how one hotel has created a way to inform guests about restaurants they recommend:

Hyatt Regency, Tokyo, uses a number system corresponding to a map.

Shinjuku Restaurant Map (Japanese Food)

	TEL	Opening Hour		Price Range
		Weekdays	Sat, Sun,Holiday	
TEPPAN-YAKI 鉄板焼き				
1 Serina 瀬里奈 (52F)	3344-6761	11:30〜21:30	Sat 17〜21:30/Sun Holiday16:30〜21:30	L:¥3,000/D:¥12,000
2 Pandora パンドラ (2F)	3344-3808	11〜15/17〜22:30	11〜14:30/16:30〜22:30	¥3,000
SHABUSHABU しゃぶしゃぶ				
3 Imahan 今半 (1F)	3345-1470	11〜15/17〜21:15	11〜21:15	L:¥2,500/.D:¥10,000
4 Suehiro 銀座4丁目スエヒロ (2F)	3356-4656	11:30〜15/Mon-Fri 17/23:00	11:30〜15/Sat Sun Holiday 17〜22:30	L:¥1,000/D:¥5,000〜
SUSHI すし				
5 Ishikawa 鮨いしかわ(B2F)	3340-3245	11:30〜14:30/16:30〜21	Sun Holiday 11:30〜20	¥12,000
6 SushiMaru 鮨丸 (1F)	3356-7077	11:30〜14:00/17〜23:30	Sat11:30〜23:30/Sun Holiday11:30〜21:30	L:¥1,000/D:¥7,500
7 Numazukou Round Sushi 沼津港 回転寿司(B2F	5321-6008	11〜22:25		¥2,000
TENPURA 天ぷら				
8 Tsunahachi つな八(B1F)	3342-2788	11〜14:30/17〜21		¥2,500
9 Tenichi 天一Isetan Park City2(1F)パークシティ	3351-7151	11:30〜21:15		L:¥2,000〜/D:¥5,000〜
UDON うどん				
10 Sangokuichi 三国一(B1F)	3346-3591	11〜22:40	Sat11〜22 /Sun11〜21:30	¥650〜
SOBA そば				
11 Daian 大庵	3352-5113	11:30〜14/Tue-Fri /17〜22:30	12〜14:30(L)/17〜22:30 Sat/16:30〜21:30Sun Holid	L:¥900/D:¥4,500
YAKITORI やきとり				
12 Toridori 鳥どり(2F)	3342-7758	11:30〜14／17〜22	Sat17〜22 Sun Holiday11:30〜14/16〜21	¥3,500
13 Imaiya 今井屋(B1F)	5326-4933	17〜23		¥5,000
TONKATSU とんかつ				
14 Wakou 和幸(1F)	3348-0610	11:20〜20:15		¥1,500
UNAGI -EEL うなぎ				
15 Wadahei 和田平(B1F)	3342-5678	11:30〜15:00/17:00〜21:00		¥3,000〜
YAKINIKU-BBQ 焼肉				
16 Jojoen 叙々苑(8F)	3340-8989	11:30〜22:15		¥6,000
17 Rokkasen 六歌仙(6F)	3348-8676	11〜4am	Sun Holiday 11〜2am	¥7,000
FUGU-BLOWFISH ふぐ				
18 Torafugutei とらふぐ亭 新宿別館	5155-2329	16:00〜3:30am	Sat 16〜3:30am / Sun Holiday 16〜23:00	¥6,500
19 Genpin fugu 玄品ふぐ 新宿歌舞伎町	5155-0329	16:00〜3:00am		¥5,000
IZAKAYA-Japanese Bar 居酒屋				
20 Hokkaido 北海道(44F)	5323-0255	16:30〜22:30		¥3,500
21 Tofuro 土風炉(B2F)	5381-0111	11:30〜14:00/17〜23	11:30〜17 /Sun Holiday 17〜22:30	¥3,000
Fish 魚料理				
22 Yakichi 八吉 西新宿	3348-8118	Mon-Thu 17〜24 Fri 17〜4:30am	Sat 16〜24:30 / Sun 16〜22:30	¥4,500〜
Dining Bar ダイニングバー				
23 Oto Oto 音音	5908-2282	11:30〜23:30	Sat Sun Holiday 〜22:30	¥4,200
24 Daidaiya 橙屋(3F)	5362-7173	17〜24		¥5,500
25 Toranosuke Hanare 虎ノ介はなれ (29F)	5324-5125	11〜14/17〜22		L:¥1,000〜/D:¥4,500〜
KAISEKI 懐石				
26 Nadaman なだ万(14F)	5381-0700	11〜21		¥7,000
27 Minokichi 美濃吉(48F)	3346-2531	11〜13:30/17〜20:30	Sat Sun Holiday 11〜19:30	¥12,000

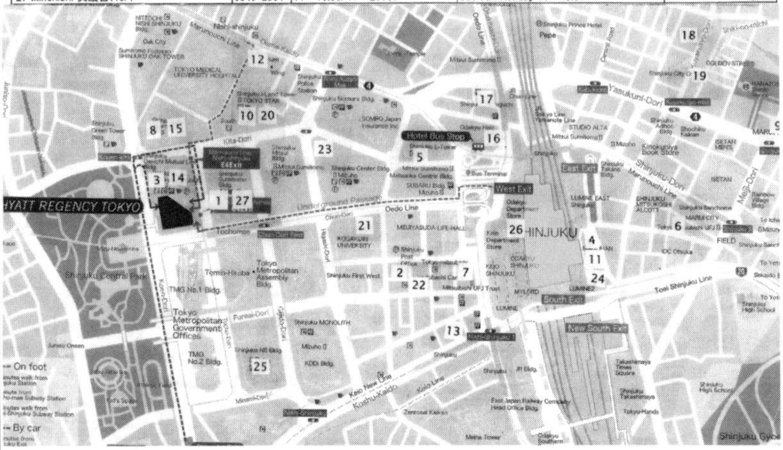

REAL-LIFE EXAMPLES

Recommending restaurants is not always as easy as simply asking questions. The concierge is often exposed to real-life human dramas. In a classroom setting, the following stories are perfect examples for role-playing exercises:

Couple Arguing

Situation: The wife wants elegance. The husband refuses to wear a tie. She wants French. He prefers pizza.

What to do? The concierge should go to great lengths to come up with a solution that pleases both parties. In real life, this isn't always possible.

True Story: A concierge I know once worked with an arguing couple for 20 minutes. She made endless suggestions. The couple could agree on absolutely nothing. After all the wrangling and protests, she finally got down to the "kicker": *Are you two actually planning to have dinner together? Thankfully, humor saved the day and invited compromise.*

Bossy and Pushy

Situation: The party is extremely demanding. They are not polite. They are accustomed to having things done for them on demand and appear not to understand the word, "please."

What to do? Take a deep breath and meet their discourteousness with politeness. Do your absolute best to make them happy. Appreciate the humor in the situation and afterward, share it as a funny "war story" with your fellow concierges.

True Story: A concierge was working with such a group and was asked to recommend the finest seafood restaurant. After making her suggestion, the guest replied: "This had better be good. We are fish aficionados."

The Challenge

Situation: A couple wants the most popular restaurant in town and the best table. They have read numerous articles singing the praises of hotel concierges that suggest: "Concierges can do *anything*!" The couple wants to test the concierge, and they ask questions, such as, "Don't you have any pull?" and "Let's see how good you really are."

What to do? Of course, do everything within your power to grant the guests' wishes. If unsuccessful, offer the next best thing. Even if they don't appreciate your efforts, take pride in a job well done.

True Story: A guest approached me on Valentine's Day, requesting a table for two at eight o'clock at one of the most popular restaurants in the city. I told him I would try, but suggested that we develop a backup plan since the restaurant was extremely busy. Rather than agreeing on an alternative, he replied, "What you need here is a good concierge." I smiled sweetly and continued with my best efforts to satisfy him.

Vague

Situation: A husband and wife from the Midwest want a recommendation for dinner. They have no special interest. Anything will do.

What to do? Ask questions and "read" the guest.

True Story: A couple approached a concierge and asked for a recommendation. When she suggested French, they said, "Oh, no. Not French." She went on to Asian. They said, "Oh, no. Not Asian." American steakhouse? "Oh, no. We don't eat red meat." Seafood didn't strike a chord, either. Finally, after many attempts and prolonged conversation, she discovered that the woman had severe asthma and multiple food allergies. She was eventually able to suggest a restaurant that offered organic, gluten-free fare.

BON APETIT!

JUST AS WORLD-RENOWN CHEFS artfully blend ingredients and techniques to create delicious dishes, so do concierges combine their knowledge, intuition and experience to create memorable dining experiences customized for each of their guests. In so doing, solid and rewarding relationships blossom with restaurateurs, maîtres d' and chefs, who become their allies in delighting guests' preferences – from peanut butter to paella. Here, there's only one thing left to say: "Bon Apetit!"

CHAPTER NINE

9 The Technical Revolution

OBJECTIVES

The following chapter will equip readers to:

Comprehend the critical role that technology plays in the life of the concierge.

Identify several aspects of the concierge role where technology has improved service levels.

Distinguish the essential equipment and software required to establish an optimal workstation.

See that technology enhances the concierge role, rather than making it redundant.

A LITTLE HISTORY

WHEN I READ OVER THE CHAPTER entitled, "Organizing the Concierge Department" in *Ultimate Service The Complete Handbook to The Concierge*, (originally published in 1992), I had to laugh. Wow, have things changed! For one, concierges no longer need to keep volumes of resource materials at the desk or thumb through drawers full of fat file folders in search of information. We are now extremely fortunate to have entered the age of high-tech.

In earlier chapters, we've seen that the concierge's primary objective is to create unforgettably exceptional experiences for their guests. We've also seen that the attainment of this goal requires information – lots and lots of information. Where does the information reside? As mentioned above, when the original edition of this book was published, it lived only on paper – stacks and stacks of paper. Imagine a concierge desk at that time. The theatre requests alone took up an entire book, not to mention logbooks for packages received, packages sent, packages held for collection, transportation requests, etc. Then, there were the books for restaurants, tours, excursions, amenities, spa services and so on. Add to this the daily logbooks with notes about VIPs and urgent requests, which sometimes were inadvertently buried in yet another logbook. And of course, there were the menu files and airline-schedule books, phone books and the list goes on. There were also letters and faxes from guests, as well as internal memoranda. In a larger hotel with a busy concierge desk, this constituted literally tons of paper over the course of a few short years. Cumbersome? Absolutely. The software systems available today have streamlined the job of concierge considerably – and saved a whole lot of trees!

If, for some reason, you're interested in reading about the "olden days" and taking a walk down memory lane, I still have some original *Ultimate Service* books in my garage, and I will be happy to sell you one. That way, you can hearken back to 1992 and learn – or remember – just how hard it was to keep track of all the information: how many notebooks we had to transfer the same information into, how many different color-coded files we needed just to store all the information, how many tabs we had to have in those giant three ring binders, how long it took to find something we needed. Then, there was the issue of how long it would take one member of the team to figure out what another member had done on a shift three days earlier.

But that was yesterday . . . Today, the paperless – or practically paperless – concierge is a wonderful reality.

WHY AUTOMATE?

When telling colleagues I was considering revising the text to bring it up-to-date, I asked specifically about ideas for approaching the chapter on technology. Here is one response:

> *I'm afraid that any concierge who isn't willing to embrace technology will no longer be effective and will surely be left behind. Our guests are expecting immediate answers and solutions, and only a computer- and Internet-savvy concierge will be up to the task. A situation like the following happens all the time: A guest is late for a presentation and realizes that he has forgotten to print out a file from his thumb drive. Rather than sending the guest to a distant business center, the concierge needs to take the thumb drive and print the document for the guest, right then and there. Another example: A concierge should be able to immediately give a guest the temperature in Celsius, as well as Fahrenheit. (This is easily done with a quick mouse click on CNNWeather.com.)*

Bottom line, if you don't embrace the high-tech digital systems, you'll be tangled up in an endless paper trail. I like the way Adam Isrow, co-founder of GoConcierge.net (a popular and highly praised concierge-software system), explains the crucial role of technology.

Who Needs Technology?

by Adam Isrow (Co-Founder of GoConcierge.net)

Does any of this sound familiar? "I was at your hotel a year ago, and your great concierge suggested a wonderful restaurant where my wife and I celebrated our anniversary. Problem is, I can't recall the restaurant's name." Or how about this one, "My family was at this resort last year, and the concierge arranged for a great babysitter, so my wife and I could have a romantic night out. I'd love to hire the sitter again. Would you have her phone number?"

Without the help of technology, some of the most basic questions guests ask the concierge can result in a panicked sense of emergency and a flurry of activity. These simple questions include requests such as, "Has my FedEx package arrived?" or "I've been in meetings all day. I'm wondering if the concierge was able to secure the four tickets to the game I'll be needing later this evening to entertain clients."

Everyone working in the hospitality industry can relate to the craziness that ensues behind the scenes, even when handling the most basic of requests. This begs the question, "Are we ready to embrace technology?" Regardless of the benefits, here are a few popular responses from people who are still reluctant:

(1) We've always done it this way, and it has worked.
(2) I have my own system for doing this.
(3) I will lose the personal touch with my guest.
(4) I am not a computer expert and feel overwhelmed by the very thought of using a computer application.

Not comfortable with technology? Fair point, but my suggestion is always: Just give it a chance. Those who have taken the journey to efficiency and "technology bliss" will attest: Do it, and you'll wonder how you ever did your job without it.

As time goes on and technology evolves, everyone owes it to themselves to at least take a look. As you would test-drive a car before making the purchase or signing that lease, give a software application a whirl around the block with an open mind. I believe you will be quite surprised once you see how a good software application can – and will – make your day-to-day operations flow much more easily and effectively.

In today's tough economy, travelers are spending less and expecting more. Hoteliers are working with fewer people per shift, who are still expected to perform the same number and caliber of "miracles" that concierges are known for. You may be a part of a wonderful team, but if you're not provided with the necessary tools, how will guests' expectations be met, let alone exceeded?

Ultimately, the question becomes, Are you equipped to succeed or fail? If your hotel has invested in technology to make team members more efficient, the answer to that question is a resounding, "Yes." However, if you tell yourself, "We have a great team that can find ways to be more efficient on their own, or "Our team is unique and already taking care of the guests in the most effective way possible," I suggest that you reconsider.

Comments from concierges are living proof that having and becoming familiar with technology is priceless. Their remarks range from how easy it is to track information, create consistency, personalize information, access information, eliminate the difficulties of deciphering illegible handwriting, all to the ultimate end of gaining more quality time to spend with guests. The unanimous response from users of the system:

"I have no idea how I ever did the job without it."

EVERYDAY MIRACLES WITH TECHNOLOGY

Paperless? *Really?*

by Jon Adler (Concierge, New York City, and fan of the concierge software system, Gold Key Solutions.

Luckily, we live in a time when a paper-based desk can be, and for many concierges around the world is, a thing of the past. This does not mean, however, that the desk is literally devoid of paper, as there will always be written or printed confirmations for guests, printed directions, handwritten welcome cards and more. You should definitely have a nice, hardbound blank book to write down funny and poignant concierge stories to share with your colleagues. You will also need to have files to keep theatre agreements, faxes from guests, limousine manifests and signed receipts for packages, etc. Most record keeping, however, which once comprised the bulk of paper at the desk, can now be totally digitized.

The following are just a few examples of how digitizing the desk has made concierges' lives easier and improved service levels available to hotel guests.

Guest Requests

The digital desk maintains all guest requests electronically. They are entered into a computer program, which tracks them on multiple levels, enabling concierges to perform at a much higher level than when using paper. One great benefit of logging all requests in the computer is that it generates printed confirmation and itinerary forms. In the pre-digital era, these documents were collated and prepared by hand. They then were typewritten or neatly handwritten and given to the guest. Today, with a few clicks of a mouse, concierges can create itineraries and confirmations – on the hotel's letterhead stationery – which can be e-mailed instantly around the world. This document can include directions, descriptions and other notes – all completed in less time than it used to take to log the requests.

At many concierge desks, the most frequent request (aside from, "Which way is the restroom?") concerns dining reservations. Concierge software enables concierges to enter dining-related requests into a system that sorts by type of request, by guest name, by restaurant and by any number of categories. It also provides a faster way to see the status of each reservation request, as they are color-coded on your screen. The on-screen colors clearly reveal the status of any entry. At a glance, one can determine which restaurant requests still need to be booked and which guests need to be advised that their reservations have been confirmed. The information is then stored in the computer, enabling the concierge to retrieve it even years later, should the guest return to the hotel and want to repeat the experience.

The same capabilities apply to theater and most other types of requests. In each instance, the entry forms within the system prompt the concierge to ask all the necessary questions related to any given request. For instance, the software will, in essence, remind the concierge to obtain every detail needed to fulfill a floral order. Additionally, the printed confirmation sheets, which are passed on to guests, will remind them of any necessary details – whether it's a penalty for cancelling a spa appointment less than 24 hours in advance or a note that their theater tickets are not exchangeable.

Gold Key Solutions

Confirmation for:	**John Smith**
Arriving:	**Thursday, November 04, 2010**
Your Request:	**Transportation**
Date:	**Monday, November 08, 2010**
Name of Company:	**A & C Limousine Service**
Time:	**1800**
Type of vehicle:	**Stretch Limo**
Amount:	**300.00**
Tip:	**60.00**
Total:	**360.00**
Confirmed With/Confirm #:	**Aviance**
Notes:	**Pickup scheduled for Hotel**

Additional Information:

A 4 hour cancellation is required to avoid any penalties.

The Concierge Staff is here to meet your every need. Please do not hesitate to call us if you require any additional assistance. Thank you.

Sincerely,

Leo Aguirre
Assist Chef Concierge

An example of a confirmation

With regard to theatre tickets and other requests that require credit-card guarantees, the software immediately generates an agreement form that the guest signs and returns to the concierge, either by fax, e-mail, or in person. These sheets can be filed and stored, which enables one to eliminate charge-backs and generally protects the concierge staff, especially in cities such as New York, where theater tickets are often frequently sold by concierges.

An example of a confirmation

Message for: Mr. Isrow

Room: 1021

Date: November 3, 2010 2:52 PM

Dear Mr. Isrow,

Pursuant to conversation, ***please complete, sign and return the following information.*** *Please note that tickets are secured from licensed ticket agencies and once obtained, tickets are non-refundable, non-transferable and non-exchangeable. The price of the ticket reflects the ticket agency's costs and administrative fees above the face value of the ticket* ***(upwards of $250 per ticket)****. The concierge will only purchase the best seat location within the first 15 rows of the orchestra or the first 5 rows of the mezzanine unless instructed otherwise from you.*

I, ______________________, hereby authorize the Concierge Team of The Pierre – A Taj Hotel to utilize the credit card information provided to secure the requested tickets on my behalf as a guest of The Pierre – A Taj Hotel. I understand and agree that should my travel plans change that I still remain responsible for the cost of the tickets.

____

Signature *Today's Date*

Credit Card No. ______________________Exp Date_____

Credit Card Security Code ______________

Billing Address ______________________________

Billing Phone_______________________________

The Concierge Team remains at your disposal and should there be any questions and/or concerns, please do not hesitate in contacting us directly at 212-940-8108 or via the hotel's main number at 212-838-8000 extension #6108.

We look forward to welcoming you to the Pierre – A Taj Hotel.

Sincerely,

Adam Isrow

Service Enhancements

Technology has allowed us to streamline service and become more efficient. Oftentimes, one person can now accomplish a task that once required two or more. For instance, with the GoConcierge system, one can turn on a message light or send an amenity order directly to the room-service department, without bothering two staff members to do one job. It's also possible to text a guest's cell phone directly from the system itself. Management is delighted with efficiencies such as these, as concierges are even more empowered to think innovatively and actively look for ways to better the department, the hotel and ultimately the guest's experience.

Guests are just as pleased as management with the results of technology. Much of the new software alerts concierges when guests check in, allowing them to shake hands with their guests and pass on itineraries in person. You can also use the arrival-date function of the software systems to know when guests will arrive, so you can have a welcome note and all the itineraries prearranged for them.

Another extremely useful benefit is that multiple users can look at identical information at the same time on their individual computer screens, which helps create impressive – even seemingly impossible – service levels. I recall a recent conversation, where I was quite involved with a guest on the telephone in preparing a very long itinerary. As I entered each request in the computer, my colleagues called the restaurants to confirm the reservations. At the end of the call, I was able to tell the guest that everything was already arranged to her exact specifications. I'm sure she thought I was a genie!

Shipping and Receiving

Logging packages electronically allows the concierge to use the same barcodes scanned by the delivery services to track packages within the hotel. The concierge in charge of receiving packages (or the package office, if you are lucky enough to have one) can use a handheld scanner to enter tracking numbers directly from the package into your software. Proper logging of the details enables one, in a few mouse clicks, to know exactly where every package is being held or when a particular package was given to its rightful owner. Faster and more accurate searching saves time for the concierge, and more importantly, for the guests. Similarly, though without barcodes, one can track faxes and items received from outside messengers through the system.

Recordkeeping and Reporting

Concierge software also enables you to track productivity and revenue. In this day and age, when the most important line is the bottom line, it's imperative to demonstrate the value of the concierge team to hotel management. Concierge software helps you accomplish this in amazing ways. End-of-month reports can be generated to quantify the value of the transactions you generate, displaying the number of reservations your department has booked for a variety of different categories, as well as the overall volume of requests. One can also see the productivity of each staff member, which helps monitor performance and pinpoint opportunities for improvement. Additionally, there are reports that show how busy the desk is over the course of a day, which facilitates proper staffing. For instance, if the bulk of requests come between 12:00 and 6:00 p.m., the creation of a mid-shift staff, in addition to the concierges assigned to the a.m. and p.m. shifts,, might be considered.

There are reporting functions that allow the tracking of the number of tables you have booked and how many covers you send to every restaurant you work with.

By showing the restaurants the exact volume you send them, they will be that much more likely to call you when that last-minute cancellation comes in at 8:30 p.m. on a busy Saturday night. Apart from the outside dining reservations, you are able to track the number of guests you send to your hotel's restaurant(s), again enhancing management's appreciation for what you do and demonstrating your contribution to the hotel's bottom line.

Another great way to track the concierge desk's revenue-generating activity for the hotel is actually through your PMS (Property Management Software). This system keeps track of every reservation and shows where each reservation came from. It's important to establish a source code, such as, "Concierge," and remind your reservations desk to use it anytime you transfer a call to them. This way, the hotel has a much better idea of exactly how much volume the concierges are bringing to the property.

Lost and Found

There are software systems that track lost-and-found items, as well. Sometimes, this can be an add-on to the concierge software already in use at the desk, while it can also be a separate program through either the loss-prevention/security or housekeeping departments. Concierges need to have access to this software and know how to use it. It's much faster than the "old-fashioned" system of calling a colleague, who has to literally read through a register to find the information, then confirm it by manually searching through countless items. Many of the programs allow you to upload photographs of all unclaimed items, which facilitates confirmation of ownership. Lost-and-found software is generally much more accurate than manual systems and enables one to generate a sheet for the receiver to sign before collecting the item. It can also be attached to a tracking form for an outgoing shipment and filed, which gives you more detailed documentation than simply a signature. It's even possible to photocopy an ID for the receivers of high-value items and file them along with the signature document.

High Tech/Soft Touch

The benefits of the computerized concierge desk are countless, yet technology also presents a challenge. Perhaps the most demanding part of computerization is maintaining the "humanness" of the experience. After all, information is just one of the many tools in the concierge's toolbox, and it is the spirit of the interaction with the concierge that creates happy memories. Therefore, it's up to each concierge to personally convey the information to the guest, so that the experience becomes personal and meaningful. I've witnessed too much customer "service," where it was clear that the information I provided was being typed, one slow letter at a time, onto a computer screen. Furthermore, the agent did not demonstrate any caring at all for the human being at the other end of the line. It was as if I was talking to a robot!

The question becomes: How exactly can tracking all this information enable the concierge to translate it into a more memorable experience for the guests? There's no one specific way to do this, but the imperative lies with the concierge to create style and fun out of every data-entry moment. Telling the guest robotically it will take you a moment to enter information into the computer is honestly boring. However, if you develop your typing and computer skills to the point where your typing improves and you understand the computer better, you can elevate the service you deliver to an art, as your fingers dance across the keyboard. In fact, keeping a connection with the guest and providing more time for personal interaction is made even more possible, once a comfort level with the system is achieved. Always remember, it's not the software, but how you use it, that creates the experience for the guest.

THE EQUIPMENT YOU'LL NEED

Hardware

First and foremost, the concierge desk requires a powerful computer, most likely running Microsoft Windows®. The majority of hotel software does not run on Apple computers at this time, although I know of one hotel that uses them with a program that creates a Windows interface. Unfortunately, it slows their operations down considerably.

Telephones

A multi-line telephone is required at the concierge desk, with at least two outgoing lines, in addition to the incoming lines. The number of lines needed depends on the number of rooms in the hotel and the level of staffing. Headsets, especially those of the Bluetooth® variety, can prevent years of chiropractic bills. Bluetooth and other wireless technology spare your neck and shoulder muscles and enable you to move around the desk easily.

It's always helpful to have a mobile number to give to guests, to ensure they can reach you, should the hotel's lines be busy. (It's also a good idea to obtain a mobile telephone number from guests, so you can contact them quickly and easily, if necessary.)

An "All-in-One" (Printer/Scanner/Fax/Copier)

This technological wonder serves four functions: printer, scanner, fax machine and copier. Ideally, one of the printer's paper drawers contains your hotel letterhead, so you can send confirmations and other documents that need to be printed on letterhead directly to that drawer. It looks even more professional if your machine prints in color. Although you may have a business center that offers scanning, photcopying and fax services, the ability to provide this service at the desk is imperative – not only for the occasional guest who refuses to go to the business center, but more importantly, for the concierge staff's use.

Software

The following software programs help make the concierge look like a star, even a miracle worker!

- Your hotel's PMS (Property Management System).
- A concierge software program, such as Gold Key Solutions, GoConcierge or similar.
- At least one other browsing program, such as Internet Explorer®, Mozilla Firefox®, Safari, etc.
- The Official Airline Guide (OAG®), which is also available as a website. This is a faster way to search for flight options on different airlines, as it enables you to search across the board – you are not limited to searching by one particular airline or alliance. OAG also helps locate airline telephone numbers, hotel information, car-rental information and so forth. The OAG was formerly contained in two bulky books about the size of a phonebook. Your subscription included fairly frequent updates. Imagine the paper that would have been used for that! You can either use the online version, which can even check flight availability, or a program in and of itself, which is updated by CD.
- You need the full version of Microsoft Office® Suite, because guests might ask you to print documents in PowerPoint® or other programs. It's always better to have the latest version of the software. (It's embarrassing to explain to the guest that your software is so antiquated that you can't open the file.)

  You will probably spend the majority of your Microsoft Office time using Outlook®, their email program, which can also maintain schedule and contact information. A great amount of communication these days occurs via email, which has largely replaced faxed requests. Whether it's a quick "thank you" from a guest's BlackBerry®, a long itinerary or request from an administrative assistant or a memo from the executive office or human resources, all emails that require a response must be processed promptly. No guest request should ever wait more than 24 hours, and technology makes it possible.

- Adobe Acrobat Reader opens PDF files. (PDF is the acronym for Portable Document Format.) PDF is a very common format used to transfer information around the Internet. A document in PDF format is more secure than a Word or Excel document, as it cannot be altered.
- Reservation-booking software, such as SpaSoft, OpenTable® and many others.

THE INTERNET

Of course, there are other important tools at the paperless concierge desk, the most vital of which is the Internet. The web has revolutionized the flow and exchange of information and concierges have countless ways to benefit. ZIP code look up, mapping and directions, metric conversions, TV and movie listings, weather forecasts, networking with other concierges, to name a few, are only a click away.

Your best friend on the Internet is probably your favorite search engine. You should set it as your browser's home page. Mine is Google.com. Through experience with the website, you will learn how to get what you need and get it quickly. Just about everything in the world can be found on the Internet through search engines such as Google™, Yahoo!® and Bing™. I used to jokingly say, "If you can't find it in New York City, it probably doesn't exist – or at least, you probably don't need it." Now, I say the same thing about the Internet. If you can't find it there, it's probably not worth finding. And this time, I'm serious!

The Internet is an extremely valuable resource for restaurant information. Most upscale restaurants have websites with digital copies of their menus. There are also websites, such as www.menupages.com. This site provides menus for just about all the restaurants in New York City. There are similar websites in other cities.

Restaurant reviews can be found on sites, such as www.citysearch.com or www.yelp.com. On these sites, the reviews are submitted by diners, rather than by critics, and can often give you a good understanding of the restaurant you are discussing with your guest. Zagat® has an extensive website at www.zagat.com, which, for an annual subscription fee, gives you plenty of wonderful information, including their ratings for restaurants around the globe.

OpenTable®

OpenTable is a very useful site on which you can make restaurant reservations at many venues around the world, anytime day or night. They have a portion of their site dedicated exclusively to concierges, which is accessed through www.ot-concierge.com. For additional information, please refer to CHAPTER 8, – "Working with Restaurants," where this software is explored more in depth.

Some Helpful Websites

While far from an exhaustive list, the following are just a few of the helpful websites available to concierges.

- **www.worldtimezones.com** – This website allows one to determine what time it is everywhere in the world.
- **www.xe.com/ucc** – *The* site for currency exchange.
- **www.faa.gov** – Use this link to the airport status page, which shows you real-time status of all the airports in the USA.
- **www.weather.com** – Provides current weather and forecasts anywhere in the world.
- Your local transit website, if you have one, can be very useful.
- **www.ticketmaster.com** or **www.telecharge.com** – Confirm tickets or performance times, with a few keystrokes.

Last But Not Least

Don't forget about your hotel's corporate intranet (internal network), where you can find important information about the corporate side of doing your job well, along with useful information about your benefits, hotel policies, etc. And for heaven's sake, check out your hotel's website periodically. This eliminates the possibility that the hotel is conducting a promotion you're not aware of. It also gives you the opportunity to spot any errors or ways to improve the website and convey them to the IT department.

MAN vs. MACHINE

Some people have voiced concern that the ease of locating information on the Internet will eliminate the need for concierges. This is upside-down thinking. Computer systems are in no way a replacement for concierges and the human touch, but a tool that helps make it easier to provide outstanding service. It's the relationships formed that keep guests coming back. This is the very reason that unattended kiosk-type concierge services miss the point entirely.

Technology is only as good as the person using it. Guests will continue to need concierges to provide a personalized recommendation, to be a confidante, wait on hold with restaurants interminably and the like. Rest assured that technology will never replace the concierge. It simply makes locating and managing information – two of the key foundations of the artistry that is the world of the concierge – so much easier.

My friend and colleague, Joanna Husk, who has a way with words, expresses it this way:

> *What the concierge creates is memorable guest experiences. This requires masterful information management, combined with empathy, flair and intuitive human interaction. Life moves far too quickly to adhere to slow, outmoded forms of recordkeeping and filing. We owe it to our guests to be on the cutting edge of tech, not only to receive information in a timely manner and be able to access it with a few keystrokes, but to also have the good judgment to eliminate the extraneous and provide exactly what the guest needs. We are the ultimate search engines and that is our magic.*

OTHER INNOVATIVE USES OF TECHNOLOGY

- The program, HotSOS™ includes a system that allows housekeeping and engineering requests to be entered into the computer by the concierge. In large hotels, such as the Bellagio and MGM, a houseman with a pager or access to the system is assigned to each floor. When a guest needs towels or a sink routed, the concierge can then directly contact the houseman or engineer assigned to that specific floor via the computer. This is much more efficient than going through a member of the housekeeping department, who then passes along the information to a houseman or engineer. Communication becomes much more effective, and more importantly, guests receive prompter service. In smaller hotels, this can be easily accomplished by giving the housemen and maintenance staff specific pager numbers.

- At the San Francisco Fairmont (and many other hotels), the bell staff has pagers and is in direct communication with the desk. That way, directly after rooming an arriving guest, they can pick up luggage from a departing guest on their way back to the lobby.

- A notebook computer or electronic notepad that is equipped with wireless Internet access and compatible with a nearby printer enables the concierge to "work the lines" during very busy times. The notebook can do most everything that can be accomplished with a desktop computer. A concierge, so equipped, can move freely to attend to waiting guests, print boarding passes and theater tickets, obtain Mapquest directions, et al. The agility and service level of this "mobile concierge" is impressive, expediting guest requests and virtually eliminating, or at the very least substantially reducing, wait times.

THE VIRTUAL CONCIERGE

One of the cleverest (almost futuristic) ways I have seen technology used to enhance service levels, remain within budgetary constraints and secure a job for a valued employee is through the concept of "virtual concierge," first designed for Anna Morris, concierge at the Santa Clara Westin. This hotel is located in Silicon Valley (where else?) – the high-tech center of the world.

The concept of a "virtual concierge" was the brainchild of Strategic Hotel Capital along with the support of IMA, widely recognized for their expertise in harnessing the power of virtual communications through videoconferencing and streaming audio/video over the Internet. Using the Sony Contact-ME Videoconferencing System and a T1 connection, Anna Morris connects remotely from her home office in Antioch, California (a three-hour roundtrip to the hotel), whereby she appears on a large screen monitor in the hotel lobby, enabling her to greet and engage guests in discussions about their needs, offer advice and take requests.

For a truly interactive experience, the dock-able pan/tilt/zoom camera feature on the Contact-ME system automatically follows Anna, as she moves around her home office, so hotel guests see more than a static image of her, making for a more personable experience.

According to her general manager, "Anna is not just our concierge, she's an invaluable asset to our hotel. We have a very loyal clientele who depend on her outstanding service. With the Virtual Concierge system IMA has designed, they are able to talk with her via a live video visit."

Personalized service from miles away? This is a great example where everybody wins, by using and leveraging the many possibilities technology affords us.

HIGH-TECH CAVEAT

IT IS MY INTENTION to be as up-to-date and helpful as possible. However, things are changing moment-to-moment. Just as I was about to send this book to the printer I heard that Intercontintal Hotels purchased iPads (which didn't exist year ago) for every concierge and has created a special concierge "app."

With the lightening pace of the evolution of technology, it's quite likely that the most popular sites as of this writing are obsolete by the time this book is in your hands. As an example, MySpace™ was "all the rage" just two years ago. Now, it seems everyone is on FaceBook.™ The same holds true of the list of valuable search engines (Google,™ Google Chrome,™ Ask,™ Bing™). Who knows what will be the latest development five, even two, years from now?

Truth be known, it's absolutely thrilling to think about all the possibilities the future holds. In the meantime, take advantage of what's here and use it to your best advantage in offering guests the most pleasant and personalized experience possible!

CHAPTER TEN

10

Netiquette

OBJECTIVE

The following chapter will equip readers to:

Demonstrate professional communication through the effective use of e-mail

GENERAL INTERNET ETIQUETTE

COURTESY, CONTENT AND CONCISENESS

THE TERM "NETIQUETTE" was coined to describe network etiquette – the "dos and don'ts" of online communication. Though technology has opened a whole new world, the traditionally held rules of common courtesy already established for all forms of communications are equally relevant to any interaction on-line. In fact, courtesy becomes even more important on the Internet, because other than video conferencing, body language, dress, facial expression and tone of voice are usually not available for interpretation. The only tangible means you have of expressing yourself are your written words.

As noted in CHAPTER 4, being gracious, behaving professionally, exhibiting good manners and being polite are fundamentals for the concierge in all situations. Because your correspondence speaks volumes about you, these same qualities should be reflected in each and every online communication. Whether it's an e-mail, social-network post or a comment on a blog, it should contribute to a polished image and create a positive impression. Remaining polite is key, even in situations when you might disagree with others.

Cyberspace is a culture unto itself. Though it has generated a language of its own and suggests an atmosphere of informality, it is still important to take special care with the quality of your writing. Sloppy grammar and spelling send the wrong impression, so you always want to put your best e-foot forward. In written correspondence, the quality of your writing is just as important as your grooming and attire are, when meeting people face to face. If grammar has never been your strong suit, you might consider taking a proofreading or copy-editing class at your local community college or university-extension program to polish your skills.

The content of your correspondence is equally important. It should be clear, concise and accurate. Accuracy is especially important. If you find yourself prefacing sentences with "I think . . . " or "It's my understanding that . . . ," you might want to delay pushing the "SEND" button until you've checked your facts. Inaccurate information can spread like wildfire over the Internet, and you don't want to be responsible for perpetuating it.

While accuracy is key, brevity is also important. Most people are stretched for time, not only because they have too much to do, but also because of all the information that's now so readily available. Many of us wake up every morning to inboxes swamped with e-mails! People appreciate when your messages are clear and concise, while paying special attention not to appear terse. The tone should always remain respectful, friendly and approachable.

BEFORE YOU HIT "SEND"

Because the Internet eliminates the need for more direct contact, one might consider it a relatively impersonal medium. To the contrary, human emotions can still run strong and the lack of face-to-face contact can make it feel more acceptable to "scream and shout." You may be tempted to write a scathing e-mail, for instance, to advise one of your vendors of a disappointing guest experience. But wait! It's always good practice to let it "rest" overnight, before an inflammatory message or post is on its irreversible way. One of the first questions you need to ask yourself is: "Would I feel comfortable saying it to this person's face?" Secondly, ask: "Do I really want this to come back and haunt me later?"

The tone of your message is so important, in fact, that a Canadian-based company, Lymbix™, has created a product that can actually gauge the emotional tone of words, phrases and emotions in text-based communication – much as the spell-check feature ensures proper spelling. Their latest product ToneCheck™ is a free e-mail plugin that flags words or phrases that may have an unintended abrupt, aggressive or negative tone and helps the sender re-write them in a more positive way.

If you've ever watched a crime drama on television, you're aware that computerized information is often retrievable, even though the sender thinks he or she has deleted it forever. The criminals are usually "busted," often due to the cyber-trail they've unwittingly left behind. Additionally, information on the Internet is easily forwarded and shared with a click of a mouse, so you never know where it might end up. Bottom line, if it's something that might lead to embarrassment later, don't send it!

You don't necessarily have to commit a crime to regret your behavior on the computer.

E-MAIL ETIQUETTE

The first question to ask yourself before sending an e-mail is: "Does it really need to be sent?" or better yet, "Will it benefit the recipient, solve a problem or lead to a greater understanding?" Most people today are suffering from chronic e-mail overload, so don't waste their time sending them e-mails they don't need. It's also helpful to keep in mind that some matters might be better discussed over the phone or face-to-face. If the situation is complicated and might involve a number of questions and clarifications back and forth, a call or personal visit may be the best bet. Another important consideration is the possible benefit a more personal mode of communication might have. It's easier to build relationships with other departments, for instance, if you actually see them once in awhile or at least have a conversation with them. It creates more of a feeling that you're on the same team. The same holds true for contacts at restaurants and other vendors.

DOS AND DON'TS

The following are some general rules that should be observed when sending an e-mail:

- Avoid designating an e-mail "Urgent," unless it truly is. (Besides, if it is truly urgent, it probably would be better handled by phone.)
- Never forward "chain e-mails."
- Use businesslike language. Be quick and concise, without appearing curt or demanding.
- Plz don't abbrvt. (Please don't abbreviate.) You can use shorthand when sending a text message to your buddies, but not on the job.
- Never use e-mail to convey confidential information. Remember, there's no such thing as a "private" e-mail.
- Avoid using ALL CAPS, as it is considered "shouting" and impolite. Some techies also contend that sending e-mails in all lower-case letters makes it appear as if you're mumbling. Even if this isn't the case, it's still bad grammar.
- This may go without saying, but never, ever send or even forward an e-mail that contains libelous, defamatory, racist, sexist or obscene content. At best, it's a bad reflection on you and the entire concierge profession, and at worst, it could result in a lawsuit against you and your hotel.
- "Smilies" or "emoticons" like this, , are punctuation marks or symbols used to signify an emotion. As with abbreviations, they have *no business* in business correspondence.
- When appropriate, add your name to the subject line, in the event that the recipient may not recognize your e-mail address, e.g., "A Question from Holly Stiel."
- Make subject lines short and meaningful, to inform the recipient

of the purpose of your e-mail at a glance.

Vague Subject Line (Avoid)	**Helpful Subject Line (Use)**
Misc.	Cirque du Soleil Tickets
Request	Request for information about your restaurant
Meeting	Meeting, 9:00 a.m., Tuesday, Hospitality Room

SALUTATION

Your e-mails should always include a salutation. When it comes to the prefix you use, every situation should be evaluated on its own. Using Mr., Mrs., and Ms. and the recipient's last name is appropriate for many situations. On the other hand, you can use the first name, if you are confident you're on a first-name basis. When replying to an e-mail, use the name that the sender has used in his or her "signature." If you are unsure of which salutation to use, always defer to the more formal option.

FORM AND CONTENT

When using e-mails for business matters, they should look and "sound" businesslike. Though e-mail is a cross between speaking and writing, it is primarily a writing tool, and like a business letter, it leaves a permanent record. The following are useful tips for composing an e-mail:

- Keep paragraphs short – preferably three to five sentences in length.
- Each paragraph should elaborate on one idea. When moving to another idea, create a new paragraph.
- Use simple sentences of reasonable length.
- Keep the message to one screen, if possible. Short, concise e-mails should provide a clear objective to which the recipient can reply.
- Avoid jargon. Use language you would feel comfortable using in a memorandum or business letter.
- Sign off with your name, title and contact information. On most systems, this can be set up as a template to appear automatically.

A Word on Attachments: Because attachments can carry nasty computer viruses, you might want to ask recipients' permission before you send them. At the same time, you'll also be able to inquire if they have the necessary application software to open it, to ensure they don't receive an error message or a lot of "gibberish."

WHEN REPLYING TO AN E-MAIL

It's always good practice to respond to e-mails promptly. If it's a complicated matter that may take more than a day, send the recipient a response to let him or her know you are working on it and will get back to him or her within "X" business days, depending upon the individual situation.

When you are out of the office for more than one day, use the "out-of-office assistant," which automatically informs senders that you are away from the hotel and when you will return. If you don't plan on checking your e-mails while you're away, be sure to include an e-mail address and phone number of a colleague who will be able to help them.

Be careful not to overuse the "reply-to-all" button. Often, after an original e-mail has been sent to you and multiple recipients, your response needs only to reach the sender. If this is the case, send your response to him or her alone, without burdening the other recipients with unnecessary e-mails.

SOCIAL-NETWORKING SITES

People are networking, sharing and collaborating with each other online more and more every day. As of this writing, the most popular social-networking or social-media sites are Facebook, LinkedIn and Twitter.

As with e-mail, cell phones, texting and other technological modes of communication, social networking seemed to emerge out of nowhere, before any "rules of the road" could be established. At least for now, there are no digital equivalents to Emily Post™ or Miss Manners™, so we are left with the task of developing guidelines "on the fly," to ensure consistently courteous, considerate and professional interactions. The more widespread technology becomes, the more the need for guidelines will arise. As we have done for the last few decades, we will make them up as we go along. Here are some basics for the polished professional to start with:

- Fill out your online profile completely, with accurate information about you and your hotel.
- Use your real name and your own photo. For business purposes, leave out photos of your dogs, backyard, etc. Business and pleasure don't mix on social-networking sites.
- Use a different account or profile for your personal connections, where pets can be proudly and appropriately displayed.
- Create a section on your main profile page, detailing who you are interested in sharing information and networking with, e.g., other concierges, travel agents, gourmet chefs, etc.

- Content is king. Always offer information of value – not "hype."
- If a screen name is required, select one that represents you and your hotel in a professional manner. Names such as, "CatWoman1" and "SurferDude36" should be reserved for personal connections.
- Don't post anything on the Internet that you wouldn't want your boss, a guest, or potential guest to read. An indiscretion here could haunt you your entire professional life.
- Never post material when you're overly tired, stressed, angry or upset. Always pause before posting.
- Compose your posts, updates and tweets on a word-processing program, which will allow you to check your spelling and grammar. Once you've perfected your message, cut and paste it to the networking site.

The social-networking phenomena is the way of the future, and the future is *now!* If you're befuddled by the very concept and don't know a "twit" from a "tweet," sign up for courses on social networking at your community college, park district or college-extension program.

OUT OF THE BLOG FOG

The world of blogging might be best described as immediate, interactive online journalism. Blogs can also be quite personal – a place for our thoughts, reflections and views on the world. Blogs have been created on every topic from soup to nuts, allowing bloggers to share information with their readers and receive feedback from around the globe.

The promotional role of blogs in business and marketing is beyond the scope of this book, as are the technical skills required to create them. I did, however, want to add a few words on blog etiquette for concierge/bloggers and those who are interested in seeing what the "blogosphere" has to offer. Whether it's relating funny stories, tips, inspirational material or travel news, the concierge/wordsmith/blogger can add a post to his or her blog at any time. One of the best features of a blog as a communications tool is that it invites comments from others, comments on those comments, et al. It is an outstanding vehicle for networking, sharing information and voicing opinions.

NETIQUETTE TIPS FOR YOUR BLOG

Your professional blog is not only a representation of you, but of your hotel and the concierge profession as a whole. Therefore, proper grammar, professionalism and courtesy are imperatives. Because the role of blogger can be similar to that of a journalist, there are a few other considerations:

- As with all communications, blog posts must be accurate. Use credible sources and always double-check the facts.
- Credit your sources, including a link to their blog or website, if available.
- Respect your sources. If you are told something is "off the record," don't post it or share it with anyone.

NETIQUETTE TIPS FOR COMMENTING ON OTHERS' BLOGS

To fully take advantage of blogging networking opportunities, it's a good idea to expand your reach by visiting other career-related blogs, enabling you to both gain and share information. Commenting on other people's blogs is a wonderful way to both make a contribution and learn from others.

When thinking about blogging etiquette, you can compare a blog to someone else's home. As a commenter, it's as if you're a guest in that home; and as a guest, you need to be respectful at all times. In other words, you can't just barge in and act like you own the place. Be polite toward the blogger and the other readers.

- Always make comments that are thoughtful, constructive and helpful, either by adding additional points, elaborating on the initial post or adding to others' comments on that post.
- Be sincere and personal with your comments. This is a place where your true personality can shine and where you can forge relationships with other bloggers.
- Be succinct. Express your ideas as clearly and briefly as possible.

HANDLING COMMENTS ON YOUR BLOG

If you are expected to be a thoughtful guest on someone else's blog, it follows that you will want to be a gracious host on your own. It's important to acknowledge and appreciate those who share their comments with you, as in reality, they are the most important facet of the blog. Without them, you're left with a one-way journal.

Respond to other's comments and show your appreciation for their contributions. While the Internet may have a language of it's own, "thank you" is still very much a part of the vocabulary.

JUST OLD FASHIONED GOOD MANNERS

WHILE I HAVE DEVOTED an entire chapter to the particulars of netiquette, the underlying principle can be summed up in just a few words: Every Internet-based communication should be helpful, professional, courteous and to-the-point. As you've no doubt noticed, these guidelines are no different than the good, old-fashioned rules we've applied to snail-mail, phone calls and face-to-face interactions for years. If anything, these guidelines become even more important in cyberspace, as communication here is vastly more accelerated, easily shared and subject to misinterpretation than ever before.

CHAPTER ELEVEN

11

Organizing the Concierge Department

OBJECTIVES

The following chapter will equip readers to:

Effectively organize vast amounts of information to maximize efficiency and service delivery

Coordinate the critical elements and day-to-day requirements of the concierge desk

THE PERFECT SYSTEM?

When I began my career as a concierge, I traveled to London for three weeks to observe other concierges in some of Europe's first-class hotels. I was in search of the "perfect system," but I ultimately found that there is no such thing. Each concierge team used a different system, ranging from ultra-efficient to shockingly relaxed. The funny thing about it is that they all seemed to work. The most relaxed system was so counterintuitive that I've never forgotten it. The concierge had worked at his five-star hotel for more than 30 years and wrote everything down on little bits of paper. At the end of the day, he threw the snippets into a box and put them in a storage room. When I asked how long he kept them, his answer was, "Ten years." I returned to America thinking, if a concierge can get by on little scraps of paper, I could surely come up with a workable system of my own. Of course, my organizational style was dramatically different, but the goal was the same: To organize information in such a way that guests can be served in the most effective and efficient manner possible.

I HAVE TO THINK THAT EVEN THE CONCIERGE, who held on so tenaciously to his little scraps of paper, would abandon his system for the high-tech organizational tools enjoyed by today's concierges. Thanks to concierge software, such as GoldKey Solutions and GoConcierge, it's dramatically easier to organize the desk, follow up on guest requests and communicate with other departments in the hotel, as well as the entire concierge team. In addition, the bulk of the information concierges need – once occupying file after file, tome upon tome and tons of storage space – now resides on the Internet and the hotel's computer.

FOR THE RECORD . . .

Before the existence of concierge-software systems, there were a variety of methods created to log information, record guest requests and communicate with other staff members and guests. As I look back on the system I created back in the 1970s,

I remember stacks of logbooks, shelves full of binders and files – lots and lots of files! Information was written on a master sheet, rewritten in a logbook and then filed so everyone could (hopefully) find it. It was a lot of work, but nonetheless, it was a key part of doing the job.

Thankfully, the physical presence of information behind the concierge desk has significantly declined. However, there's no less information to contend with – in fact, quite the opposite. There's more information today than ever before, and it's no less important to meticulously record all guest transactions. The information is still logged, but now it's done on the computer. Today's software programs organize it, make it available to others who need it, and even prompt the concierge to make sure he or she has entered all the necessary information.

It is the responsibility of the concierge to log every transaction, no matter how seemingly trivial, into its proper field on the computer. Computers and concierge software have made it amazingly easy to ensure that every request and every booking is recorded accurately and completely, and then stored where it can be easily found. When a team works together, each person must be able to follow on the heels of the others. When requests are properly logged, any concierge on the team is able to retrieve and fully understand the information, no matter who did the original work.

Communication among staff members is extremely important, and there is often precious little time for one concierge to communicate with another without interruption. The concierge is constantly engaged with guests and with vendors or other departments on behalf of guests. The system must, therefore, be simple and efficient. It should never be necessary for one concierge to ask if a task has been completed. A glance in the right place should supply complete information on everything that has been done and all that is pending. This is the epitome of seamless service, empowering one team member to take charge, where another left off.

While technology can do amazing things, all bets are off if the information entered isn't clear and accurate. The same attention to detail that was required when using logbooks and daily master sheets is just as important today. Additionally, each shift is responsible for reading all the notes that the preceding shifts have left.

In the event of a computer "crash," it's important to back up all information stored on the computer. While printing out a hard copy is one way to do this, the hotel's IT department or the manufacturer of your concierge software should be able to provide more effective and efficient options.

WHAT TO LOG?

Every request a concierge receives – from the mundane to the magnificent – needs to be logged. While the methods of recordkeeping have changed significantly, the types of information that need to be logged have remained the same. This includes:

- Restaurant Reservations
- Airline Transactions
- Hotel Reservations
- Spa Services
- Tickets
- Shipping
- Floral Requests
- Limousine Services
- Auto Rentals
- Tours
- Airport Transportation
- Charters
- Messengers
- Babysitters
- At resorts, Golf, Tennis and Boat reservations are essential.

CONFIRMATION CARDS

Many of the above guest requests will require confirmation cards. Confirmation cards are given to guests to verify airline bookings, restaurant reservations, theater and hotel bookings and many other requests handled by the concierge. They give guests a sense of security and help assure them that their requests have been handled successfully. They also supply supportive details, such as directions, cancellation policies, etc. Today, in most cases, concierge software automatically generates confirmation cards at the same time the reservation or the arrangements are being made.

Concierge software has the capability to create professional-looking cards, customized with the hotel's logo. In the past, a duplicate copy was filed at the concierge desk. Today, the record of the transaction is always available to the concierge on the computer database.

Some concierge prefer the look and "feel" of handwritten cards, which can add a warmer touch. Be sure to have blank cards readily available at the desk.

PASSING THE TORCH: COMMUNICATIONS WHEN CHANGING SHIFTS

Evening, morning and any interim shifts must communicate with each other with absolute regularity. Every night, notes must be written to the morning shift and vice-versa. Notes between shifts should clearly explain what needs to be done and what to expect. This type of communication is often necessary when booking theater tickets, for instance. Because some tickets must be purchased during normal business hours, the nightshift may need to hand over the task to the dayshift. It is of the utmost importance that all the information is conveyed clearly and completely to the following shift, including the guest's second choice of dates/times/seating, etc. As another example, packages that may have been left for someone to pick up need to be flagged, so that they don't become confused with packages to be shipped.

The software system should have a special field to enter time-sensitive requests that need to be fulfilled immediately by the next shift, such as floral requests and early-morning spa requests.

Leave only those tasks that absolutely cannot be handled on your shift. It is very poor teamwork to burden colleagues with work that could have been accomplished on the spot.

The public-messaging function of concierge software allows all intradepartmental communications to be keyed into the computer and easily accessed by other team members. This is a great opportunity to lend a soft touch to high tech, by adding something *personal* and *kind* to start your colleague's day with a smile. This makes it possible for the new shift to get off to a pleasant start and also serves as emotional "glue," helping to cement relationships among members of the concierge team.

I made it a practice not only to impart important information at the end of my shift, but also to include "something nice" every day for the shift to follow. If all one is able to muster is, "Have a nice day," then so be it. I still firmly believe that a nicety of some kind should be included. One of my colleagues drew little pictures, to the delight of the next shift to arrive. It was always a treat to arrive early in the morning to one of her illustrated notes! Even in this digital age, a handwritten note or a hand-drawn picture is greatly appreciated.

THE PAPER CHASE

Of course, not all the information that needs to be shared is in digital form. The concierge still receives printed materials, such as letters (snail mail), tour brochures, maps, notes, group prospectuses, announcements and schedules. Every member of the concierge team needs to read, assimilate and know how to readily find this information going forward.

To distribute "To-be-Read" materials, it's helpful to have two file folders. One is marked "To Read Immediately," which can be created for all team members daily. To ensure the entire team has had the opportunity to read its contents, a sticky note should be attached that each member can initial as they finish. When everyone has reviewed the information, the paperwork can be filed away in the appropriate place or discarded, depending on its importance and availability elsewhere. Examples of information that belong in the "to-read-immediately" category include store openings or closings, restaurant specials, changes in schedules and upcoming events. Previously, this file often contained memos from management or human resources, but today, most inter-department communication is sent via the computer.

Another file, marked, "To Read at Leisure," can be created to pass along items such as thank-you notes and information of a less critical nature. This might include updated brochures from frequently used vendors, which contain no major changes, brochures from new vendors for consideration, and interesting articles about the profession, theater, local restaurant, or attraction reviews. This file should be read at least once a week.

STAFFING

Staffing is a very sensitive area between concierges and general managers. As discussed in CHAPTER 4, general managers are often unaware of the sheer volume and diverse nature of the situations that arise during a concierge's day. Too often, the perception is that concierges do nothing more than make dinner reservations. The truth is that concierges strive to give personal attention to all guests – helping them plan their stay and solve problems of all kinds. This requires working with all other areas of the hotel, as well as a multitude of vendors. This kind of personal attention requires time. The best, most experienced concierge cannot perform well if he/she is overloaded with requests and telephone calls.

The size of the hotel, the services the hotel provides, the standard of service and guest expectations all contribute to determining the proper amount of staffing. As a general guideline, a five-star hotel requires at least two concierges on duty at all times, regardless of the number of rooms. Any hotel with more than 250 rooms also needs two concierges on duty. During the height of tourist seasons, hotels with more than 300 rooms need three people on duty during peak hours, especially on Friday and Saturday evenings. Some large hotels have attempted to provide concierge service with one person in the lobby per shift. The result of this type of understaffing can be summed up in one sentence, "May I please place you on hold?"

NOT JUST A NUMBERS GAME

It is difficult to staff according to hotel occupancy, because the concierge department is affected differently than other areas of the hotel. For instance, the hotel might be booked at just 40 percent occupancy, but if the majority of the guests are transient (not part of a group or convention), the concierge is used more frequently in attending to each individual guest's needs. The remainder of the hotel business may well be slow, but the concierges are overwhelmed. At other times, the hotel may be 95 percent occupied by groups that have outside coordinators who keep them busy with activities and banquets. These guests seldom use the concierge services, so the traffic at the desk will be slow, in spite of the high occupancy.

It's difficult to predict staffing needs in all circumstances, although computers have made it easier to forecast staffing needs from year to year. In general, it is optimal to have two people assigned to each shift and then reduce the hours when it's obvious the desk is slow. Of course, in special circumstances, such as the arrival of a Saudi Prince or a concert by Elton John, staffing needs will increase considerably.

There is additional information on staffing the concierge desk, including desirable qualities to look for in prospective candidates, in CHAPTER 18 – "Managing the Concierge."

THE BACK-OFFICE ADVANTAGE

To provide ever-increasing guest satisfaction, some well-run hotels have embraced the idea of adding a back-office for the concierge team. It has been found to increase service levels and decrease concierge burnout. The back-office staff operates behind the scenes to return phone calls, answer e-mails, make follow-up calls, handle paperwork, etc. In general, they provide a vital support function, which enables concierges in the lobby to devote their undivided attention to the guests at hand.

Rotating staff between the back office and the bright spotlight of the hotel lobby helps reduce the stress of being constantly "on stage," with all systems go. Changing every couple of hours has been shown to keep the job fresh and concierges on top of their games. The back office is also an ideal spot for communication between switching shifts. All in all, it provides a nice variety for concierges, and it is my strong belief that it elevates service levels for guests and potential guests exponentially.

The back office can double as a storage room, where supplies, guests' packages and outgoing mail can be stored. It is also a perfect place to communicate during the shift switch.

DESK HOURS

In Europe and a few hotels in the United States, the concierge desk is staffed 24 hours a day. However, most U.S. hotels offer concierge service between 7:00 a.m. and 11:00 p.m. If a hotel is truly committed to providing comprehensive concierge services, it is necessary and appropriate to keep the desk open during these, or similar, hours.

At night, if the concierges are off duty, the front-desk staff typically logs requests they're unable to satisfy, leaving notes for the early-morning concierge for follow-up. In this case, the front-desk staff will need access to the concierge software, which allows them to serve as a seamless extension of the concierge department.

DESK LOCATION

The concierge desk should be located in the hotel lobby, easily accessible to all guests and within view of the front door, if possible. The concierge is the hotel's ambassador and should be positioned in a highly visible, central location. If at all possible, the desk should be in view of and adjacent to the hotel's front desk.

The concierges' services should be readily available to all hotel guests. Offering concierge service to only a few select guests on special floors is not considered true concierge service by Les Clefs d'Or.

DESK TYPE

There are two basic types of concierge desks: standing and sitting. In 1976, when I was creating the job of concierge at the Grand Hyatt San Francisco, I assumed I'd take my place at the desk, seated. After eight years of sitting, however, I changed my mind. My back was always in pain, because of all the twisting I did to locate brochures, reach for menus, retrieve stamps, etc. Furthermore, I realized that I offered more efficient and personal service when I spoke to guests at eye level. Finally, I determined that the job was just too active to be handled in a seated position. Surprisingly, I also discovered that staying on my feet actually increased my energy, thus raising the quality of service I was able to deliver.

While a sit-down desk may appear more gracious and indicate a more laid-back approach, the concierge desk simply isn't a laid-back area. After all, concierges need to "think on their feet!" In addition, the appearance of a seated concierge can tempt guests to linger, which generates a waiting line of other guests. Lastly, a sit-down desk prevents any sort of "dancing" through the day – one of my favorite stress relievers – which is fully explained in CHAPTER 12.

An example of a typical sit-down concierge desk

Here are a few more advantages of using a standing desk:

- Guests can approach the concierge eye-to-eye, rather than gazing down.
- The concierge is free to move around, reach into drawers, retrieve information, get packing materials, lift packages and perform tasks easily.
- Paperwork may easily be hidden on a lowered work surface.
- A more professional and "at the ready" image is projected.
- Working in tandem with another concierge is infinitely easier.

THE IDEAL CONCIERGE DESK

A team can spend as many as 16 hours a day behind a concierge desk, working consistently and hard. If one is lucky enough to be able to design one's own desk, the ideal standing desk would measure 3-feet, 6-inches high, with ample room for two people to comfortably function. There should also be a lowered workspace, which creates a false top to keep the desk's surface looking neat, while providing sufficient space below. General managers expect the concierge desk to be spotless and the best way to keep the tools of the trade neatly tucked away is using a well-designed stand-up desk.

The actual size of the desk depends on the size of the lobby. Proportion is very important. When designing a desk, one must also be acutely aware of its functionality. Most people who specialize in designing desks have no experience with the tasks that face the concierge every day. Therefore, they frequently recommend a sit-down

An example of a typical stand-up concierge desk

model with one small drawer. This might work if guests approached the concierge one at a time, at leisurely intervals, with simple questions. But as revealed in previous chapters, this is far from the case!

The desk itself is an important tool, and a cluttered desk can cause undue stress. Space must be allotted for equipment, storage and workspace. I remember a desk in a beautiful new hotel in San Francisco that looked sleek and wonderful, but was sadly too narrow to accommodate even one computer terminal. Plus, there was no room to keep any kind of materials on file. When it comes to the concierge desk, it is essential to think about both form and function.

Computerization aside, the reality is that the concierge department still needs room for supplies, maps, brochures, packing materials, travel guides and, of course, an assortment of telephones, computers and printers. A computer terminal for each concierge on duty is strongly recommended. The desk itself will be able to hold only a portion of all that is required, so it's advisable to have file cabinets and a storage room/back office that is easily accessible.

Everything Old Is New Again

When I began my concierge career in the late seventies, I had a sit-down desk with comfy chairs that were located within the lobby, but a bit off the beaten track of the main lobby. It was an ideal place for guests to "hang out " and chat with the concierges about San Francisco. I even made scrapbooks to share my own personal experiences and walk guests through my favorite places.

It seems as if hotels are now returning to this concept of placing desks away from the crowds and the front desk. As a result, sit-down desks, comfortable chairs,

An example showing sit-down desks in a livingroom-type setting.

overseen by several concierges on staff, are making a comeback. The intention is to offer more personalized and well-paced service just outside the main lobby. (Many still recognize the value of having at least a view of the main lobby activity, however, to monitor bell and door activities.) The benefits of this placement include reducing the length of lines to answer the routine questions that could be answered by any staff member, such as the location of a meeting room, sales office or restroom. This frees the concierges to gain a deeper understanding of their guests to help personalize the perfect experiences for each of them.

In the hotels that have transitioned from stand-up desks to the sit-down format, the feedback is generally good. Both the concierges and the guests seem to appreciate the experience. For older, experienced concierges, the benefits include less wear and tear on the body, which allows them to better serve their hotel and its guests.

People still tend to line up, as this new configuration tends to encourage lingering. To help alleviate the problems associated with this, the concierges I interviewed told me they have become masters at body language. Acknowledging waiting guests with their eyes and a gesture, silently indicating, "I will be right with you," clues the lingering guest that someone is waiting. In most cases, this is all that's needed for the present guest to realize it's time to move on.

If the more casual approach of the sit-down desk is used, staffing considerations need to reflect the same atmosphere. Ideally, phones should be answered behind the scenes, and there needs to be an adequate concierge staff on hand to serve the guests in a calm and connected manner. Three concierges on a shift is optimal.

Though it is a set-up where the guest is seated, it's a good idea to stand and greet the guest as they enter the space.

At one of the hotels testing this approach, they turned the concierge area into a living-room-type setting, with a huge table that doubled as an interactive map of the city!

A WORD ON LIGHTING

Appropriate lighting at the concierge desk is an important factor. The concierge desk should have lighting that creates a pleasant ambiance and welcoming warmth. While harsh lighting should be avoided, there does need to be adequate light for the concierges and guests to see printed materials and computer screens clearly – especially the "fine print!"

OTHER CONSIDERATIONS

- There should be enough space for two people to function well and move freely.
- Adequate counter space is needed to accommodate a computer terminal for each person, preferably two printers, a copier/scanner, phones and fax machine.
- Shelves and drawers are needed to accommodate all the supplies that are needed at the desk.
- There should be enough outlets to accommodate all electronic equipment, including small electronics such as cell-phone chargers and pencil sharpeners.
- Drawers must lock. This is important, because concierges keep valuable items, such as theater tickets, stamps, and cash on hand.
- It's nice to have file cabinets built into the design of the desk.
- Brochure slots are recommended.

- Space is needed for incoming packages and flowers, as well as for outgoing packages.
- The sign(s) indicating, "CONCIERGE," should be clear and readable from a distance .
- Nearby seating is needed for guests awaiting bus, limousine and touring services. This allows guests to wait comfortably, while the concierge can keep an eye out to ensure they board the correct vehicle.
- At least one side of the desk should be open for easy entrance and exit, allowing the concierge to easily greet guests and shake hands.
- The back of the desk is best kept flush with a wall, preventing guests from approaching from all sides at once.
- The desk should be deep enough to allow for easy workability, but not so deep that it positions the concierge too far from guests.
- There should be space for at least one wastebasket.
- A built-in mail drop is advisable.
- When designing a new concierge desk, if space allows, at least one surface should be low enough for wheelchair access, to be in compliance with the Americans with Disabilities Act.

THE HIGH-TECH DESK

As mentioned earlier in this chapter, computers and the latest in concierge software have maximized concierges' organizational skills. As a result, today's concierges are able to perform more magic than ever before! In CHAPTER 10, I outline the hardware, software and peripheral devices recommended for the high-tech concierge desk.

Have at least one monitor that can swivel freely, so guests can easily view the computer screen. It is also helpful to have an adjustable-height computer terminal for the comfort of all members of the concierge staff.

TELEPHONES

Concierges and telephones are inseparable. A great deal of a concierge's time is spent on the phone – both communicating and inevitably, waiting on hold. A good rule of thumb is to have one phone for every concierge on duty, and then add one more. In other words, if three concierges work on a shift, four telephones are needed. Even if only one concierge is on duty, there should be two phones at the desk.

Multi-line telephones are required at the concierge desk, with at least two outgoing lines, in addition to the incoming lines. The number of incoming lines needed depends on the number of rooms in the hotel and the level of staffing. Three to five incoming lines are standard. There also needs to be a dedicated line for faxes. (Some people still send faxes.)

Due to the nature of the business, a separate line, not connected to the hotel, should be established for incoming calls from frequently used vendors, such as limousine and tour companies and restaurants. This takes some of the burden off of the communications department and helps ensure that important vendors' calls get through. This number should be considered "sacred" and given out to only a selected few.

Lastly, headsets, especially those of the Bluetooth® variety, can prevent years of chiropractic bills. Bluetooth and other wireless technology spare your neck and shoulder muscles, while enabling you to move around the desk easily. When all members of the concierge team are sporting headsets, the department typically functions much more effectively.

It's always helpful to have a mobile number to give to guests, to ensure they can reach you, should the hotel's lines be busy. (It's also a good idea to obtain a mobile telephone number from guests, so you can contact them quickly and easily, if necessary.)

THE WELL-SUPPLIED CONCIERGE DESK

The concierge desk should be set up and organized to best serve both hotel guests and the concierge team. Stress is significantly reduced for all concerned, when the necessary supplies and information are at the concierge's fingertips. The following is a list of items that belong at the concierge desk.

OFFICE SUPPLIES:

☐ Envelopes & Stationery	☐ Pencils & Pens	☐ File Folders
☐ Plain Paper	☐ Pencil Sharpeners, Erasers	☐ Hanging File Folders
☐ Hotel Stationery	☐ Highlighters	☐ File Tabs
☐ Note Pads	☐ Ruler	☐ Plastic Binder Sheets
☐ Legal Pads	☐ Scissors	☐ Binder Dividers
☐ Clipboards	☐ Tape Measure	☐ Binders
☐ Scotch® Tape & Dispenser	☐ Postal Scale	☐ String & Rope
☐ Shipping & Masking Tape	☐ Shipping Labels	☐ Three-Hole Punch
☐ Paper Clips (Large & Small)	☐ Toner Cartridges for Copier	☐ Rubber Bands
☐ Stapler & Staples	☐ Ink/Toner Cartridges for Printer	☐ USB "Thumb" Drives

Concierge-Related Supplies:

- ☐ Maps
  - ○ of the Surrounding Areas
  - ○ of the City for Walking
  - ○ of the City for Driving
  - ○ of the Country
  - ○ Transit Maps – Buses, Subways
- ☐ Direction Cards
- ☐ Bus Schedules
- ☐ Train Schedules
- ☐ Ferry Schedules
- ☐ Direction Cards
- ☐ Theater-Ticket Vouchers
- ☐ Overnight Express Supplies (all Shipping Companies)

"As if by Magic" Items:

- ☐ Bow Ties
- ☐ Regular Ties
- ☐ Cuff Links & Studs
- ☐ Socks (Black, Brown and White)
- ☐ Safety Pins
- ☐ Collar Stays
- ☐ Electric Razor
- ☐ Disposable Razors
- ☐ Reading Glasses
- ☐ Eyeglasses Repair Kit
- ☐ Lint Rollers
- ☐ For Children
  - ○ Crayons & Coloring Books
  - ○ Small Toys
- ☐ Cellphone & Mp3 Player Chargers
- ☐ Combs
- ☐ Toothbrushes & Toothpaste
- ☐ Hair Dryer
- ☐ Curling Iron
- ☐ Hair Spray
- ☐ Feminine Hygiene Products
- ☐ Clear Nail Polish
- ☐ Polish Remover
- ☐ Cotton Balls
- ☐ Tissues
- ☐ Nail File
- ☐ Hand Cream
- ☐ Airline-Approved Zip-Lock Bags
- ☐ Luggage Keys (obtained from repair shop)
- ☐ Note Cards
- ☐ Dictionary
- ☐ Assorted Small Vases
- ☐ Umbrellas
- ☐ Plastic Bags
- ☐ Wooden Package Handles
- ☐ Chewing Gum
- ☐ Mints
- ☐ Band-Aids
- ☐ Name Tags
- ☐ Sewing Kits
- ☐ Matches
- ☐ Hand-Sanitizer
- ☐ Super Glue®
- ☐ Flashlights

IF YOU'RE THE LAST, REPLACE IT FAST

I love this acronym, TEAM: "Together Everyone Achieves More." It applies to all facets of the concierge's job, including keeping the desk properly supplied. A well-supplied desk functions efficiently, and it's up to everyone to contribute to that efficiency. While this might seem like a small matter, it's very frustrating to reach for a Band Aid for a guest, only to find an empty box. It doesn't make a very positive impression on the guest whose finger is bleeding, either.

A good rule of thumb is to simply designate the person who uses the last of anything to take a trip to the storeroom and replenish the supply at the desk. So, when the last Band-Aid is given out, the concierge who used it refills the supply. When the storeroom stock gets low, it should be noted on a supply-requisition form or requested from the purchasing department online.

If the team members have difficulty diligently and consistently making this happen, one staff member can be assigned to be in charge of the supplies, rotating that responsibility every three months or so.

ORGANIZE, ORGANIZE, ORGANIZE

Concierges are constantly fielding information – undoubtedly one of their primary strengths. At the same time, information overload can be a significant source of stress. Though e-mail inboxes can't literally overflow, the sheer volume of messages can be downright intimidating. Thanks to concierge software, important messages, documents, spreadsheets, databases and links to websites can now be organized, cross-referenced and stored in the computer. Websites that are frequently used can be designated as "Favorites," allowing access with a click of the mouse.

Though a great deal of information is now communicated and filed electronically, the concierge desk still receives its share of paperwork. After all members of the team have had the opportunity to read it, some of the information can be discarded, while other more important material that can't be found elsewhere will need to be filed. It's important that this information is well organized, so all team members can easily access it. Organizing information can be time-consuming, but it is absolutely necessary. It's impossible to handle this task while engaging with guests, so it's best scheduled for afterhours. The extra effort is well worth it, paying off in the smooth operation of the entire department.

Organization is an ongoing process. New materials need to be added and old materials purged. Since information is forever changing, the system will always need updating. When organizing, it's useful to divide materials into general categories, and then subdivide those categories. It's important to be absolutely clear about what each folder or binder will contain, i.e., "a place for everything, and everything in its place." Even if there's one measly item for a given category, so be it. The primary objective is that everyone can retrieve information quickly.

It's helpful to use colored hanging files and matching colored file folders and tabs, with each color representing a different category. Every city will have a different set of files. A hotel in Hawaii, for instance, might have separate files for boating, fishing, surfing, whale watching, kayaking, etc., while a landlocked city might get by with one file designated, "Water Activities." If the concierge desk itself does not have a built-in file cabinet, one should be located as nearby as possible. In spite of all of the digital filing systems available today, there still needs to be a manual filing system to store information.

While it might be tempting to create a file for "Miscellaneous" topics, try to avoid it. There's nothing worse than rifling through an overflowing file folder that contains everything from soup to nuts.

Keep a small pocket tape recorder on hand for notes and quick messages. This is very helpful when guests make requests, and it isn't possible to make a note at the time. It is especially helpful when approached away from the desk and is an excellent tool when out of the hotel. Notes can be made on the recorder and later added to the computer database.

Create an ***adopt-a-drawer program!*** Each member of the concierge team can be responsible for a particular set of drawers and/or cabinets. Each person is responsible for keeping his or her area tidy, well supplied and well organized, which contributes to maintaining an orderly department, with everything in its proper place.

No little pieces of paper! Notes that you scribble down on haphazard scraps of paper are frequently lost, misplaced or overlooked, especially when you're feeling overwhelmed. Place the information in a notebook or file folder or transfer it to a database. Put it in its proper home, where you and others will be able to find it.

There is a direct relationship between having readily accessible information, a concierge's confidence and guest satisfaction. However, you don't want too much of a good thing. To keep the desk clean and manageable, it's best to keep only frequently used printed materials that aren't available on the Internet. (Menus are one exception.) You also want to keep hard copies of frequently used material on file, in the event of a computer crash.

Because concierge software programs organize and cross-reference information so efficiently, it's best to make use of this technology, if possible, rather than creating elaborate file systems.

BOOKKEEPING

Records are kept for all charges that come through the concierge department. In most cases, this process has been computerized. Precise logging is important for tracking any charges to guests' rooms for limousines, flower orders, tours, purchases, and other services. The hotel's accounting department should provide basic procedures to make these transactions as simple as possible. Normally, one computer file for each major category will suffice, as long as it contains the guests' name, room numbers, descriptions, and exact dollar amounts. Not only is this practice imperative for recordkeeping, it also helps the concierge department track how much revenue they're contributing, both within and outside the hotel.

THE PETTY CASH BANK

The concierge desk requires a petty-cash bank, which should serve in the best interest of both the concierge and accounting departments The bank is used for the purchase of tickets, for tips to special messengers, odd purchases for guests and a host of other incidental purchases that keep the department well supplied. The amount of the bank is typically determined by the size of the hotel, the volume of business and the types of purchases that are required.

It' an excellent idea to make contact with the accounting department and ask them to help establish a simple system for the concierge department that coordinates with their own system. In that way, reconciling the account will be a simple matter. It is mandatory for the concierge to retain all receipts and keep precise records of all service charges and messenger fees. Everything relating to the bank – especially the cash – should be kept in a locked drawer or strongbox (along with other valuables, such as tickets).

The accounting should be reconciled regularly: Daily in large hotels and weekly for smaller properties. This reconciliation should be made according to the accounting department's specifications. Normally, reconciling a petty cash bank is as simple as adding up the receipts and subtracting that amount from the total bank. The remainder should be the amount remaining in the bank.

PLANNING AHEAD: PRE-PREPARED, PERSONALIZED ITINERARIES

When working behind the concierge desk, it's impossible to plan ahead for every contingency. There are simply too many quirky requests from "out of the blue," requiring quick thinking and creative problem solving. On the other hand, there is some degree of predictability when it comes to frequently requested itineraries.

Preparing personalized itineraries for popular activities, such as what to do with children on a rainy day, is an opportunity to get a jump on demand, work efficiently and provide excellent service to guests.

> *In Hawaii, at the Lodge at Koele, the concierge department was continually getting questions from guests about what to do on the island. Since there were only about six activities available, the team was able to prepare an interesting three-day itinerary, which included every possibility from basking on the beach, to an exploration (with a map) in a four-wheel vehicle.*

At the Grand Hyatt San Francisco, we created an itinerary for a day in the wine country, with our personal favorites in wineries and restaurants. This sample will give you a good idea how to prepare an itinerary that you can generate efficiently, while still giving it a very personal feel. It was nicely printed on hotel stationery and looked something like this:

A Day in the Napa Valley

After reaching Route 29, the main artery of the Napa Valley, you can begin your wine country adventure! Of course, it's fun to explore on your own, but we wanted to offer a few of our favorite spots as suggestions.

For the first-time visitor, a stop at Robert Mondavi Winery is a good choice, as they have one of the most informative tours available. After you've taken the initial tour, you'll have learned a great deal about wine making, so any future visits can be dedicated to the fun of tasting it!

A winery with a good self-guided tour is Sterling Vineyards, which is known for its views and spectacular setting. Across the street from Sterling, you'll find an architecturally interesting winery called Clos Pegase. We also recommend a stop at Domaine Chandon, because the process for making sparkling wine is different and quite interesting.

Parallel to Route 29, you'll find a lovely road called the Silverado Trail, which has less traffic than Route 29. There is a vineyard off Silverado called Rutherford Hill Vineyards, where it's interesting to tour their "caves." Next door to Rutherford Hill is a beautiful inn called Auberge Du Soleil. We suggest that you sit on the verandah at Auberge and have a glass of wine or champagne, while overlooking the beauty that is the Napa Valley.

If you want to taste wine from boutique vineyards, a great place to stop is Vintners Village on Route 29 in St. Helena. There are tasting rooms for several small wineries in this clever complex of shops and restaurants.

If you are enjoying a meal in Napa Valley, there are several good restaurants from which to choose: Mustards Grill on Route 29 in Oakville, Tra Vigne on Route 29 in St. Helena and The Diner in Yountville.

For a picnic, you can stop at the Oakville Grocery in Oakville on Route 29, pick up yummy goodies, and then retrace your steps back down 29 to the Robert Pepi Winery. You couldn't picnic closer to the vineyards unless you were *in* them! Though they don't have a formal picnic area, you can spread your blanket on the grass in front of the vineyard. You can purchase wine for your picnic here, too, and then sit back and enjoy this lovely spot!

We hope you have a great day!

In the spirit of "in service through friendship," itineraries like this one can be shared with concierge colleagues – even those outside of your city.

> *After working as a concierge in San Francisco, Jeannie O'Reilly founded the first concierge desk on the Monterey Peninsula, at the Monterey Hyatt. She was inspired by our idea of preparing itineraries in advance and created a wonderfully useful three-day itinerary for her new "neck of the woods," including directions from San Francisco. Graciously, she shared the information with us, so we could give our guests interesting and useful information when they asked about Carmel/Monterey.*

In fact, thanks to today's technology, pre-prepared itineraries for your city can be shared with concierges all over the world in a click of a mouse, empowering them to help their guests plan their next trip! Many hotel websites have a section highlighting their concierges, so it's easy to request these pre-printed personalized itineraries from around the world.

IT'S A SMALL WORLD

In addition to becoming intimately familiar with one's immediate area, concierges should be knowledgeable about popular destinations elsewhere in the country and around the globe. Brochures should be kept for guests who ask about activities in other nearby cities they may be planning to visit in the future.

> *When working in San Francisco, I kept brochures and travel information on file for Hawaii, Las Vegas, Los Angeles, San Diego, Yosemite National Park, Sacramento, the California coast and dozens more destinations. I even maintained files on European cities, Washington, D.C., New York, Chicago, Florida and Mexico. While all this required upkeep and storage space, it was worthwhile, because I was frequently asked for travel advice and used these files consistently.*

Keeping information on file gives it a more personal touch than simply searching the Internet for a Guest. Of course, it's not practical to keep literature on file for every location on the planet, but fortunately the Internet now helps concierges serve guests who inquire about even the remotest of locations.

A FEW LAST (BUT IMPORTANT) WORDS ON ITINERARIES

Creating pre-planned itineraries requires a commitment of time and effort, perhaps even afterhours, but it's a practice that pays off handsomely. The efficiency of the concierge desk improves dramatically, as does the quality of service to guests.

Formulating special itineraries for various interest groups can be very helpful. For instance, you might come up with lists of fun activities for:

- Children
- Seniors
- Antique Enthusiasts
- Shopaholics
- Daredevils
- Active folks
- Singles
- Romantics
- Museum Junkies

While it requires a lot of work, the fun of getting creative with these itineraries can be almost as much fun as actually following them!

One of the best examples of this is Joie De Vive Hospitality. The clever folks at Joie de Vive have put together ideas tailored to many different tastes, including advice from local luminaries. It is worth checking out at http://www.jdvhotels.com/hotels

A critical caveat: Though itineraries designed in advance can be generated quickly and automatically, by no means is the process static or robotic. Be sure to review all information regularly to ensure it's complete, accurate and up-to-date. You don't want to send a family on their Christmas vacation to an attraction that's closed during the winter or a young couple to a "hot club" that closed three weeks ago.

Last but not least, in no way should an itinerary be a replacement for personal interaction and individualized attention. As with direction cards, handing a guest a sheet of paper and saying, "Here ya' go," is unacceptable. All tools designed to increase efficiency are most importantly intended to enhance the level of personalized service – never to replace it.

THE ORGANIZING PRINCIPLE

AS I WROTE THIS CHAPTER, I was amazed at how much has changed behind the concierge desk since the first edition of this book was written in 1991. Technology has come a long way in streamlining processes, improving communications and enabling concierges to serve guests more efficiently. Dog-eared Rolodex files have been replaced by computers and "smart phones" and stuffed-to-the-gills file folders reduced or eliminated entirely. One thing, however, will never change. The concierge desk should always be philosophically "organized" around the underlying principle of working cooperatively as a team to provide outstanding service levels for each and every guest.

CHAPTER TWELVE

12

Transforming Complaints Into Compliments

OBJECTIVES

The following chapter will equip readers to:

Explore the essence of what it takes to be an exceptional Les Clefs d'Or Concierge.

Utilize various practical techniques to transform an irate guest into a loyal ambassador

Diffuse guest conflict before it becomes potentially abusive

Consider the personal fulfillment that can be obtained from resolving challenging guest situations

If one were to categorize complaining guests, they might fall into two general categories:

- **The guest with a reasonable complaint, who is upset and disappointed about a situation.**
- **The guest who doesn't have a logical reason to complain, but does it anyway. This might stem from an aspect of his or her personality, an ulterior motive to gain something, the need to be right, or some inscrutable cause the concierge may never fully understand.**

One of the mysteries of human nature is that some people just seem to like to complain!

AT THE CONCIERGE DESK, working with a variety of personalities and behaviors is part of the challenge. Concierges are there to serve, and service is an equal – opportunity proposition: The same high level of service is afforded to the pleasant and the unpleasant, the right and the wrong, alike.

Concierges are fortunate that most of the people they serve are agreeable, polite and happy. When there are complaints, they are typically legitimate, understandable, and if not completely correctable, at least mitigable. However, there are exceptions, and it is vital that the concierge master the art of handling difficult situations with grace and finesse.

A MATTER OF PERCEPTION

When working with irate or disgruntled guests, there are two important principles related to perception:

- The guest's perception is the guest's reality. Guests' perceptions can be difficult to change.
- Concierges can always improve the situation by changing theirs.

TAKE A WALK IN THEIR MOCCASINS

It may be difficult at times to understand why a guest would become so upset over something seemingly unimportant, but one must consider the situation from the guest's point of view. Travelers often feel insecure and out of their element when visiting an unfamiliar place. As a result, they might overreact or act somewhat irrationally in response to seemingly minor problems. They are often tired, disoriented and so uptight from the stress of travel, that even the slightest inconvenience could be the last straw.

Hotel employees have an entirely different perspective. They're familiar and comfortable with the "beat" of the hotel and their city. Situations that arise are "all in a day's work." Easy as pie. To gain perspective, concierges should always stop to consider what it might be like to be in their guest's shoes. Did you ever find yourself lost in a strange city? If you are an itinerate traveler who navigates the world with ease, can you think of another situation where you were "a fish out of water?" Were you ever so "over your head" in algebra class that you felt as if you were drowning? Though the details may differ, we've all been there.

From this perspective, it becomes easier to identify with the guest's fears and frustrations and provide solutions that will not only take care of the problem, but also help give them a sense of safety and comfort. There is no perfect way to work with dissatisfied guests, which covers all circumstances and all behaviors. By putting oneself into the guest's shoes, however, it is possible to meet their overt and emotional needs most of the time.

The next time you encounter a difficult guest, remember: Not only is it your job to serve this type of customer, at some point in your life, you have probably been this type of customer!

A LITTLE PSYCHOLOGY

Theirs . . .

One of the most important points to remember when working with irate guests is to *deal with feelings first and solve the problem second.* It is important to the guests' self-esteem that they feel they are being understood and taken seriously. When people feel valued, it is infinitely easier to take the necessary actions to solve their problems, because you gain their trust and cooperation.

. . . and Yours

In tense situations, concierges' feelings are just as important as those of the guest. Before they're able to clearheadedly address the feelings of the guest, they need manage their own feelings and attitudes. This way, one can serve the guest consciously, without interference from reactions, emotions and judgments. Concierges with high self-esteem will feel confident that they have the capabilities and the resources to solve the problem at hand. They will also be able to recognize that the guest's venting is not directed at them personally.

There is almost a spiritual aspect at play, when the self-possessed concierge can silently forgive the guest for his or her behavior, with a degree of humility and a willingness to serve. At this point, the energy of the concierge becomes elevated to the extent that he or she is not affected by the tirade.

WOULD YOU RATHER BE RIGHT OR HAPPY?

Try repeating this question to yourself, whenever you're wrestling with your attitude about a complaining guest: Would you rather be right, or would you rather be happy? Accepting that being right does not guarantee a successful outcome makes it easier to tolerate complaints. In fact, in many cases, holding on tenaciously to being right guarantees only misery. Giving up the need to be right all the time is a giant step toward genuine humility and greater emotional maturity.

As a rule, guests repeat themselves when they are angry and upset. As you honor the guest's need to vent (and vent some more), you can simultaneously remain conscious of your feelings and reactions and get them under control.

IT'S NOT ABOUT YOU . . .

Before reacting to an upset customer, bear in mind that *it is not personal.* This is very difficult to remember when someone is yelling and screaming at you, but it is absolutely crucial not to take it personally. Irate guests are not directing their complaints at any person in particular. The buck has simply stopped at the concierge desk, and the guests want solutions.

If you begin to feel personally attacked, repeat to yourself: "This is not personal, this is not personal . . . " to restore calm to your mind.

At a concierge conference, a speaker from the airline industry gave an example of one of her most difficult passengers. She described a few of his behaviors, later adding that he was in the shoe business. At least 20 concierges gasped in recognition, as they had encountered this very same gentleman at their hotels. He was an equal-opportunity curmudgeon, which reminded everyone at the conference to not take things personally.

. . . BUT BE SURE TO MAKE IT PERSONAL FOR THE GUEST

The concierge working with an aggravated guest should immediately begin to establish a personal bond by making eye contact and using the guest's name, rather than "sir" or "ma'am." The concierge's entire focus should be devoted to the guest, tuning out all other distractions. Remain engaged, caring and personal, to convey to the guest that he or she is being taken seriously and is a priority. Remember it's a human being you're facing, not just another complaint.

AGGRAVATION VS. ABUSE

While the well-known phrase, "The customer is always right" applies to most situations, the truth of the matter is that abusive behavior is never right. There is a distinct line drawn between "angry" and "abusive," which should be clearly drawn and documented by hotel policy. Generally speaking, the use of obscenities or any act that even approaches physical violence is considered abusive. Sometimes, the concierge can quickly defuse the situation with statements like the following:

- "I understand you're angry about this situation. This is the first I've heard of it, so please help me, so I can help you."
- "I really want to help you, but I can't be of help while you're speaking to me this way."

Avoid the directive, "Calm down!" When was the last time anyone actually did calm down when you told them to?

If the situation continues to escalate, it's time to call in a member of management, or even security.

> ***I was told of an instance when a concierge was trying their best to help a guest, who just couldn't seem to calm down. When he picked up (a relatively large) "Concierge" sign and threw it across the room, I calmly continued to apologize, while at the same time, dialing security for backup.***

THE ART OF APOLOGY

A sincere apology is one of the most disarming and useful tools in the concierge's toolbox. It both acknowledges the guest's problem and shows caring and empathy. An apologetic attitude also helps the concierge better empathize with the feelings of the guest.

Here are just a few examples:

- I apologize for this. We have ruined your morning, and I am sorry.
- I apologize. I'd be upset, too, and I'm so sorry you had this experience.
- I apologize for the oversight and I'll make it right.
- I am so sorry you feel this way and will do everything I can to find an alternative that works for you.

Notice that I refer to a sincere apology – one from the heart, which is expressed in a way the guest will understand. A rote or off-handed apology serves only to throw more kerosene on the fire. A robotic, "We apologize for the inconvenience in this matter," or a casual "Sorry 'bout that," will only serve to aggravate the guest more.

GATHER FACTS; GAIN ALLIES

Listen, Listen, Listen

It's important to make every effort to interact personally and empathize with the guest. However, it's equally important to stay in a rational, problem-solving mode and not get "caught up" emotionally. Ask yourself: Why is the person so upset? What is it that he or she wants? What can be done with the resources at hand?

Listen without interrupting, and listen with the total self: heart and mind. Take in the guest's version of the facts and pay attention to the nuances that lie beneath the surface of his or her words. Listen for any key phrases that might provide important clues as to what it is they *really* want.

Of course, listening is about more than simply gathering facts. The primary aspect of dealing with any guest, especially an angry one, is listening. Most guests appreciate having someone to talk to and empathize with them. It restores the guest's composure and helps defuse the entire situation. Convey the feeling that your guest has found an ally (you!) – someone on his or her side who is eager to help. Once an atmosphere of trust has been established, you've won half the battle.

Before I became a concierge, my background and previous job experience had been in special education. I learned early on, that the skills I had used as a behavior-modification specialist in the school system were not all transferable to the hospitality industry. In the classroom with 8-year-olds, it's acceptable to ignore negative behavior and reinforce positive behavior. It was the only way I knew of to handle difficult situations, but when I was confronted with my first irate customer, I discovered I needed a new approach.

Mr. and Mrs. X were waiting at the concierge desk for their tour. The tour bus was late, which upset Mr. X quite a bit more than seemed appropriate. I explained that the bus was making pickups at various locations in the city and that it would arrive soon, but for some reason, Mr. X only became more irate. He literally threw a temper tantrum!

Using my skills as a behavior-modification teacher, I chose to ignore the outrageous behavior and even said to his wife, "I'll speak to you, because you are the only one who's behaving like an adult. Your husband is out of control, and I'll ignore him until he regains his composure." Needless to say, this didn't work well . . . at all.

Paraphrase what the guest has said, without necessarily agreeing. This helps clarify the problem and lets the guest know that he or she has been understood.

ADDITIONAL TIPS FOR WORKING WITH AN ANGRY GUEST

- Remain calm and patient. The last thing you want to do is escalate the situation.
- Feel confident. There's no need to fear contact with an irate guest.
- Don't become defensive or intimidated.
- Never be condescending to a guest.
- Avoid offering excuses. Irate guests are seldom interested in why something occurred or didn't occur.
- Don't blame other departments or individuals for the problem.
- It is never appropriate to argue with a guest. This accomplishes nothing positive and just fuels the fire.
- Avoid asking too many questions until the guest has had an opportunity to vent.
- Remember: ***It's not about you. Don't take it personally!***

When guests are upset, getting to the root of the problem can be a process. Most dissatisfied guests will vent their anger first, before getting to the facts, however disjointedly. Be on the lookout for bits and pieces of important information between the angry words. If you pay attention and listen carefully, the truth will come through. As the guest calms under the concierge's caring and competent demeanor, more and more information will seep out. Once a problem has been acknowledged, apologized for and softened by empathy, the concierge can move on to solving it.

While concierges are experts at smoothing over rough situations, there are occasional instances when management will need to get involved. If a guest is becoming so disruptive that he or she is causing a disturbance that's affecting other guests, it's time to call a member of management, so the problem can be resolved away from the hotel lobby.

LIVING IN THE SOLUTION

One of the best solution-oriented tactics is offering realistic options that will make the situation "right." For instance, you might say to a guest: "I'm so sorry you've been kept waiting for your room. I can offer you complimentary cocktails at the bar, or perhaps you'd like to take a brief tour until the room is made ready."

In addition to offering possible alternatives, the concierge might ask the guest what he or she wants. If they don't seem happy with any of the solutions offered, nicely ask them for a suggestion that would work better for them. Usually, they don't have a better idea and gradually come to accept the solution offered. On other occasions, it may prove surprising to hear the response, because it is often quite simple.

> *One of my favorite examples of this came from a very upset guest who'd asked that the room be cleaned early for a business meeting. When her request wasn't met, she angrily phoned the concierge desk to complain. I assured her that I would personally dispatch a housekeeper. I apologized profusely and asked how we might make up for our error. Without hesitating, she said she wanted a bowl of nuts, a dry martini and a vodka tonic with lots of ice delivered to her room at 5:00 p.m. Obviously, my response was, "Of course!" We were more than happy to make that happen. The apology was given, the room cleaned and the guest had a little smile on her face all evening, I'm sure.*

Sometimes a small touch can move mountains. Nice little gestures, such as a couple of conciliatory cocktails, can sometimes completely erase the memory of the unpleasant occurrence and replace it with a pleasant memory of something special. Involving the guest in the creation of solutions can often lead to just such an outcome.

Satisfying guests doesn't necessarily involve a cocktail, a free room, a free meal, or free anything. Those options are merely icing on the cake and are not, in themselves, part of a solution. Nice gestures from the hotel are fine, but it takes a caring heart with a sensible mind to solve problems and mend relationships.

After gathering the facts and ensuring the guest that you are his or her faithful advocate, act on the problem immediately. Be especially careful to only make promises that you can keep and provide the guest with a realistic time period in which to expect a solution. If another department or an outside vendor is involved in clearing up the problem, take into consideration the time it will take to work with them. Consider all angles and take special care not to overlook even the tiniest detail. Think before making any promises, as adding insult to injury when resolving complaints can be devastating.

I've talked about the importance of using creativity when working with guests, and sometimes the difficult guest requires all the creativity you can muster. The following story illustrates this:

> ***A woman, who had just checked in to a hotel, was upset about the bed. She had requested a king-size bed, and the one in her room obviously wasn't. After several hotel employees assessed the situation, they came to the only possible conclusion: It was, in fact, a king-size bed! The concierge gently informed the guest that her bed was king-sized, but she would have no part of it. She insisted on another bed. The concierge thought for a moment and came up with a solution: The maintenance department removed the bed from the room, and a few minutes later, put the same bed back in. The guest was happy and enjoyed a good night's sleep. Problem solved.***

"THE WINGS OF NO"™

A number of articles have been written in the popular press suggesting concierges can do anything. While this is flattering (and very often true), even concierges have their limits and have to deliver the bad news of "No" at times. When the guest is upset or irate, this becomes especially difficult, but "The Wings of No" formula is amazingly effective.

To help make "No" fly, I recommend giving it "wings." In my earlier books, I have shared "The Wings of No" strategy, not only with hotel concierges, but also with many people on the firing line in other service industry. Essentially, "The Wings of No" is a technique of bookending the "No" between the "wing" of a sincere statement of caring and a second "wing" of at least one alternative.

The conversation may sound something like this:

> *Guest's Question:* "Can I bring my pet into the hotel?"
>
> *Wing I – Statement of Caring:* "I love traveling with my pet, too. I understand how important that is."
>
> *The Bad News:* "We're not able to let pets stay in the hotel."
>
> *Wing II – The Alternative:* "There's a wonderful kennel close-by. If you'd like, I can call them for you or give you their number.

Wing I

Beginning with a caring statement lets guests know you are truly interested in their wellbeing and want to resolve their issue. It's vitally important to preface "No" with a caring statement, because mentioning the "No" word right off the bat can dramatically affect a guest's willingness to listen to alternatives.

Here are a few good examples of caring statements:

- "I can see how frustrating this must be for you."
- "I wish there was more I could do to help."
- "This must be so disappointing. I'd love to find a way to help."

Your body language and tone of voice can speak as loud as your words, so show attentiveness by leaning forward, making eye contact and using a warm tone of voice. Leaning back, arms crossed, a blank gaze and hollow tone of voice sends the wrong message and calls into question every word you have said.

Wing II

Providing options reinforces the fact that you care, and though they may not be the guest's first choice, they may well solve the problem. Coming up with alternatives often requires creativity, as demonstrated by the example of the "replacement" king-sized bed. For more common requests, such as the one presented by the traveling pet-lover, the concierge should be prepared with an arsenal of alternatives. In this example, the concierge should have had a brochure for the kennel at her fingertips and their phone number within reach. She might also have pulled up the kennel's website, swiveling the monitor toward the guest to view.

Avoid the explanation, "It's our policy . . . " both as a complete sentence and as a preface to a sentence. This statement annoys and sometimes even enrages people, who frankly, could care less what your policy is. Use explanations, such as, "We're no longer permitting pets in the hotel, as so many of our guests have had allergy problems." If you must refer to hotel policy, lead into it, rather than leading with it.

FOLLOW-UP

It's very important to follow-up on guest complaints by touching base with any other department(s) or vendors that have been involved, to ensure that their part of the bargain has been fulfilled and the guest has been completely satisfied.

The concierge should also follow-up with guests personally, to verify the problem has been resolved to their satisfaction. A brief call or personal note may be appropriate, depending on the situation. People really appreciate the concern and extra attention. Often, the caring demonstrated by a follow-up will entirely erase the negative experience from the guest's memory.

ALWAYS LOOK ON THE BRIGHT SIDE

HANDLING COMPLAINTS and soothing angry guests are all in a day's work of a hotel concierge. It may not be the most enjoyable aspect, but it certainly is challenging and can be appreciated from the perspective that there is much to learn and much to gain by resolving difficult situations successfully. Make it a personal challenge to turn an angry guest into a very satisfied one. It is deeply gratifying to overcome obstacles, and it allows the concierge to grow continually in the profession.

> *A friend of mine has a special award called "The Turn-Around Award." Whenever her staff turns an angry guest into a satisfied one, they document it. They also keep a doll strategically placed in the back office, which they physically turn around with each victory. Each turn is worth prizes. This focus on transforming a potentially negative situation into a positive one has given the concierge staff a new perspective on their job purpose.*

When all is said and done, learning how to cope effectively with irate guests is an example of "everybody wins." Remaining calm, apologizing, listening, allowing the guest to be right and finding creative solutions creates a favorable outcome from all points of view. The guest is satisfied. The hotel has retained a valued customer. The concierge has solved another tough problem successfully. Gold stars all around!

CHAPTER THIRTEEN

13 Sailing Through Stress

OBJECTIVES

The following chapter will equip readers to:

See the value of investing in their health and wellbeing.

Detect the methods of self-sabotage and ways to avoid it.

Use several tips and words of advice to relieve the burdens that cause stress.

STRESS . . . WHAT STRESS?

AS IS THE CASE WITH MOST SERVICE PROVIDERS, stress is a very real job hazard, never ending for the concierge. A guest can show up behaving rudely, which can later manifest, quite literally, as a pain in the neck. Swollen feet and ankles can also take their toll from standing for long periods of time, while gastrointestinal problems can arise after a hectic day in the lobby.

The following is a typical example of what 10 minutes in the life of a concierge might look like. (In fact, this all really happened!)

> *A gentleman tripped and fell down in front of the concierge desk and began screaming for someone to call an ambulance. Just then, at that very same concierge desk, Cody Anderson, who was driving a bicycle across the United States for an organization called CARE, was holding a press conference. Simultaneously, a concierge from a hotel across the street called to borrow an adapter, another guest was searching for a place called the Page Brown Mansion that had no address, another needed rooms in Napa Valley for the weekend, four more wanted restaurant suggestions and the Barbershop Quartet Convention was bringing in risers for their show that evening. This is not exaggeration. Rather, it is typical of the activities that are involved in a concierge's workday.*

Concierges are called upon to be in the eye of the hurricane in days like these, while at the same time juggling their home responsibilities, family, school, etc. Fortunately, there are ways to live with this type of stress, relieve it and sail through it gracefully.

THE ART OF SELF-CARE

**Most service providers possess the nature to nurture.
We simply need to nurture that nature.**

The important thing to remember is that the single most powerful investment you can make is an investment in yourself. You must take time to care for yourself, or the well will eventually run dry. At that point, all areas of your life suffer. While there are thousands of books, CDs and classes on the subject of self-care, I am including it in this book, because I firmly believe it's an essential tool for the concierge.

If you're not taking good care of yourself, chances are you will be ill equipped to take care of others. All great concierges have the qualities and skills needed to do the job, or they would not have been hired in the first place. However, what it takes to successfully continue in the job are the important concepts of self-care and self-renewal.

For some concierges, self-care may not come naturally. Many people who serve others for a living have a deep-seated need to be needed and consequently, feel more comfortable giving than receiving. It often takes a shift in thinking to realize that giving to yourself is the very best thing you can possibly do to be available to give to others.

When it comes to self-nurturing, the obstacle most often mentioned is the lack of time. Let's look at that for a moment. I believe it's not simply about the actual amount of time that's available, but rather your attitude regarding time. For instance, take a look at your behavior and notice if you always tend to make time for others, but not yourself. If so, a great technique to counteract this tendency is to actually schedule time for yourself. I'm serious. Make an appointment with yourself, record it on your calendar or in your "smart phone," and by all means, keep that appointment! If you think you absolutely can't find time during the day, make your day a little longer by waking up 15 minutes earlier than usual, then dedicate that quarter of an hour to yourself only.

There are so many ways to renew yourself. Here are a few ideas you can use easily, without even leaving your house.

- Play your favorite music and dance to it.
- Take a hot bath with aromatic oils.
- Read a book.
- Putter in the garden.
- Arrange flowers.
- Meditate

Always make it a priority to find a moment for yourself. I'm saying "a moment," because I'm realistic and sensitive to the fact that many of us lead busy lives – above and beyond our hectic jobs. You may not have two hours to go to the gym or even 45 minutes to take a walk, but you can usually find 5 or 10 minutes – even if it's in your car – before you tackle the next item on your agenda.

During your "me time," don't answer the phone just because it rings. Let voice mail handle it. Hang a "Do Not Disturb" sign on your door, lock it and revel in the silence.

THE SIX PATHS TO SELF-SABOTAGE

When you're not taking care of yourself, you become vulnerable to all kinds of self-sabotage. Beware of these six classic paths that lead to your own undoing and derail them immediately with self-care:

The critical voice. This is a voice inside your head that has one purpose and one purpose only – to make you doubt yourself. While healthy self-esteem is paramount when serving others, self-doubt is a deadly enemy. Deal with it immediately! I call my own inner critic "the man with the whip." Here's how I handle him: As soon as he opens his mouth, I send out squads of cheerleader voices to drown out his constant whip-cracking banter. He sounds something like this: "You're not good enough, you didn't do this well enough, you're not really that smart," and on it goes . . . This critical voice, which is the opposite of self-care, can and should be overridden with endless streams of positive self-talk: "You have so much to offer, you did a great job today, how smart of you to solve the guest's dilemma." Now I need to add here, that learning to be a friend to yourself is not an overnight process and the "man with the whip" may never disappear altogether. However, if you continue to call in the cheer-leading squad, his voice will become more and more distant, as the volume of the encouraging voices increase.

Comparison. Simply put, comparison is a one-way street to misery and it's an ongoing process to resist the temptation to compare yourself to others. I am a member of the National Speakers Association, a group of very outgoing, highly accomplished professionals. While I truly enjoy going to meetings and growing in my chosen profession, the hardest work for me is to be comfortable with myself and my own path, instead of comparing myself to everyone else. It's not always easy, but it's definitely worth working on, because comparing oneself negatively with others is so damaging – and futile!

Resisting the Good. This pitfall is so subtle, you may not even realize you're doing it. For instance, by not accepting compliments. you are, in essence, rejecting your personal power. I was in the Seattle airport going up on an escalator, and as a woman on the down escalator passed me, she paid me a compliment: "Your hair is so pretty. What do put on it?" For reasons still unknown to me, I casually replied, "Chlorine." I even surprised myself with such a curt response to such a kind compliment! I've since realized that we sabotage our self-care (and can even hurt other's feelings) by not accepting a compliment.

Unclear Boundaries. This is a trap many people-pleasers fall into. They so want to please, that they find it very difficult to say "No," even when "No" is clearly the answer and saying "Yes" interferes with their self-nurturing. Using my technique, "The Wings of No," is helpful – both in one's personal and professional life. (For more information about using "The Wings of No," see CHAPTER 11.)

Not Asking for What You Want. It's safe to say that most people you meet don't have psychic abilities. Consequently, you need to ask for what you want. Whether you get it or not, the very fact that you have asked for what you want is a step in the right direction. You always win, when you are brave enough to take the risk; and you'll never get it if you don't ask at all!

Remaining in Toxic Relationships. One of the primary signs of a toxic relationship is that you always feel worse after you've been with a person. Granted, some of these relationships are inescapable (particularly in the case of a family member or co-worker), in which case you need to walk softly and set firm boundaries. Eliminating toxic relationships whenever possible and creating positive, meaningful connections are critical to well being.

FORGIVENESS IS PART OF TAKING CARE OF *YOU*

Who's perfect anyway? Striving for perfection destines you for a disappointing life. Why is it that, although we manage to please and receive compliments from guest after guest, the one person who "blows up" becomes the focus of our attention? This certainly happened to me a lot, and I'm assuming it happens to you, too!

When I worked at a hotel and felt responsible for a customer's negative experience, I obsessed about it for days. I don't know why we do this. Even now, I struggle with this issue. If I'm giving a lecture and most of the room is attentive, but one person is falling asleep or looking at his watch, I have to resist the urge to obsess about the one watch watcher! The key is to concentrate your energies on the people who are with *you*, instead of becoming distracted by the isolated negative disturbance.

When faced with rudeness and hostility in the lobby, the key to minimizing stress is to remain calm and focus on the positive steps you can take to solve the problem and satisfy the guest. The other part of managing your stress levels is to work "behind the scenes" (in your mind, that is) on forgiving the guest for his or her behavior. One can never be sure what guests have gone through before they reach their boiling points. Regardless, sending out "vibes" of understanding and compassion will help you feel better, even if the guest is incapable of absorbing it at the time.

For concierges in particular, it's even more important to *forgive yourself,* acknowledging that you can never be all things to all people. Of course, forgiveness is only possible when you are honestly doing the best you possibly can. There's so much freedom in doing one's best, because it allows you to forgive any imperfections and concentrate on all the wonderful things you've done so well.

NAME YOUR STRESSOR

Once while on the telephone, a concierge in San Francisco was suddenly interrupted by a car crashing through the front door of the hotel and landing in the lobby. After quickly checking for injuries, he rushed back to his desk and continued calmly with the duties at hand: three people waiting for a tour, a car rental to reserve and a Federal Express box to be wrapped. It was all in a day's work! Of course, a car crashing into the lobby is an exception to the rule, but he handled it with such aplomb, no one would ever have guessed it wasn't a daily occurrence.

Runaway cars are just one type of stressor. Doing three things at once for hours on end is another. In addition, everyone has their own little "pet peeves" that always get their goat. Maybe it's aggressive guests, who say things such as: "What's the matter, don't you have any yank?" or "Use your influence," or "Tell them I'll give them a big tip if they give me a table." For others, it's guests who want to make multiple reservations for the same evening, so they can make up their minds at the last minute.

The potential for stress at the concierge desk is enormous. Consider the nature of the location alone: no walls, no office, no privacy, no door to close, no place to go and nowhere to vent frustrations. Being constantly available – not just to guests, but to outside vendors, outside callers and other hotel staff – is stressful.

During my concierge years, there were times I just couldn't handle another question. I would take a very quick break, run down to the kitchen, tear into the freezer, close the door and scream at the top of my lungs. Hey, it was safe! No one could hear me, and the temperature helped cool me down – in more ways than one. Very refreshed, and only moments later, I returned to the frontlines, grateful to be cheerfully serving guests once again.

I've mentioned it before, but it bears repeating here that having a back office both improves service levels and lowers stress. Rotating staff between the hectic lobby and the relative peace of the back office is a huge stress reducer. It's also a great place to "run and hide" for a moment when the going gets tough at the desk.

Don't let this be you! At the time of this writing, a flight attendant made national news when he blew his top after a passenger swore at him and delivered a blow to his head with her luggage, as he tried to assist her. He completely stunned passengers, as he cursed at the entire aircraft, grabbed a couple of beers and made his dramatic escape down the emergency exit hatch.

This story brings to light the enormous expectations and resulting emotional toll placed on concierges and all direct service providers. His news-making departure from the plane – and his entire airline career – create a perfect metaphor. Those who work with the public, and are thereby subject to rude behavior, really must have our own "escape hatches." We should all be aware of the limits of their abilities to cope and have the necessary tools to change direction, before we "lose it" on the job.

Wouldn't it be great if, instead of feeling trapped as prisoners of our white-knuckled personal politeness, we each had our own individual escape hatch? For me, it is accepting all of the people, places and things that I cannot change, maintaining a spirit of playfulness and spending time standing in awe of the mysteries of a redwood tree. I encourage you to find your own personal escape hatch, so you can be free to enjoy connecting with others, instead of continually suppressing the urgent need to escape them.

How do you cope? What are your escape hatches?

COPING

Relief Is As Close As Your Next Breath

One very simple, but often forgotten, concept is breathing to relieve stress. It sounds silly, but when people get busy and the pressure is on, their breath becomes shallow. Sometimes, it even stops altogether! The first step in learning to de-stress with the breath is noticing when your breath becomes rapid, labored or non-existent. Awareness is half the battle. When this happens, taking a few minutes to breathe deeply is the quickest, most effective, least expensive and most readily available stress reliever going.

It's important to learn how to breathe properly, which means deeply and diaphragmatically. If possible, it's advisable to get away from the desk and do a few deep-breathing exercises. Proponents of yoga and meditation are well aware of simple and highly effective breathing techniques. For instance, you might focus on breathing slowly and deeply. As you inhale, slowly count to five, hold your breath for five and then exhale out on five counts. Repeat this process three times or so. You can do this anywhere – even at the desk – if you're able to do it subtly enough. It's a guaranteed stress reliever!

Here is another very effective breathing technique that will need to be done in private:

Alternate-Hemisphere Breathing

1. *Sit or stand with your spine straight. Gently rest the right thumb on the right nostril, the ring finger on the left nostril and exhale through both nostrils.*
2. *Now, hold the right nostril closed with your right thumb. Slowly and deeply inhale through the left nostril to a count of five.*
3. *Then, press the left nostril closed and count to five. Now, open the right nostril only and exhale to a count of five. Without pausing, inhale through the right nostril to a count of five.*
4. *Open the left nostril and exhale through it for five counts.*
5. *Repeat five to ten times.*

Practicing alternate-hemisphere breathing will allow you to return to the desk feeling refreshed and energized, ready to smile and calmly ask the next guest, "How may I help you?"

THE POWER OF GROUNDING

Most of us, especially when we are busy, have all our energy spinning around in our heads. We have become detached from our bodies and become scattered and fragmented. Taking the time to re-group and ground yourself quickly changes the energy, and most importantly, gives you the ability to get in touch with your intuition and higher self.

Grounding is the ability to be fully present and responsive, which enables you to make sound choices. When you're not grounded, your mind is swimming and you become reactive. In over 20 years of searching, attending seminars, consulting healers and exploring self-care options, the following technique is the most efficient and effective grounding tool I have ever encountered.

Grounding and Centering Process

The following Grounding and Centering process was created by Aimee Lyndon-Adams, a very talented teacher of energetic healing, as well as an expert in customer service. When I first learned the technique, I considered it to be one of the best gifts I had ever received.

1. *Sit in a chair, with your legs uncrossed and feet on the floor, about a foot apart. Place your hands, palms down, on your thighs and gently close your eyes. Shift your awareness to the base of your spine. Take a deep breath in through your nose and as you slowly exhale (out through your mouth with an audible "ha"), imagine you are sending a cord from the base of your spine down to the center of the earth. This exhalation should be twice as long as the inhalation. Then, return your awareness to the base of the spine and "breathe" that cord down again – this time, imagining it is 50 percent thicker and stronger.*

2. *Return your awareness to the base of the spine and as you take another deep breath, exhale a similar cord down each of the legs and out through the bottom of the feet, all the way down to the center of the earth. Imagine that the earth's center is red, hot and molten. Using a "pumping" breath (quickly in through the nose and out through the mouth, with inhalations and exhalations of equal length), imagine that you're drawing the earth energy up into your feet and ankles with each exhalation. You may start to feel a warm and tingling sensation, as you continue to bring it up into the knees and thighs – filling every cell with revitalizing earth energy. Draw it up, until it reaches the base of your spine and notice how it continues to rise of its own accord, filling every cell of your body with earth energy.*

3. *Now, to protect your energy field, take a deep and grounding breath, while imagining a layer of protective blue energy all around you. Begin above the top of the head and sweep it down in front of you, underneath your feet and back up behind you, making a complete circle at above the top of your head. Then, sweep another layer down both sides.*

4. *Sit quietly and experience how it feels to be grounded and centered and imprint it, so you can call upon this feeling anytime you need it.*

The more you practice it, the more you will develop the "circuitry," and at some point, you'll be able to ground yourself in just one breath!

I recommend that you commit to this practice at home twice a day – morning and evening. As you become proficient with the practice, you will easily be able to ground and center yourself throughout the day, by taking deep breaths, bringing awareness to your abdomen and imagining the protective blue energy all around you. You'll feel refreshed and ready to face whatever challenges the day may bring!

MOVEMENT AS MEDICINE

The next best stress reliever is movement. Whether it's, dancing, walking or jumping, nothing breaks up tension quite like movement. It's a great way to release stress, as it literally "works it out." The most effective activity depends on the person doing it and can range from fast walking, running, bike riding, weight lifting, aerobics, to swimming.

One of the best ways to discover what activity best nurtures you is to ask yourself, "What did I love to do as a child?" What were your favorite games and pastimes?

> *At one point in my concierge career, I was so stressed, I knew I had to do something to bring balance and self-renewal into my life. I remembered that in my childhood, I had loved to swim, so I gave swimming a try. Now when I swim, I think of it as "me time." I even call it my swim. It's not about counting laps or competition, but moving, relaxing and enjoying. Taking the time to take care of myself renews me and provides the "juice" I need to serve my clients, my family and my friends.*

The best exercise is the one you will actually do.
So just do it!

STRESS REDUCTION STRETCHING EXERCISES

Another form of physical activity that's highly effective for stress release is stretching. Here are just a few suggestions:

1. Clasp your hands together behind your back, squeeze your shoulder blades together and begin to lift your hands as you simultaneously lower your head. Bend forward as far as you can. Hold for 30 seconds. Repeat three times.
2. Make a fist. Keep your arms straight at your side and lift your shoulders up to your ears. Squeeze very tightly. Take a deep breath and scrunch your face into a small ball. Hold for 30 seconds. Exhale deeply and let go of the muscles in your face, shoulders and fists. Repeat three times.
3. Take three deep breaths and then just hang loose like a rag doll.

DANCING THROUGH THE DAY

Busy people can create a "rhythm" to their work, and that very rhythm can be harnessed into positive energy, by imaging and expressing it as "dancing." There is both a personal rhythm and a collective rhythm that's created behind the concierge desk. I'm not talking about drumming or toe-tapping, but an energy that's created when you're in the flow of your work – whether it's logging information into the computer or escorting a guest to the conference room.

Many people who work in restaurant kitchens are well aware of this phenomenon. In a restaurant with an open kitchen, you can observe the chefs dancing their own way while preparing their dishes, as they orchestrate the many elements of the process. Whether it's one chef coordinating all the components or a team working together, it's magical to observe this rhythm in action. Most concierges are unaware that this rhythm even exists. I know I was, until a colleague of my brought it to my awareness.

> ***An associate and I were standing at the concierge desk on a fairly slow day, when suddenly a tour bus pulled up and a sea of humanity poured unexpectedly into our lobby. Michael turned to me, leaned over and whispered, "Let's disco concierge!"***

I've never forgotten that! What a wonderful response to a potentially overwhelming situation. I was on my feet in a moment, following his lead and "dancing" with an imaginary rhythm in my step. I was handling the hectic pace with a smile on my face. The results of making the conscious choice to dance through this challenge were amazing. Not only was there no stress, we were having fun! We were in control, and most importantly, our guests were served in the most positive way possible. Turning what might be considered a negative situation into one that is totally positive is exhilarating. "Dancing" accomplishes this.

It's possible to bring subconscious rhythms into the conscious, and there is tremendous personal power in understanding and practicing this concept. The greatest benefit of being in touch with your own rhythm is that you can always retrieve it once it's been broken and continue gracefully with the work at hand.

The benefits of being in touch with your own rhythm go far beyond getting concierges through crunch time. This understanding can quite literally keep a bad moment exactly that – a bad moment. It doesn't have to turn into a bad day, a bad attitude you take home with you, or a bad week. Why waste all this time and all those opportunities to shine?

> ***A friend of mine had a doctor's appointment at a very busy clinic – so busy that there were two receptionists handling the patients in the waiting***

room. One of the doctors was delayed in surgery, so all of the appointments had to be rearranged. My friend was fascinated by the behavior of the two receptionists who were navigating the exact same situation. One handled it with compassion and style, while the other was overwhelmed and rude. My friend asked the busy-yet-helpful of the duo what her secret was. She said she gets into the rhythm of the situation and dances through it. Dance or be miserable – you make the choice.

When the pressure is really on, it's time to take out the dance card and move through the situation joyfully. Rise above the stress – don't be a victim of it. The concept of "dancing through the day" might be the single most valuable tool for the concierge to master. It is the very essence of the fundamental "attitude adjustment" necessary for turning overwhelming energy into pure fun.

If you can relate to the metaphor of dancing through your day, great! If not, create your own metaphor to describe your individual rhythm, whether it's flying, sailing or swimming. It doesn't matter what it is; the important thing is that you have a rhythm and are aware of it.

BRING YOUR SENSE OF HUMOR TO WORK

Humor is stress management in its highest form. However, at times (especially the stressful ones), developing a sense of humor takes practice. First, you need to be willing to look at situations differently. Make the decision that you're going to look for the "funny," and it will actually become fun. It only requires two tools – a pen and a notebook, teamed up with a positive attitude. You are now armed for creating a humor journal and adding levity to the workplace.

I always kept a small notebook at my concierge desk. In it, I would record funny incidents, as they occurred. The entries ran the gamut from stories, to one-liners, to incredible moments. Keeping a "humor journal" will not only help you remember these occurrences, but also sets you up to "look for the funny." Mine became so treasured that I would measure the success of my day by the number of entries in it. Without this life-saving strategy, I don't think I would have survived frontline service for very long.

Once you have your journal, you need to get into the practice of using it. It may require some motivation. If adding levity and laughter to the workplace isn't enough incentive, try rewarding yourself and other team members with a prize for the best journal entry of the month. Read them aloud and share the joy!

I remember a seminar attendee telling me she got very annoyed when customers would ask her, "Do you work here?" It was a toy store, and more

> *often than not, she was on the top rung of a ladder, dressed in an orange vest with the store logo on it! I suggested she bring her sense of humor to the top of that ladder and find the "funny" in the situation.*
>
> *I was working with three people in front of me, with two telephone calls on hold, when a man stormed right up to the concierge desk. He very gruffly and aggressively stated, "Hey lady, I need a room for tonight."*
>
> *Because he did not appear to be a regular guest, I hesitated to send him to the front desk, so I asked him exactly what it was he needed. He replied, "Well, I haven't slept for four days and I have three dollars. Where can you send me?"*
>
> *Not wanting to upset him or the other guests, I acted as if this request was all in a day's work and took out some maps and a highlighter. I wanted to handle the situation with dignity, so I quietly marked the location of the nearest homeless shelter. Off he went – another satisfied customer.*
>
> *But this is not the end of the story! Three days later, I looked up, and there he was again! He looked at me and said, "Hey lady, do you remember that shelter you sent me to? Well, I didn't like it. What else you got?"*
>
> *Instead of becoming aggravated, I remember thinking: "Only in San Francisco would the homeless use a concierge and then come back to complain." Needless to say, this story won the "best-entry prize" in the humor journal for that month!*

Do whatever it takes to find the humor in life. When you work with people, there are always stories. Write them down! They're just too good to risk losing. It takes commitment and consistency to look for the magic in the face of adversity. The results are well worth it, though, in the happier, more hilarious environment you'll be creating for yourself and those around you. Why be annoyed, when you could be amused. It's your choice!

It probably goes without saying, but concierges must always treat guests with respect and take their requests seriously. So, be sure to wait to savor and share the humor, until after the guest has left the desk!

SERVICE IS A PERFORMING ART

It's show time! The hotel lobby can be considered a "theater" and the concierge desk the "stage." One's neatly pressed uniform is a costume and the concierge is the consummate "actor." The guests, of course, are the audience.

Disney does it. Every park and hotel employee at a Disney property has been trained to be on stage – in a costume, a part of the cast and performing in front of an ever-changing audience. This includes everyone – those behind a counter, at a ticket gate or tending the grounds. In uniform, they are in costume. At work, they are on stage.

It's the concierge's responsibility to behave in an exemplary manner at all times, to project professionalism and never allow negative feelings or personal problems to interfere with guest service. As the concierge approaches each day, the curtain's up and it's Show Time!

I encourage all concierges to develop acting skills. Look for an acting class – an "improv" class, ideally. You'll learn how to be spontaneous and in the moment within a framework. In the hotel lobby, it's the guests' framework – it's their play. You are the actor. As you become more adept at this, you will move up to the director's chair. It becomes your play, as well.

You might be asking yourself, "What does this have to do with the stress of the job?" Well, it really comes into "play," when giving the same answers to the same questions over and over again. The repetitive parts of the job can be viewed as a long-running Broadway show with the concierge as the star.

> *In Hello Dolly, Carol Channing repeatedly sang the same songs and the same lines every day and night for years – all the while acting as if it was the first time she had ever done it. When asked how she was able to do it, she replied, "Why, that's my job. The people have never heard me sing it before, so my job is to sing it like I never sang it before."*
>
> *When I was asked for the ten-thousandth time "Where are the cable cars?" I allowed myself to be in the moment with the guest and challenged myself to say it like I'd never said it before.*

If a guest were to remark that it seemed as if I've answered this question a million times, I'd know I'd failed in my job. I should appear to be saying it all for the first time, with excitement and enthusiasm. The game is to take things that could drive you crazy and turn them into a wonderful challenge. Acting works!

OTHER STRESS BUSTERS

- If possible, take two days off in a row, which allows time to unwind.
- Trade places and be the one who is served. Get a massage, manicure, facial, or pedicure. It's necessary to nurture oneself when constantly serving others.
- Be like Teflon.® Let the negative energy of others roll right off.
- Don't become a victim of the stress. Remember, dance through the day!

If possible, wear a headset. This technique helps to relieve tension in the neck and shoulders, keeps hands free and is a major help when waiting on hold (which can consume a large part of the day). The drawback of wearing a headset is that people can't tell when a person is actually using the phone, so they just start talking to you. It's also a bit disconcerting when guests become confused as to who is being spoken to – the guest or the party on the other end of the telephone. Non-verbal communication helps. It's easy to point to the phone and whisper, "I'm on the phone" or "I'll be with you in a moment."

DON'T SWEAT THE SMALL STUFF

WHEN IT COMES RIGHT DOWN TO IT, it's not the stressors themselves that get us down; it's our reaction to them. We all have different ways of coping with the stressors in our lives; the key is to actually use those coping skills – providing they are healthy ones. The next time you're feeling as if you're in the lion's den, take the time to be aware of your feelings, pause and breathe. During times of stress, it also benefits me to accept what I cannot change, change what I can and ask for the wisdom to know the difference. I also try to put things in perspective. Usually, I have forgotten what was worrying me the week before, which tells me the following words of wisdom are true: This, too, shall pass.

CHAPTER FOURTEEN

14

Uniforms And Grooming

OBJECTIVES

The following chapter will equip readers to:

Appreciate the value of portraying a professional appearance at all times

Make use of a variety of tactics to enhance their personal style

As stated in Les Clefs d'Or *Code of Ethics and Professional Standards*, concierges should "always maintain a professional appearance and unless told otherwise, wear professional attire to all concierge-related functions." This standard also applies to one's attire when representing the hotel in any way, including taking in a complementary theater production or enjoying a complementary dinner.

CONCIERGES, INCLUDING CHIEF CONCIERGES, are always in "uniform" when they are on duty. There are no "Casual Fridays" for concierges, as they need to look their absolute best at all times. The style of the uniforms will vary from hotel to hotel, but should always convey a sense of professionalism, sophistication and style. They should also be distinct from those worn in other areas of the hotel.

In the past, in some hotels in Europe, concierges wore formal uniforms with military-type hash marks (stripes), denoting rank. The chief concierge, for instance, would have four hash marks, while the second in command had three and the other members of the team had one or two. Even today, some European concierges wear formal frock coats.

Depending on the hotel, a tuxedo, a morning suit, or a simple but elegant business suit are appropriate for men. Tuxedo shirts obviously go well with a tuxedo or a morning suit. Over the years, the styles for women have changed. While some hotels still require coatdresses, many now opt for more feminine styling and flattering designs. Conservative, standard white shirts or blouses are recommended for a business suit, both for men and women. Whatever form your uniform takes, it should always be clean and well pressed. If you live with pets, be sure to have a lint-roller at home to remove any traces of Fido or FiFi before you leave for work.

Regardless of the uniform style, there should be a lapel or another appropriate spot to accommodate the Cross Keys pin, designating membership in Les Clefs d'Or. Members have worked very hard for this distinction, and there should be a prominent place where they keys can be displayed with pride.

ACCESSORIES

Specific standards are established by each hotel, including any restrictions as to body piercing and body art (tattoos), but in general, a conservative touch is recommended with regard to accessories and jewelry.

> *I once visited a hotel in New York City, where the concierge was dripping in diamonds. The only thing missing was a tiara. I was uncomfortable, because I think a concierge's uniform should be business like. The image projected should demonstrate ability and professionalism. It should not be flashy or gaudy.*

Remember, less is more. A nametag and, when the time comes, Les Clefs d' Or Cross Keys pin can be sufficient. In general, earrings should be no larger than a quarter, and dangles (often more comfortable for telephone work) should be discreet. A simple, conservative wristwatch can round out the look.

A trend in some smaller hotels is to eliminate nametags, as management feels it helps guests feel more at home. I think wearing a nametag helps guests remember whom they have talked to and encourages the concierge to take personal responsibility. I also like the idea of adding a second line to the nametag, indicating the concierge's hometown or an interesting tidbit of information, such as their favorite movie. It's fun and a great conversation starter!

The concept of "less is more" applies to fragrances, too. Especially since some people are allergic or sensitive to fragrances, perfume and cologne should be worn sparingly, if at all.

HANDS

Because a concierge's hands are often upfront and "center stage," it is imperative that they are well-groomed. Men's nails should be buffed and a weekly manicure is necessary for women. When it comes to the color of nail polish, again a conservative look is always preferable. Of course, rings are acceptable, as long as they are in keeping with the overall look of professionalism. Two rings per hand should be the limit.

Keep hand lotion at the desk and use it often, to keep hands looking their best.

HAIR AND MAKEUP

All hotel companies will have their own etiquette and grooming standards, including any guidelines as to hair length. In general, it's recommended that hairstyles and makeup be professional looking – in keeping with basic fashion – but not too "trendy". A simple, classic look is always best.

Kathleen Fitzgerald, Les Clefs d'Or Concierge, Carmel, California, is shown wearing a perfect example of a professional concierge uniform.

A PROPER HANDSHAKE AND SMILE ARE A PART OF THE UNIFORM

Many people make an immediate judgment about others, based on their handshakes alone. A firm (not crushing) handshake is an integral part of the concierge's calling card, though concierges should always wait for the guest to offer his or her hand first.

For the proper handshake, use the right hand and a complete grip (palm to palm and web to web). It should constitute approximately one – three shakes, with a medium level of vigor, held for no longer than two to three seconds.

Your handshake should be accompanied by eye contact, a warm, natural smile and a polite greeting – preferably using the guest's name. Actually, a smile on the face – and in your voice – is an integral part of the concierge's uniform and should be worn at all times (unless, of course, you are discussing a serious matter).

It has been scientifically proven that, if you subtly raise your eyebrows (no more than 1/16″) for a split second when greeting someone, it gives them the impression you are more open and available to them.

DRESSING THE PART

AS I'VE DISCUSSED IN CHAPTER 12, putting on your uniform is tantamount to putting on your "costume" before entering the "stage" of the hotel lobby. It acts as a symbol that it's time for "Lights, Camera, Action!" By the same token, taking off the uniform when you return home after your shift can powerfully symbolize a transition to a little downtime. When the uniform comes off, you can leave the busy lobby behind and soak up some greatly needed R&R!

Uniforms can run the gamut from a simple tailored suit to a formal tuxedo complete with morning coat. This photo shows an example of a formal concierge uniform, worn proudly by Abraham Guzman, Maurice Dancer and Francisco Andeliz of The Pierre New York, A Taj Hotel.

Photo courtesy of Philip Allport

CHAPTER FIFTEEN

15

Tales From The Front

OBJECTIVE

The following chapter will equip readers to:

Appreciate authentic stories that highlight examples of what can be expected in the concierge role

> *Being a concierge is about making the seemingly impossible possible, as long as it's legal and kind.*
>
> —Holly Stiel, 1978

MAKING THE IMPOSSIBLE POSSIBLE

THE CHIEF CONCIERGE at The Park Hyatt Chicago, Karen Giobbia, believes that maintaining the concierge edge is simple: While anyone can do an "OK" job, she and her staff always strive to go above and beyond. Of course, you can't actually go above and beyond with every single guest every single time; but it is the idea, challenge and the possibility of doing so that has sustained her enthusiasm for many years. It is one of the greatest joys of being a concierge.

"At the same time, guest expectations have risen, mainly due to increased competition and the fact that most are experienced travelers," says Simon Hudson, endowed chair in tourism and economic development at the University of South Carolina. "Good hotel managers and employees know that the only way to guarantee loyalty is to constantly exceed those expectations."

As a result, the life of a concierge is so filled with the odd, the adventurous and the "unobtainable" that it can seem more like a research project, scavenger hunt or surrealistic movie than a day on the job. The following real-life experiences from concierges throughout the profession demonstrate just a few of the unexpected twists and turns that constitute both the challenges – and the joys – of being a concierge, I've included this chapter of stories – not only because some are humorous and entertaining – but also because they give you a good idea about the types of situations you might actually experience firsthand in the hotel lobby.

I'll begin with the following real-life events, which were listed in an internal Fairmont Hotels document. A Toronto spokesman for Fairmont Hotels confirms the legitimacy of the list, which spans three or four years of truly exceptional requests.

A concierge was asked to fill in on a blind date.

At The Plaza Hotel in New York, a guest who'd had a falling out with his daughter requested that a Native American reconciliation ceremony, complete with feathers and peace pipe, be performed in his room by a chief – who, incidentally, had to be tracked down in neighboring New Jersey by the concierge. That same hotel had a guest ask for a dinner of roasted tarantulas.

In San Francisco's Ghirardelli Square, the Fairmont Heritage Place had someone request a hyperbaric chamber.

A concierge at the Copley Plaza in Boston located a pair of velvet-lined handcuffs at 11 p.m., at the urging of a female guest – a bizarre request that nonetheless paled in comparison to the time the hotel was asked to track down a highly specific model of incubator in time to save a guest's ostrich eggs.

A guest at the Fairmont in Chicago requested 30 pig eyes on ice for an ophthalmology conference.

The following are still more true stories lived out by one of my concierge friends, who played the starring role in taking every opportunity to make the impossible possible.

My friend at the Four Seasons in Chicago remembers the time a guest wanted to surprise his daughter on her birthday and solicited her help. He asked that her to purchase a candy-apple red Miata for him and have it wrapped and waiting outside the front door. Her only dilemma was the wrapping, so she added a teddy bear in the driver's seat with a huge bow.

This same concierge helped a gentleman whose luggage had been delayed and needed clothing for a particularly important meeting. The man's wife supplied sizes and explained that he had very expensive tastes. She was instructed to buy only the finest garments. The concierge had a wonderful afternoon choosing an Armani suit, Gucci shoes, a Hermes tie and luxurious silk underwear – all at very hefty prices. When the gentleman got to his room, the complete outfit was waiting. He was very pleased and happily added the purchases to his permanent wardrobe.

Another of her challenges took her on a whirlwind of planning for the wives of several Italian businessmen who were meeting in Chicago. The ladies had heard of Niagara Falls and asked Abigail to arrange a trip for the day. They had no idea, of course, that the attraction was so distant from Chicago, and wanted to be back in time to meet their husbands for cocktails and dinner. An impossible feat? Not at all. She managed to arrange special limousine service to get them to the plane, have them met in Niagara, taken on the "Maid of the Mist" tour, taken to a private luncheon and returned to the plane, where they were picked up by limousine to arrive at the hotel in time to change for their evening on the town.

OUCH! NEXT . . .

These are great success stories. On the other hand, concierges should always be prepared for the times when events don't quite unfold according to plan. The following is a collection of tales demonstrating the occasional woes faced by concierges across the country.

A concierge at the Copley Plaza in Boston handled a group of fifteen Saudi Arabians who wanted to return home on the same flight during their religious holy day, Ramadan. All flights to Saudi Arabia were full, but the concierge and his associate spent two entire weeks tracking down airline representatives and consulates to fulfill the request. Triumphantly, he called the group leader to tell him the good news, only to be greeted by the curt response: "Oh, we changed our minds. Never mind." Ouch.

A concierge in Seattle remembers a distraught couple crying at the desk because they'd left a bag of heirloom jewelry on a local bus. She made a mad dash to a taxi, with the instruction to the driver: "Follow that bus!" After an adventurous journey through the city, she finally caught up with the bus and was able to find the jewels. Breathlessly arriving at the desk with the prize in hand, she discovered that, not only were the people not guests of the hotel, they didn't even say, "Thank you." Ouch.

A concierge at the Mayflower Hotel in Washington, D.C. rushed home at the last minute – on foot and in the rain – for his personal cufflinks, studs and cummerbund to lend to a high-ranking member of government for an inaugural ball. The items were returned the next day, but when they arrived, their boxes were missing – so was a note of thanks.

At a major hotel in Seattle, the concierge tells an outrageous story of a guest who lost a "valuable" diamond ring while dining in an outdoor cafe. The concierge went to great pains, calling the city sanitation department and had them remove a manhole cover to retrieve the ring. The ring was retrieved, but the concierge's efforts were met with disdain and displeasure. It turns out the ring wasn't at all as "valuable" as the guest had described and the concierge could only assume that the guest had planned on an insurance settlement, rather then the return of the item.

Another concierge remembers an administrative assistant calling to reconfirm a complex itinerary on the day of arrival of a crown prince. Unable to locate it, the concierge assumed that the original arrangements had somehow been misplaced. So, he frantically made all the plans necessary to accommodate the VIP – including securing the presidential suite, hiring limousines and providing a police escort. Shortly before the prince was due to arrive, he discovered that the administrative assistant had mistakenly called the Ritz-Carlton in Naples, Florida when she had meant the one in Laguna Niguel in California. Ouch! Next . . .

In each of these cases, there was no time to wait and bemoan the "ouch incident" that had just transpired. There were people waiting, so the disappointing and frustrating circumstances were followed – just a split second later – by the same highly professional concierges greeting the next guest in line and asking with a smile, *"How may I help you?"*

BE PREPARED . . . TO MANIFEST MIRACLES

The Boy Scout's motto, "Be Prepared," is a good one for concierges, as well. Concierges are always on the ready to expect the unexpected and create the miraculous:

A concierge at the Willard Hotel in Washington D.C. was happy to have a camera close at hand when one of his guests surprised his wife with a red Jaguar convertible for her fortieth birthday. When the Jag was delivered, Michael discretely arranged for the guest to take an imaginary telephone call, which took him away from lunch with his wife, so that he could sign for the car. When lunch was over, the maître d' notified the concierge, who was able to meet the couple at the front door and forever capture her surprise and elation over the extravagant gift.

A concierge at a five-star hotel in San Francisco received a request for a jar of Pacific Ocean water for a child's science project. Undaunted, he took the house limousine, went to the ocean, rolled up his pants and got the jar of genuine Pacific Ocean water. Easy.

A concierge at the Peninsula Beverly Hills arrived one morning to find an enormous grandfather clock waiting. A guest had checked out, leaving a note requesting that it be shipped to his office. The guest apologized to leave such a daunting task, but had no other choice. He'd admired the clock at a friend's home and the friend said he could have it, as long as he took it with him. The concierge had it professionally crated and shipped. Simple.

The same concierge remembers a panic-stricken guest calling with an urgent plea for help. He wanted to buy shoes at 7:00 a.m., when no stores were open. He said that he desperately needed a pair of size 8 shoes within the hour for a breakfast meeting, since he'd forgotten all but his sneakers. All the men near the desk wore sizes that were too large, and even housekeeping couldn't produce the right size. Mercifully, the concierge's plight was overheard by the reservationist, who did have the right size and the right color. Wonder of wonders, they were stylish as well! The clerk and the guest exchanged shoes and changed back when the meeting concluded.

A gentleman from the nearby suburbs was attending a business meeting at the hotel and had just sat on his glasses. The poor soul was nearly blind and didn't have an extra pair. Not only was he unable to participate in his meeting, but he couldn't even see to drive himself home. The concierge on duty, who could commiserate because of his own poor vision, made the gesture of offering his glasses. The man tried them skeptically, since his prescription was very strong and unusual but a miracle happened: He could see! Off he went to his meeting, leaving Robert to fumble blindly through the rest of the day, but early the next morning the specs were returned by a very appreciative fellow.

THE UNUSUAL BECOMES THE USUAL

Not all requests before the concierge are all that complex or difficult and can be taken in stride without a second thought. For the concierge, they're all in a day's work, even though they would definitely be considered oddities in any other context:

A concierge desperately needed to buy a leash for a famous person's dog, just as he and his canine companion were en route to the hotel from the airport. Naturally, it needed to be done at an odd hour – and immediately. The concierge, using his powers of detection and logic, located a pet-supply store, contacted the owner and asked if the store could be opened. The request was granted and the leash was ready at the hotel before the guest (and his dog) arrived.

A distraught guest approached a concierge at the San Francisco Ritz-Carlton in tears with a plea to find her dog, "Muffy." The guest had placed the pooch in a kennel and then had forgotten the name and location of the place. It took a several telephone calls, but the dog was united with the owner before the sun set that evening.

In such cases, people can say hurtful things. On one occasion, a guest was so irritated that I couldn't grant his wish, he turned on his heel, saying: "What you need here is a good concierge." A great tool to use on such occasions is to silently say to yourself, "Bless them, change me." After all, the only person you have control over and can change is you. A concierge friend of mine once told me that when he arrives at 7:00 a.m. in California and is contending with a heavily caffeinated personal assistant in New York (where it is already 10:00 a.m.), he uses this tool to handle the situation with style and grace.

ALL IN A DAY'S WORK

OCCASIONALLY, THE CONCIERGE IS CALLED UPON to act as a father confessor, an intermediary, a peacemaker, a hand holder, or even a paramedic. Concierges have been asked to deliver condoms, tie ties, dry tears, zip tight dresses and even perform wedding ceremonies. (In Florida, a notary can officiate at weddings.)

> *A guest at the Sheraton at Fisherman's Wharf in San Francisco confided to the concierge that her traveling companion was so hairy that he disgusted her. She asked for his help in ditching the "hairy monster," and the concierge immediately made arrangements for the lady to be accommodated at another hotel.*

In such cases, as with all guest requests – from peace pipes to pigs' eyes – the concierge is called upon to manifest the miraculous with discretion, respect, grace and style.

CHAPTER SIXTEEN

16

The Evolution of the Concierge Phenomenon

OBJECTIVES

The following chapter will equip readers to:

Appreciate where the role of the Concierge originated.

Be aware of a brief introduction to the history of Les Clefs d'Or.

Understand the role of the Concierge model outside of the 5-star hotels.

Visualize the potential for the Concierge role into the future.

The Past

THE RICH HISTORY OF THE CONCIERGE PROFESSION is not easily described linearly, as there appear to be various times and places in world history when the predecessors of today's concierges began shaping the profession. Among other titles, those who came before us were called "house porters," "gatekeepers," "prefects" and "royal governors."

In 1937, Marcel Cacciolato, chef concierge at the Plaza Athenee, published his book *Le Hall*. In it he states: "The first story in Greek literature is where a master complains about his house porter. It's found in the book of the Odyssey where Telemachus bemoans the fact that Pallas Athena was kept waiting at the palace gates on the grounds that she had not been recognized." Gatekeepers were also mentioned in writings about lodgings for sailors in Piraeus. If seamen at that time were as robust as they are today, surely the doormen needed to be mighty strong.

"Writings from the Roman Empire left clearer traces of the role of gatekeepers. Their job was an unattractive one at the outset, to that of current day concierges who may derive special satisfaction from realizing that they are heirs to a job that has risen in dignity and status through the ages."

The more modern interpretation of the concierge and the concept of the "hotel" appeared somewhat later. The emperors Augustus, Domitian and Aurelian organized stations (stopping places) along the Roman roads where hostelries were maintained. The Roman Prefect in charge of vehicles may have been the first to hold a position similar to that of the concierge today. Prefects had to provide relay mounts and were responsible for the supervision of the stations.

In the Middle Ages, monks continued the tradition of hostelries. Every abbey had guest quarters and one monk was usually assigned to see to visitors' needs. Because castles were prone to attack, gatekeepers or lookouts were posted with instructions to keep the door closed unless the person desiring entry was recognized. He may also have had other less odious duties, such as tolling the hourly bells, hanging tapestries, lighting bonfires, keeping the entry tidy and registering the name and title of visitors.

The chef concierge in a hotel in San Francisco found great joy in taking on one of his responsibilities of winding the grandfather clock in the library each day. It gave him such a sense of satisfaction, as it reminded him of the history of his profession, dating all the way back to the original gatekeepers.

As early as the twelfth century, the title concierge began to see regular use. The concierge of the Palace in Paris had become elevated in stature considerably, also enjoying the title of Royal Governor in charge of the palace, its grounds and the nearby parish of Saint James. He presided over courts, hearing infractions committed within the palace and disputes regarding contracts that originated there. That same century, a decree listed the numerous monetary and honorary privileges associated with the position of concierge.

In Paris, housing evolved into dwellings where several families lived together and a new category of caretakers, also called apartment concierges, emerged to guard the door and handle maintenance. They gradually acquired rights and shared some duties with today's concierges. Unfortunately, these pioneering concierges have suffered a poor reputation. Spending days in a cubbyhole by the door didn't foster a service mentality and they tended to engage in petty, tyrannical meddling in other people's affairs. Apartment concierges have often been accused of simply being nosy. It is interesting to note here that the evolution of the concierge runs the gamut between noble and nosy. Fortunately, the position of the concierge has evolved, after its lowly beginnings, to the present, where the concierge in a modern hotel has earned significant responsibilities and respect.

In Europe, the process of becoming a concierge was evolutionary. Often, concierges begin as children performing page duties and gradually working their way through the ranks of uniformed services to become a member of the concierge team. Eventually, they might have had the opportunity to become a chef concierge, but this process took many years. In Europe, the profession is time-honored, and many people have devoted their lives to it – as have many concierges worldwide.

As I've discussed in CHAPTER 1, one etymological theory is that the word concierge is derived from the Latin *conservus*, meaning "fellow slave." Some believe, however, that it comes from the French *comte des cierges* or "count in charge of candles." This interpretation might elude to some ecclesiastical function of the porter in the Middle Ages, such as lighting candles in monasteries and churches. Either way, the title was gradually borrowed until gatekeepers everywhere began to use the term concierge.

The symbol of the concierge is the crossed keys. The Swiss Guard of the Roman Catholic Church has also the crossed keys as their symbol. Rumor has it that the origin of the crossed keys may have come from the Parisian prison, the Conciergerie, whose most famous prisoner was Marie Antoinette. The prison warden, obviously the keeper of the keys, was known as the concierge: hence the symbol of the keys.

With the development of grand hotels in the late nineteenth century, a concierge was posted at the entrance to welcome guests and distribute the keys. Few of today's American concierges actually give guests their room keys, but it remains a function European concierges value. They claim that it helps them quickly learn the names and recognize faces of their guests. They also get to know the comings and goings (not in a nosy way, of course!) and guests soon learn to depend on them.

By the twentieth century, every good hotel (in Europe) had a concierge, but it was not until 1936 that a social law was passed to pay them. Up to that time, they worked for no wages, handling such duties as the dry cleaning and laundry services for gratuities only. So you can easily see that our predecessor's viewed their jobs with the same spirit as today's concierges: They certainly did not take on the job for a paycheck only!

The Creation of the Society of the Golden Keys

You will learn more about the Les Clefs d'Or in the following chapter, but I wanted to include a brief history of it here, as the organization has played a vital role in the evolution of the concierge profession.

The first section of Les Clefs d'Or was created in France in 1929. A visionary, Ferdinand Gillet, saw the need for concierges to "network," thus helping to found the first association. Later, he envisioned a European society that would provide concierges access to detailed information – country by country – and he worked tirelessly through the 1930s and 1940s to create the association Les Clefs d'Or (The Society of the Golden Keys).

The symbol of the crossed keys on the lapels of concierges became symbolic of the power to open doors unavailable to the average traveler. A large part of the ability to open doors came about because of the networking opportunities within Les Clefs d'Or. It was after World War II that more people began to travel and access to information from other countries became more important.

The Society of the Golden Keys USA which later became Les Clefs d'Or USA was founded in 1977 by Tom Wolfe, of the Fairmont Hotel in San Francisco. Tom had been trained in Europe and hoped to start a network of concierges in America similar to the UIPGH in Europe. This was an ambitious undertaking, considering that only a handful of hotels employed concierges. In fact, the concept itself was still quite alien to the American hotelier. Howard Storm of the Stanford Court, Laurence Allport of the Clift, Shelby Topp of the Fairmont and myself were among the first supporters of a national concierge organization. Believe it or not, my qualification for membership was in question back then, simply because I am a woman!

> *The actual minutes from one of the earliest meetings (1977) state: "The matter was raised as to whether or not female members should be allowed, in particular since the Hyatt Hotel Union Square has a female concierge who is trying hard to provide first-class service to their guests. It was therefore moved and carried that females should not be excluded and it was further moved and carried that Holly Stiel should be invited to our next meeting as a guest."*

When I heard that the motto for Les Clefs d'Or is "service through friendship," I was deeply moved because I believed then, and still believe today, that with such high spiritual qualities, one can do anything. It certainly took more than enthusiasm to create this huge society across the entire United States. It was an enormous struggle emotionally, physically and professionally, taking from 1976, when Tom first started making phone calls, to 1981, before we were able to realize our first national meeting (held in Dallas). This historic meeting brought together under one roof the greatest number of concierges ever assembled in the United States.

THE PRESENT

The Proliferation of the Concierge

There's a saying that imitation is the highest form of flattery. If so, the concierge profession should feel very flattered, indeed. The concierge concept has far transcended the hotel lobby and made its way into office buildings, department stores, retirement communities, airlines, convention centers, sports arenas, health clubs, corporate headquarters, law firms, hospitals and shopping malls. Why? Because the term concierge is synonymous with service; in fact, it is the paradigm of service. In an article called "Cloning the Concierge," printed in his magazine *The Service Edge*, Ron Zemke, co-author of Service America, says: "Every front line service person today must strive to replicate the concierge model."

> *Louis Patler, co-author of* **If It Ain't Broke, Break It**, *states: "A significant area of challenge and opportunity is found in new models for and applications of customer service. In my research of the most innovative and successful examples of unparalleled customer service, I have identified the hotel concierge as the one model of excellence in both approach and practice widely applicable to other industries. Concierge quality levels of customer service are no longer just for five-star hotels. On the contrary, a wide variety of industries and organizations now use concierge training to enhance customer service approaches."*

I couldn't agree with Mr. Patler's statement more. In fact, in my consulting and training work, I have successfully adapted concierge approaches and practices to organizations ranging from NASCAR to Audi to Nordstrom. In an excerpt from a white paper written by Marlene Sinicki, she speaks to the necessity of providing top-notch service in today's competitive economy:

> *"Business transactions have become conversations and customer service has become a competitive advantage for many companies. Beyond offering*

personalized and customized services to manage and deliver consumer needs, businesses are increasingly interested in developing relationships with their customers. Technology has made available a wide range of customer service tools that allow for the gathering of data and exchange of resources, but quite often 'the human element' is required to 'touch' people's lives and create personal connections . . . In an age of competitive fever and instant communication, customers have learned to expect a customer-service system that's so proactive that it anticipates a customer's every need. Who, but a committed concierge, is best equipped to make this happen?"

In the hotel lobby, the concierge is noticeably "up front" and visible. Other industries have recognized this and realized that the addition of a concierge is a highly effective way in to show customers immediately that they are taken seriously and cared for. It is a distinguishing mark of a service leader. But even beyond actually providing a concierge desk in a business, the phenomenon of the concierge goes much farther. The concept of the concierge as the paradigm of service can be adapted in a myriad of ways. The possibilities for the concierge concept are endless, and the following represent only a few of the more popular.

Apartment Buildings

One of the first applications of the concierge was in apartment buildings. It would be rare indeed these days to see an ad for an elegant apartment building in a big city that did not boast concierge service.

The Corporate Concierge

This concierge is prominently featured in office buildings and is often a major factor in attracting tenants. Employees in office buildings who are able to take advantage of the concierge's services are better able to manage their time, thus increasing their personal job productivity.

Financial Concierge Services

Banks and credit unions are now keenly focused on providing members with superior service.

Credit Card Companies

Some credit card companies provide concierge services that range from buying gifts to making reservations. They are able to provide complimentary personal assistance – anytime, anywhere. From last-minute restaurant reservations to planning ahead for a special occasion, they are always on hand to make it easy for their customers. Experts can help you with almost anything, including: restaurant recommendations and reservations; travel arrangements; entertainment planning, including ticketing;

business-related assistance such as conference and hospitality services and everyday needs, from finding doggie daycare to a reliable plumber.

Law Firms

I was hired by a prestigious and very old, conservative law firm in California to consolidate their reception desks into one cohesive concept, offering a full range of service and hospitality. Although I had been a consultant in all other areas of the applications I've mentioned here, I was unsure of how the concierge service would translate in this instance. I was amazed by the fact that the concepts and qualities of the concierge were so easily adapted to the environment of a law firm. The philosophy of the concierge proved to be inspirational to people who had never thought of "going the extra mile" in the context of their own job descriptions. I left them with the understanding that even with routine tasks, the opportunity exists to make a significant difference.

Concierge Healthcare

As a general rule, for a fixed annual fee, these practices offer a limited number of patients special services and amenities that are not now provided by most medical practices. These services may include, among other things, the following: nicer and less crowded reception areas; priority/same day/guaranteed next day/extended/Saturday appointments; 24-hour pager, cell phone, home phone access to the physician; house calls and out of office care, possibly including accompanying patients to appointments with specialists; preventive care/weight loss/nutrition/wellness advice and programs; telephone and email consultations; spa-like amenities and décor; free check-ups; physicals and other normally uncovered services.

Hospital Concierge Services

Concierge service in the hospital setting personalizes the hospitalization experience by surrounding the patient – and their family – with embracing support, practical guidance and complete compassion.

Personal Concierge Services

A personal concierge service runs on the most basic of premises. People want things done but don't have the time to do them. They're happy to pay someone to take care of their business efficiently and with a touch of class.

Retailing

Many retail stores and shopping malls offer concierge service. I remember a very successful use of the concept at Nordstrom in San Francisco. Some of the services included coat and package check, stroller and wheelchair availability, umbrella covers for wet days; store deliveries; opening courtesy accounts; store information resource service and store tours.

Apple Computer is known for legendary service. The real secret behind the success of the fastest-growing retail chain in history is their commitment to the customer. When Apple was considering opening their retail stores they conducted extensive research into the field of cutomer service. Today, Apple's retail stores offer one of the best customer service experiences and one of the most impressive applications of the concierge concept I've seen to date. When you first enter the store you are greeted by the "Concierge" – the go-to person who will help you find products and purchase them without waiting in a line. You may also be directed to their "Genius Bar," inspired by the concierge concept, which offers a very helpful service and most importantly, the answers you need.

Here is a quote from an article about the transformation of the Apple stores that appeared in *Fortune* magazine, written by Jerry Useem:

> *"When we launched retail, I got this group together, people from a variety of walks of life," says Johnson. "As an icebreaker, we said, 'Tell us about the best service experience you've ever had.'" Of the 18 people, 16 said it was in a hotel. This was unexpected. But of course: The concierge desk at a hotel isn't selling anything; it's there to help. "We said, 'Well, how do we create a store that has the friendliness of a Four Seasons Hotel?'" The answer: "Let's put a bar in our stores. But instead of dispensing alcohol, we dispense advice."*

Here's an excerpt from Apple's job description for their concierges, which is indistinguishable from that of a hotel concierge:

A candidate we'll love:

- You exude warmth, energy and charisma.
- You love meeting and inspiring new people.
- You have mastered the art of conversation.
- You get people, and people get you.
- You nurture all budding technology crushes and lifelong Apple love affairs.
- You thrive on the unexpected.
- You're an expert at juggling multiple tasks.
- You work just as enthusiastically behind the scenes as you do on center stage.

A position you'll love:

- Warmly welcoming customers to the store and ensuring a great experience and fond farewell.
- Orchestrating the store adventure in the best possible way.
- Understanding the needs of customers and connecting them to the right person at the right time.

- Providing every customer with a superlative experience.
- Looking for every opportunity to shine with our customers.
- Anticipating customers future needs.
- The ideal opportunity to be a people person.

A job at an Apple Retail Store is a chance to:

- Use your knowledge and experience.
- Contribute meaningfully to people's lives with your warmth and enthusiasm.
- Delight, Enrich, Impress, Engage, Inspire.
- Use your hands and heart.

THE NATIONAL CONCIERGE ASSOCIATION

Concierges are now enhancing service levels in so many different industries, that an association has been organized to encompass them all. In 1998, The National Concierge Association (NCA) was established in Dallas, Texas, to create a format for networking on a local, national and international basis with other concierges from all industries. Today, the NCA has members worldwide representing the corporate, hotel, retail, entertainment, academic, civic, medical, residential and privately owned sectors of the hospitality industry.

Their founding principle is to provide unlimited and unparalleled networking and educational opportunities to its members, both concierges and affiliated businesses, as well as to promote the concierge profession worldwide.

FUTURE

EXPANDING THE CONCEPT OF THE HOTEL CONCIERGE

Within the hotel concierge profession itself, there are endless opportunities for creativity and expansion. As just one example, some of the Four Seasons Hotels have hired teen concierges during the summer and school holidays to suggest what their peers might do for fun and recommend places they might visit.

THE SKY'S THE LIMIT

AS MORE AND MORE INDUSTRIES become aware of the value of providing concierge skills and training to their staffs and offering clients and customers concierge-caliber service, the possibilities are endless. Customer service representatives in all industries, postal employees, entertainment venues, the list goes on, can all reap the benefits of the concierge model. Customers, business owners, employees and shareholders alike emerge as winners. Truly, the gatekeepers of yesterday have become pacesetters of tomorrow.

CHAPTER SEVENTEEN

17

Les Clefs d'Or

OBJECTIVES

The following chapter will equip readers to:

See the value in being connected to an Association of like-minded professionals.

Inform others of the history and philosophies of Les Clefs d'Or.

Inform others of the requirements necessary for Les Clefs d'Or membership.

Distinguish the various components that make up the Association.

Outline the profile of a Les Clefs d'Or Concierge.

> "*In Service Through Friendship*"

OF COURSE A BOOK ON THE PROFESSIONAL CONCIERGE should include a chapter devoted to Les Clefs d'Or, the professional concierge association. It has always been my strong belief – and actual experience – that membership in Les Clefs d'Or can be the single most valuable asset in the life of a professional concierge.

To work in the capacity of concierge and not participate – first in your local association and later when you qualify as a member of Les Clef d'Or – is to deprive yourself of one of the richest and most rewarding experiences of the profession. It is well worth the time and effort – if for no other reason than the collective power of the local branches to gather information and attract educational speakers. My colleague, Kathleen Fitzgerald, makes the trip from Carmel to San Francisco, California every month (a two-and-one-half hour drive each way) to attend the local meetings. She finds them so valuable that the trip seems inconsequential. I will explain a bit more about the benefits of involvement in local associations later on in this chapter.

The opportunities that membership in Les Clefs d'Or presents through the connections to other members, participation in Congresses, the lifelong friendships, the world travel and unsurpassed international networking, are limitless – and priceless. The value of this kind of network is rare and is the envy of many international businesses. For me personally, it has enriched my life beyond measure and opened so many doors – in both my business and personal life – that would never have been available to me otherwise. Membership elevates the work from a mere job to a profession that connects us with many other like-minded professionals all around the world.

These benefits don't automatically happen with membership alone, however. As with most any endeavor in life, you receive in proportion to what you give. For me, the real benefits have been realized, because I am an active member who is passionate about the work and willing to give of my time and talent. I've enjoyed my participation in bettering the association through board membership and relentless dedication to the belief in the artistry of the concierge and the sacredness of service, in which I deeply believe.

The following is a portion of a speech I wrote to capture the truly sacred nature of the values that lie at the heart of Les Clefs d'Or and its members.

> *It's no accident that the Golden Cross Keys, signifying membership in Les Clefs d'Or, are also a papal symbol that can be seen on stained-glass windows in churches across the world. This became very clear to me as a young concierge, when I attended our gala event at an association meeting. The gala was held at The Windows of the World on top of The World Trade Center. At that party, I felt total gratitude and awe for being a part of something that was so much bigger than myself. It was, in fact, a spiritual experience.*
>
> *Of course, the fact that this occurred in the very place that would later be the site of worldwide transformation was unknown to me at the time and remains incomprehensible for me even today. I was quite surprised by the intensity of my feelings about this, which I shared with Jean Gillet, the son of Ferdinand Gillet, the founder of Les Clefs d'Or. He understood completely, responding, "For me, my dear, Les Clefs d'Or is a religion."*
>
> *As I see it, it is not so much of a religion, but I do have the deep understanding that thinking and behaving like a world-class concierge is firmly based in spiritual principles. Every major religion has a component of service at its core. In Judaism, it is called "Rachamim" – the love that motivates us to serve with empathy and care. In Islam, the word "Mahaba" means to express love for others, as well as love for the divine. In Buddhism, it is known as "loving kindness," while in Christianity, the word "agape" denotes the act of serving unconditionally. The Cross Keys we wear on our lapels help us to remember that we are to be of service every day – to our employers, customers, vendors, to each other and to ourselves.*
>
> *I was the last to leave the gala that night, as I never wanted the party – or the feelings I had – to end. As I stood alone, gazing out at the teeming streets and lights of New York City, I wanted to hold on to the sprit of unity with people from all walks of life, cultures and religions. It was a sense of wonder and oneness that only a spiritual deepening can make possible.*
>
> *I believe this is the true key to the success of the concierge – the connectedness through our relationships and our commitment to serve. Without this spiritual component, any replication of concierge services will fall short. The belief in something greater than yourself – be it working for the common good, achieving excellence in a worthy endeavor, performing ordinary tasks in an extraordinary way or providing memorable experiences for your customers – requires more than cutting-edge thinking. Concierge thinking is absolutely based on principles rooted in the ancient, yet ageless, spiritual traditions of all time.*

Suffice it to say that, in addition to the business, networking, educational and professional benefits, the personal joy of being a Clefs d'Or member is beyond measure.

Longtime San Francisco concierge, Jim McCasland and I are all decked out to attend a ball at the Les Clefs d'Or Congress in Vienna in 2007, where we laughed until our faces hurt, connected with colleagues from around the world and had the time of our lives.

A picture speaks a thousand words as Kathleen Fitzgerald joins the festivities.

While it makes excellent business sense to invest in the professional development and networking opportunities offered by Les Clefs d'Or, hotel management may not completely understand its true importance for the concierge team – or the hotel's bottom line. In such situations, it behooves every concierge to do his or her very best to communicate the benefits, not only to management, but also to their colleagues and the hotel's guests.

THE HISTORY OF LES CLEFS D'OR

(Excerpted from Les Clefs d'Or USA website)

In the beginning of the 20th century, the international tourism industry experienced a tremendous boom, in large part due to the increasing popularity of rail and steamship travel. In working to satisfy the needs of these travelers, Switzerland's "grand hotels," created the "Hall Porter" position. These first-ever modern concierges were responsible for everything from meeting the guests at the station in a horse-drawn carriage to assisting them with every detail of their stay.

With time, these Swiss concierges relocated to other cities throughout Europe as a means to stay at the constant disposal of their traveling clientele. In October 1929, three of the more prominent concierges met in Paris to exchange service tips and ideas. They found that, together, they could more effectively network and enhance guest services throughout their cities. As a result, many European countries created national concierge "societies."

The end of World War II sparked a renewed interest in the need for these societies. Concierges throughout Europe created a chain of mutual assistance and friendship to help smooth the journeys of their clients who were traveling in post-war Europe. On April 25, 1952, delegates from seven European nations met in Cannes to hold the first ever "Congress" and create "L'Union Europeene des Portiers des Grands Hotels" (UEPGH). Ferdinand Gillet (then concierge at the Hotel Scribe, Paris) masterminded this effort and is considered the "father of Les Clefs d'Or." Mr. Gillet served as president of this association until 1968.

In 1970, with the acceptance of Israel as a member country, UEPGH became UIPGH (Union Internationale des Portiers des Grands Hotels) signifying that not just Europe, but countries from around the globe, were joining forces.

Today, the UICH acronym stands for Union Internationale des Concierges d'Hôtels "Les Clefs d'Or." The word concierge appears in the name as a way to strengthen the brand-name recognition of UICH as a society of professional hotel concierges. The USA section of Les Clefs d'Or was formally recognized on

November 22, 1978, when the United States became the 19th member of UICH (Union Internationale des Concierges d'Hôtels) at a meeting in Vienna, Austria.

From their humble beginning of just a few concierges assembling in 1952, there are, as of this writing, 40 member sections (countries) and 3,500 members of UICH. In the USA alone, the Les Clefs d'Or members represent over 275 thousand hotel rooms nightly, at primarily four and five star hotels.

THE VALUES OF LES CLEFS D'OR

The values of Les Clefs d'Or are both as profoundly simple as they are simply profound:

- In service through friendship
- Our word is our bond
- My guest today is your gust tomorrow

These simple values, as well as the Les Clefs d'Or "Code of Ethics" and Professional Standards are fully outlined in CHAPTER 1. It bears repeating here, however, that living these values in thought, word and action strengthens the fabric of each individual concierge, as well as the profession as a whole.

LES CLEFS D'OR USA
KEYS TO EXCELLENCE

(Excerpted from Les Clefs d'Or USA website)

The Purpose

To foster the professional development of concierges in the hotel industry by promoting tourism and the highest standards of service for hotel guests.

The Motto

"In Service through Friendship"

The Creed

Members of Les Clefs d'Or USA will:

- Uphold the professional and ethical standards of the association.
- Coordinate, promote and assist the activities and interests of fellow members.
- Mentor individuals entering the concierge profession.
- Promote and improve the technical skills of the profession.
- Foster friendships and communication networks within the USA and abroad.

- Respond to the needs of fellow members quickly, courteously and professionally.
- Uphold the motto, "In Service through Friendship."

Les Clefs d'Or literally means "keys of gold" in French. The crossed gold keys are the international symbol of the organization. The keys displayed on a concierge's uniform lapels assure travelers they are dealing with a seasoned professional, one who is dedicated to serving the guests' every need. The crossed-key logo is internationally trademarked, and individual member countries trademark their own, customized versions of it. For example, the USA logo displays the American flag behind its crossed keys.

Getting your keys comes with a great responsibility. Over the years Les Clefs d'Or has become its own brand – with a distinction that members are quite proud to be affiliated with. The name has cache, and membership is coveted. It represents many years of dedication to the profession – in some cases, careers that span 30 to 40 years of working diligently to develop the brand. When concierges wear the keys, it's important that they fully support the ethical and moral fiber of the concierge profession and the Clef d'Or brand in each and every situation they encounter.

Local Associations

Most major cities and many smaller tourist venues, such as Napa and Monterey in California, have their own local associations. Because most of the questions asked of concierges involve local information, the local associations are important and valuable educational and networking resources. By attending local meetings and networking with local colleagues, one's learning curve increases exponentially.

Usually there are several social events a month, along with a monthly meeting. It's a great opportunity for vendors, as well, because they can provide information about their products and services to many concierges at once. The local associations are also usually very philanthropic and give back to their communities in many ways.

Les Clefs d'Or is especially supportive of participation in local associations. In fact, to become a member of Les Clefs d'Or, one first must become involved with the local association and community, as well as be recommended by colleagues in one's hometown. Each year at Les Clefs d'Or Congresses, the local association presidents meet with other local associations to get to know each other and exchange information. Sometimes, there are regional meetings, as well, and both are very valuable resources for the working concierge.

International Congresses

The purposes of the International Congresses are to:

- Conduct the annual business meeting and allow for open-forum discussions, giving members the opportunity to participate in the association on an international level.
- Impart new knowledge and provide continued training for our members through symposiums and guest speakers.
- Showcase the host cities, allowing concierges to experience first-hand the services and venues they are regularly called upon to recommend to guests.
- Enjoy the social aspects of the congress, cement old friendships and create new ones, ensuring our networking efforts continue to flourish and grow.
- Display and exchange hotel sales and marketing materials.

By attending International Congresses, Les Clefs d'Or members gain an endless network of acquaintances, friends and colleagues from around the world. These connections are of immeasurable value in helping them meet and exceed guest expectations. Thanks to these contacts, concierges have become well known for their personal and priceless databases, placing them in the enviable position of being able to recommend destinations, businesses, companies and/or products to thousands of business and leisure travelers throughout the world.

It is the very solidarity of its members and participation in congresses that provides Les Clefs d'Or Concierges the network and knowledge to accomplish the impossible and maintain the highest possible standards of service to our guests. The networking opportunities are world class and literally unsurpassed.

Several hotel companies have established an excellent networking practice: Each member of LCD that represents the particular hotel brand, such as Four Seasons or Intercontinental, takes an extra day at a congress, either before or after, to meet together. This kind of internal networking within the brand is priceless. Not only do the concierges share best practices, they also increase business throughout the brand. For instance, knowing that a guest is going to Budapest, a concierge in Washington, D.C. can contact their LCD colleague in Budapest and pave the way for a personalized and outstanding guest experience. While this has always been the practice of LCD concierges, the extra networking time that is set aside is a great boost in maintaining esprit de corps and loyalty within the brand.

It was especially sweet to celebrate the 30th anniversary of Les Clefs d'Or USA at the congress in Vienna – the very place the U.S. had been accepted as a member country, as well as the site of the first meeting I ever attended. I was privileged to cut the celebratory cake thirty years after this historic date.

I have been attending these congresses since 1978, at which time the first women ever attended a Les Clefs d'Or meeting.

CHARITABLE ENDEAVORS

Clefs d'Or concierges are community conscious. Working within their local areas, many host extravagant fundraising events that have helped to raise hundreds of thousands of dollars for local charities, as well as for Les Clefs d'Or Foundation of the Americas. This foundation was established to assist concierges and/or their family members who are no longer able to work due to catastrophic illness.

Les Clefs d'Or Foundation of the Americas

I am including information on The Les Clefs d'Or Foundation of the Americas in the chapter on Les Clefs d'Or. While the name Les Clefs d'Or appears in its title, it is not officially the same as Les Clefs d'Or. It is its own separate entity with its own board of directors.

The foundation is very near and dear to my heart, as I was instrumental in creating it in 1990 and have served as a member of the Foundation Board ever since. As concierges, we are aware that we can't entirely lift the financial burdens of our colleagues going through catastrophic situations, but we can always stand as a symbol of friendship and lend a helping hand. Over the years, many concierges – both members and nonmembers of les Clefs d'Or have received much appreciated assistance through Foundation Grants. It is a representation of kindness, care and service, and it is something we are very proud of.

Les Clefs d'Or Foundation is a tax-exempt, volunteer, nonprofit organization founded in 1990 to respond to the suffering of concierges and/or their significant others, affected by catastrophic or life-threatening illnesses. While it began as a U.S. entity, the Foundation today is a Pan-American effort, combining and benefiting the UICH sections of the United States, Canada, Mexico and Brazil.

Les Clefs d'Or Foundation provides financial support and in-kind donations of goods and services to persons who are no longer able to work, due to the life-threatening illnesses, as well as to individuals who find themselves in financial need through no fault of their own. Those who will benefit include hotel concierges, former concierges in the USA, Canada, Mexico, Brazil, Argentina and significant others of the above stated.

The Clefs d'Or Foundation and its members appreciate the continued generosity of all donors, with whom we pledge to continue our Foundation expanded mission of service and care.

QUALIFICATIONS FOR MEMBERSHIP

The following are qualifications for Les Clefs d'Or USA. While requirements vary slightly from section to section, similarly high standards for membership extend worldwide.

- Applicants shall be at least twenty-one years of age, of good moral character and employed in the hotel lobby-level for at least five years, three in the position of concierge and active within their local concierge community.
- The final year of these five years of employment must be worked continuously as a hotel lobby concierge.
- The membership of this Corporation shall be limited to concierges who are employed by hotels and resort hotels having a transient clientele and who work full time at a desk located in the main lobby of such hotels, from which they provide services to all the guests of the hotel.
- Concierges employed to provide services to certain guests on VIP floor "towers" or on any other floor other than the main lobby of the hotel shall not qualify for membership in this Corporation.
- Concierges employed in any other type of establishment other than a hotel, even if they house a transient clientele, shall not qualify for membership in this Corporation.

In addition to these requirements, letters of recommendation are needed from two Les Clefs d'Or colleagues and from a present and former general manager. Finally, there are two forms of tests that must be passed – one involving test calls and another a written test. The following questions are samples from one of the written tests:

Sample Test Questions

1. Time zones. If it is 12:00 noon in New York, New York, what time is it in the following cities?
   - Cape Town, South Africa
   - Wellington, New Zealand
   - St. Petersburg, Russia
   - Hanoi, Vietnam
   - Caracas, Venezuela
   - Barcelona, Spain
   - Miami, Florida
   - Colombo, Sri Lanka
2. A guest forgot his Rolex and insists that he has to have it returned to him the same day. He is now in San Francisco and your hotel is located in Miami. What are your options?
3. How many local concierges associations are there in the United States?
   - ☐ 30
   - ☐ 25
   - ☐ 32
   - ☐ 19
   - ☐ 38
   - ☐ Other
4. What would your dream desk look like and contain if you could design it yourself?
5. What information do you need to obtain from a non-guest to place a flower order for a guest at your hotel?
6. Your guest would like to place a call to the following locations. State the locations' country codes and city codes:
   - Mar del Plata, Argentina
   - Baku, Azerbaijan
   - Jaixing, China
   - Madras, India
   - Abu Dhabi, U.A.E
7. "The Passport Dilemma." A guest has just told you he needs to travel to Australia for a family emergency. He asks you to find out what he needs to process a passport and if he needs a visa. He needs to travel within 48 hours. State the requirements, forms and time frame needed for obtaining a U.S. Passport and what you would do as a concierge to assist your guest.
8. "Cash Flow Crisis." A regular guest has lost her handbag. It

contained her credit cards, driver's license, identification and money. State in detail what steps you, as a concierge, are going to do to help her with this tragic situation.

9. What is the tallest hotel in the United States?
   - ☐ Waldorf Towers (New York)
   - ☐ Hotel Inter-Continental (Chicago)
   - ☐ Fairmont (San Francisco)
   - ☐ Westin Peachtree Plaza (Atlanta)

10. What is the minimum postage required (all mail originating from the United States) for the following items?
    - Letter to Alaska
    - Postcard to Hawaii
    - Letter to Canada
    - Letter to China
    - Postcard to Europe
    - Postcard to Canada
    - Letter to Europe

A PROFILE OF A LES CLEFS D'OR CONCIERGE

The following was excerpted from the Union Internationale des Concierges d'Hôtels (UICH) website and provides a comprehensive and inspiring profile of a Clefs d'Or concierge.

- Clefs d'Or concierges will accommodate every guest request so long as it is morally, legally and humanly possible. Their services run the gamut from the mundane to the extraordinary, yet each request is fulfilled with vigor to the guest's full satisfaction.
- Clefs d'Or concierges handle all duties with zeal: mail and messages, recommendations and reservations, travel and meeting planning, personal shopping and professional communications. They are also supreme social advisors, business expediters and personal confidantes.
- On those rare occasions when guests' requests cannot be fulfilled single-handedly, Les Clefs d'Or concierges have the necessary back-up: a never-ending network of acquaintances, friends and colleagues from around the world to see to it that guests' demands are met.
- Les Clefs d'Or members have dedicated many years of hard work and training to the concierge profession. They are pleasant and welcoming in appearance, they remain calm in a hectic environment, and they always display integrity. Indeed, discretion is the hallmark of a Clefs d'Or concierge.

- Les Clefs d'Or concierges have their fingers on the pulses of their cities, able to advise guests on restaurants, night life, sporting and theater events, sightseeing tours, shopping, etc. They can direct guests to any location, to any product, at any time of day or night.
- Les Clefs d'Or concierges are motivated by a genuine desire to serve. They are prudent, patient, kind toward guests and staff alike, self-confident, tenacious, persistent, adaptable, ingenious, disciplined and flexible.
- The global environment of today's business world demands that concierges be able to converse with all travelers, from Albania to Zaire. Many Clefs d'Or members are multilingual and most are well-versed in many cultures.
- Les Clefs d'Or concierges have worked hard to obtain their keys. Whether requesting something simple or complex, you can be sure they are trusted resources to business travelers and vacationers alike, always keeping guests' safety, enjoyment and satisfaction in mind.

THANK YOU *VERY* MUCH!

THE PRECIOUS NATURE of the deep friendships forged within Les Clefs d'Or cannot be overemphasized. With today's modern technology, it's easier than ever for concierges to remain in touch with their colleagues from all over the world. (Concierges love Facebook!) Fellow Clefs d'Or members make great traveling companions and often become lifelong friends – friends who can count on each other through thick and thin, both personally and professionally. The membership and experiences we share connect us for a lifetime of friendship and dedicated service – both to ourselves and others.

A special thanks to Les Clefs d'Or USA and the Union Internationale des Concierges d'Hotels (UICH) for their permission to reprint material from their websites:

www.lcdusa.org and www.uichlesclefsdor.org, respectively.

CHAPTER EIGHTEEN

18 Managing the Concierge

OBJECTIVES

The following chapter will equip readers to:

Identify the key elements of concierge recruitment.

Understand the most important skills and tools required to manage the concierge team effectively.

See the importance of two-way communication and mutual understanding between the concierge and hotel senior management.

Recognize the most important areas to focus on when producing successful reports.

WHILE THERE ARE AN ENDLESS NUMBER OF BOOKS ON LEADERSHIP, hiring and management, I feel it's important to include a chapter on these topics that's specifically written for the chief concierge. There are a few reasons I believe this chapter is important. First, the combination of skills and personality traits required to be a good concierge are unique and often not always easy to find. Secondly, concierges need to be managed differently, as they are required to function independently and sometimes break away from "standard operating procedure" (even to bend a rule or two) to satisfy a guest. There are also other special considerations, including working with hotel management.

HIRING

In CHAPTER 1, I detailed the characteristics of concierges who excel in their field and enjoy every minute of it. In brief, these fundamental qualities include:

The sincere desire to give to others, basic native intelligence ("street smarts"), creativity, the ability to multi-task, problem-solving skills, patience, empathy, compassion and the utmost professionalism. The following passage appears in CHAPTER 1, but it bears repeating here.

> *Begin with an outgoing nature and professional demeanor. Combine it with a deep desire to serve and be appreciated. Top it off with one's comfort zone at center stage, and throw in a love for excitement, a voracious drive to organize, the patience of Job and the soul of a private eye. Combine these characteristics, and you have the makings of a good concierge.*

I've repeated "The Six Cs" found in CHAPTER 1 here, as their importance cannot be overstated.

THE SIX Cs

Marjorie Silverman, former hotel concierge and Honorary Past President, Union Internationale des Concierges d'Hotel, Les Clef's d'Or, has identified these six characteristics that define the top professional concierge:

Curiousity: Concierges are curious about people, the world, travel and tourism. They explore every nook and cranny of their locale – its history, restaurants, tours, architecture, culture and subcultures.

Creativity: Concierges are innovative and proactive. They anticipate guests' needs and generate new/fresh ideas for every challenge. They look for new and better ways to operate and constantly adapt to the marketplace, new technology and changing preferences of guests and management.

Confidence: Successful concierges are self-assured and confident, not tentative. Today's guests generally come to the concierge, having done their own basic research. They are looking for a local authority they can trust for accurate knowledge of the "up-to-the-minute" local scene.

Charisma: The word "charismatic" comes from the Greek definition and means that a person has the gift of grace. This is a beautiful way to describe the ultimate concierge, who projects an image of charm, poise and enthusiasm.

Competence: Concierges are effective and efficient. They understand their role and exactly how it fits into the hotel's service mission. Guests can put their full trust into the hands of the competent concierge.

Courteousness: Concierges are kind, understanding, gentle, diplomatic and giving. They always demonstrate civility in their interactions with guests, staff, management, vendors and their concierge colleagues.

TEAM CONCIERGE

Remember, TEAM stands for "Together Everyone Achieves More." Whenever you see the word "concierge," you should automatically think "team." The dynamics of a concierge team are of the utmost importance, as each member must work closely with the others if their guests are receive outstanding service. All members must be supportive of each other and willing to freely share information. Typically, if a candidate possesses the qualities mentioned at the beginning of this chapter, he or she will complement the existing staff perfectly. Particularly important is the desire to give.

This desire should extend, not only to guests, but equally to fellow concierges.

When selecting a new concierge who will best serve the team and hotel guests, it's also important to take into consideration the personalities and talents of the current staff. How will the traits, talents and knowledge of the candidate complement those of the existing team? Pay attention to the additional assets candidates might bring to the desk, for instance fluency in a language, business savvy, or a background in international travel.

SEASONED OR GREEN?

The biggest difference between experienced concierges and those who have never done the job is the likelihood that the former already understand the essence of the job. This typically makes it easier for the rest of the team to integrate them into the fold. If they have solid prior experience, the experienced new hire can bring the best of what he or she knows and share it with the team. The only aspects that remain to be taught are the culture and procedures of the particular hotel.

On the other hand, inexperienced hires that have a can-do attitude and the right spirit for the job can also be a great choice. First, they have no preconceived ideas of how it's "supposed to be." Secondly, they are typically more open to new ideas and can bring enthusiasm and "heart" to the team. Newcomers to the profession can be a breath of fresh air, infusing the existing team with renewed enthusiasm.

GETTING TO KNOW YOU...

When sitting down with job candidates, it's important to have a list of strategic interview questions that will help reveal whether or not a candidate has what it takes to be a valuable member of your concierge team. While the following is not a comprehensive list of questions, it can offer excellent insight into prospective job candidates.

Suggested Interview Questions

1. What strategies do you have for coping under pressure?
2. What has been your greatest achievement to date?
3. What has been your greatest challenge and how did you deal with it?
4. What strengths do you bring to a team?
5. What are your expectations of your manager?
6. What can your manager expect from you?
7. What are your developmental opportunities?
8. How do you manage a work/life balance?

9. If you had to organize the most unforgettable four-day guest itinerary in your town, what would you arrange?
10. What leadership qualities do you possess?
11. What motivates you?
12. What would your previous co-workers say about you?
13. What professional organizations do you belong to?
14. What irritates you?
15. What book are you currently reading?
16. What is your greatest childhood memory?
17. If you could be a brand, what would you be and why?
18. Why should we hire you over the other applicants for this position?
19. If you were a product, what would you be and how would you position yourself?
20. If there was one thing you could bring to this organization or the role, what would it be and how would you make it happen?

MANAGING

TRAINING THE NEW CONCIERGE

Orientation

Introducing the new concierge to the other members of the team is one of the first steps in the orientation process. During the first 30 days, it's important that the new concierge – whether seasoned or brand-new to the field – feels comfortable behind the desk. Even when new hires have had previous experience as hotel concierges, there is still a great deal of information to absorb. New members should be given a sense that they are not alone and can trust that the team is there for them every step of the way.

During the first week, assigning new concierges to read the first three chapters in this book is an excellent orientation tool. The material contained in these three chapters explains the qualities concierges are expected to bring to the desk and the manner in which guests are to be treated.

During the first 30 days, remind new concierges to first focus on the guest, instead of immediately looking down and searching the computer or scrambling for files. Though there are bound to be new-on-the-job jitters, new concierges should be encouraged to look the guest in the eye confidently and specifically connect with them before taking any other action. After establishing this initial rapport, he or she can then proceed to locate the information or ask a colleague for assistance in accessing it.

During the initial 30 days, it's helpful to require new hires to alternate shifts between mornings, evenings and weekends. This way, the new person becomes familiar with the questions that arise on each shift, involving both business and leisure travel. Additionally, they will learn firsthand the types of information the next shift needs to properly serve guests.

Each day of the first 30 days, the new concierge should devote at least two hours to becoming comfortable with the computer system.

Routine Requests and Frequently Asked Questions

Teaching new concierges the necessary hotel- and region-specific information can be divided into four general categories:

- The hotel itself
- The six-block radius around the hotel
- The entire city
- Any areas of interest outside of the city, such as the wine country outside of San Francisco or the Hill Country outside of Austin, Texas.

The techniques for teaching hotel- and region-specific information include conducting one-on-one training, shadowing other team members and leading informational sessions each day with a few targeted topics. After instructing on each section, it's helpful to give a quiz to ensure the new concierge knows how to confidently and accurately answer the important frequently asked questions.

Topics for the sessions might include:

- Hotel logistics and locations, such as restrooms, meeting rooms and guest rooms
- Hotel operations, such as paid-out forms and charge slips
- A glossary of terms
- A review of the literature in the hotel rooms
- Shipping options and courier services
- Museums
- Maps (state maps, walking maps, area maps, et al)
- Transportation, including public and private (limousines)
- Theatres/Box Offices

- Forms and Waivers
- Neighborhood services, such as banks and pharmacies
- Restaurants/OpenTable software/websites for menus
- Preprinted Itineraries, such as children's activities, the best barbeque establishment and fun outings for a rainy day. These should be preprinted for efficiency and consistency.
- Tours and walking paths
- The technology system
- The phone system and telephone manners
- Providing directions
- The particulars of the desk itself (e.g., where supplies are located)

To properly educate new hires about the resources outside of the hotel, it is important (and fun!) to send them on "field trips," where they can have experiences just as a guest would. For instance, they need to walk to the bank, the box offices, shops, etc. They should ride a trolley, visit museums and check out other points of interest. It is also fun to conduct a "scavenger hunt" of sorts, where they can actually experience traveling the distances between the hotel and popular destinations, interpreting signage and encountering any challenges first hand. One person I interviewed keeps this process alive by asking her staff to bring in new discoveries to share with the team every month – a sort of "city surprises show and tell." This turns the initial training into a dynamic process that continues to expand the horizons of all staff members. Of course, these discoveries are entered into the computer and also discussed at monthly meetings.

MANAGING THE EXPERIENCED CONCIERGE

The more seasoned concierges at your hotel need to be continually re-educated, re-inspired and reviewed.

Clear and consistent communication is a necessary part of managing a concierge team. In management, there are five simple questions to keep in mind when communicating with your staff. Each member of the team will need to have a clear understanding what the answers are to the following questions:

- What do you want me to do?
- Why do you want me to do it?
- How do I do it?
- How do I know how I'm doing?
- How can I do better?

These questions pertain not only to the technicalities of the day-to-day tasks, but also in a more general sense to the manner in which the concierges approach their jobs as a creative art form. Aspects that fall into this category are empathy, patience, enthusiasm and creativity.

Thinking like a concierge sometimes requires the ability to cut through the red tape, even bend a few rules. When a guest's satisfaction is on the line, concierges need the flexibility to work "outside of the box." Due to the nature of the job and the nature of concierges themselves, they cannot be micro-managed or "whipped into submission." Because their work is an art form unto itself, an atmosphere that encourages responsible creativity should be fostered. The chief concierge must be able to trust that the members of their team have and will practice good judgment. This confidence in the team's sound decision-making abilities should also be passed along to hotel management, so they, too, understand the need for flexibility.

Accentuating the positive is empowering, while harshness and negativity can be disheartening – stifling spirit and creativity. I've heard supervisors admonish their staff members by asking rhetorically, "What were you thinking?" This kind of confrontation is especially counterproductive with concierges, because in order to think like a concierge, you have to be thinking all the time. Rather than discouraging concierges from thinking freely and creatively, it's better to review the situation and brainstorm for ways it might have been handled better. This process of discussing the occurrence, re-training if necessary, testing and ongoing coaching is far better than harsh, punitive or demeaning techniques.

As an example, let's draw comparisons between two managers, as they work with a staff member who consistently neglects to wear his nametag:

Manager One browbeats, insults and harshly points to the concierge's chest and demands, "You must wear your nametag."

Manager Two asks, "How will our guests write all those wonderful letters about you, if they don't know your name?"

Both responses are possible ways to address the problem, but which do you suppose actually prompted the concierge to wear his nametag.

Even the areas outside of the box have limits, however, which an overzealous concierge might mistakenly cross from time to time. In such cases, the supervisor constructively explains the difficulties arising from the choice the concierge has made by revisiting the last two of the five questions listed above: "How am I doing?" and "How can I do it better?" These situations need to be addressed in a manner that clarifies the pitfalls of the concierge's decision, but does not discourage creative thinking in the future. The best approach is a collaborative one, best described as coaching, in which the concierge participates in exploring alternatives.

COACHING, LEARNING AND MYSTERY SHOPPING

COACHING IS KEY

After teaching the values, standards, procedures and hotel-specific information, the ongoing process of *coaching* comes into play. The process of coaching addresses the last two questions listed above: "How do I know how I'm doing?" and "How can I do better?" The three highlights to remember about the coaching process are:

- That it is positive and constructive.
- It fosters self-discovery.
- It focuses on asking questions.

The most important factor about coaching is simple: It's about asking questions; not telling people what to do. When I first started managing others, I learned my lesson the hard way. I thought getting results was a simple as knowing what I wanted, stating it and expecting people to comply. When they didn't, I was perplexed, frustrated, annoyed and occasionally angry.

> ***After hour upon hour of explaining that a map should accompany any and all directions given to a guest, a concierge on my team refused to do it – time and time again. After I witnessed this many times, I reacted badly and actually screamed, "Give them a map!" as I lightly swatted her arm. I can tell you now that it's not a good idea to hit and scream to get your standards understood and applied. It is much wiser to coach, ask questions and encourage the employee to come up with the answers themselves.***

When it comes to letting members of your staff know how they're doing and discovering ways to do their jobs better, a once-a-year performance appraisal simply isn't enough. Continuous coaching – not only asking questions, but asking the *right* questions – fosters insight, creativity and a feeling of empowerment.

An effective method of coaching is to first ask a question that prompts the concierge to focus on their strengths, what has worked, and what they feel good about in a situation they have recently handled. You might ask, "What are you proud of about the way you handled that irate guest?", "What positive elements did you bring into working with the guest to book his airline reservation?", or "What was most effective about the way you took care of that request?" The answer is followed up with the second question, which prompts the staff member to consider how to improve upon his or her performance in the future. Examples might include: "What might you do in the future to be even more effective?" or "Thinking back to what you learned in your training, what other steps can you take to make the experience more memorable for the guest?"

> *In my consulting work, I had the opportunity to work with baristas in a luxury hotel. When I asked them about the positive aspects of their day, they mentioned the quality of the beverages they'd made and the quick service they had provided to their hurried guests. After acknowledging these strengths, I then asked them what they might have done to be more effective. This prompted them to realize that each cup of coffee was given to the guest with an off-handed, "Here ya' go." This process of self-discovery led them to consider and practice more personal ways of ending the transaction, such as, "Enjoy your latte and have a great day!"*

Effective coaching empowers "coachees" to tap their innate knowledge and gives them confidence in making well informed decisions – in the moment and going forward. Coaching is not about demanding outcomes, "writing up" or berating people into compliance, but encouraging them to find within themselves the encouragement and background information necessary to achieve sustainable results.

LEARNING IS LIFELONG

The profession of concierge involves lifelong learning – continuous and ongoing. There are as many ways to learn as there are topics to learn about, but here are just a couple of ideas to provide concierges with ongoing education.

Jeanne Mills at the MGM Las Vegas regularly invites visitors to speak to her staff at pre-shift meetings. For example, it might be a chef from one of the MGM restaurants to talk about his or her specialties and how they procure ingredients. Maybe the pasta is handmade or the cheese comes from a tiny farm in Italy. This type of additional information can then be passed along to guests, which makes the recommendation of the concierge more personal, knowledge-based and interesting. This, in turn, translates into a deeper, richer and more meaningful experience for the guest. It strengthens both the relationship between the guest and the concierge and the relationship between the concierge and the chef.

Visiting speakers can also be selected from areas outside the hotel, including experts on customer service, representatives from outside vendors/restaurants and technicians from concierge-software companies.

Not all learning takes place on the part of the concierges, however, as management can learn a great deal *from* the concierges. They are precious resources on your frontline and are constantly in touch with your guests, other departments in the hotel, the local community and the world at large. Their antennas are always up – not only picking up signals from guests, but also collecting valuable information from their network of colleagues around the world.

MYSTERY SHOPPING

Follow-up is an important tool to assess the success of the initial training, ongoing education and coaching. An excellent way to determine firsthand if the concierge team is applying what they've learned to the everyday demands of the concierge desk is mystery shopping. Mystery shopping is the practice of sending "plants" to the concierge desk with requests, keeping a careful eye and ear out for how the request is handled. These internal "shops" are very important, as they not only give feedback on the basic skills, but can also assess a specific attribute or attitude the mystery shopper may be targeting. Perhaps you want to determine if the concierge is insightful. For example, did he suggest walking shoes for a tour that's primarily on foot? Was she aware of a possible change in weather and offer the guest an umbrella? Here, it's important to make the distinctions between what is actually insightful versus what is simply informed, especially in today's information-rich world. Because most guests have all the information they need in their handheld devices, why would they even talk to a concierge in the first place? It is precisely because of their invaluable *insight* and trusted opinions.

A good manager will internally "shop" the staff routinely as an assurance that guests are receiving the absolute ultimate in service. At the MGM in Las Vegas, the supervisors are assigned to do four mystery shop calls a week. Since there are four supervisors, this amounts to 16 "shops" a week. It is also excellent fodder for sit-down coaching sessions, allowing the supervisor to offer help with areas that need improvement and give accolades when accolades are due.

Mystery shoppers are on the lookout for attitudes and behaviors, such as:

- The use of professional verbiage.
- Specific offers of assistance that goes beyond, "Is there anything else I can help you with?" (e.g., " I see by your reservation that you are here for two additional nights. Might I suggest a dinner or a show for those evenings?)
- Suggesting the services of the hotel, up-selling and "buck stopping." (Remember, the buck stops at the concierge desk!)
- Creative problem solving.

MANAGING "UP"

SHOW AND TELL

Lack of awareness and support on the part of management is an all-too-common issue for concierges. Without it, they might as well be operating with one hand tied behind their backs. Unless there is clear, direct and regular communication with the hotel's management staff, chances are the resources the team needs will be limited. Limitations might include inadequate staffing, insufficient continuing education, lack of the proper technological tools, as well as deficits in the other types of support required to serve hotel guests. Inadequacy in any of these areas directly results in the inability to measure up to the service standards – required not only of members of les Clefs d'Or – but of the hotel's management, as well.

Show . . .

As I've discussed in CHAPTER 6, general managers need to understand and appreciate the complexity and workload their concierges face, so the department can be adequately supported on all counts. A great way to demonstrate this is to freely offer concierge services to members of management, treating them as well as one would a guest. This allows the GM to experience the level of service provided firsthand and gain an appreciation of the complexities dealt with on a daily basis by the department. Even if some execs go a bit overboard, fulfilling their requests is time and energy well spent. It's also an excellent idea to have the general manager spend time at the concierge desk to familiarize him/herself with the realities of the job.

An Important Note: The concierge desk is best managed by the rooms division manager or better, the general manager of the hotel. Sometimes, the concierge team reports to the front-office manager; however, this typically is not the ideal reporting relationship. The concierge staff plays a valuable and vital role in the operation of the hotel, which requires the vision of an executive staff member whose purview encompasses the "big picture." Conversely, because concierges are the "eyes and ears" of the hotel, they are valuable sources of the critical feedback upper management needs to advise their top-level decisions. Another primary advantage to this reporting relationship is that a member of the top executive staff is more empowered to allocate the resources necessary for the smooth functioning of the concierge department.

And Tell . . .

Communication with management includes more than simply a general understanding of the concierges' day-to-day activities, however. It is of equal importance to report, in quantifiable terms, the extent to which the concierge department is a profit center and a tremendous asset to the hotel.

The goal of communicating to management might be to convey information, such as the revenues generated, or make a request for additional resources or permission to attend a professional event. Regardless of the objective, it is the responsibility of the chief concierge to communicate with management clearly, effectively and compellingly.

It is vitally important to report the business the concierge desk generates and quantify its contributes to the bottom line. Some of the concierge department's contributions are difficult to measure, such as the number of returning guests and referrals of new guests that result from the great service at the concierge desk. On the other hand, there are other significant financial contributions that can be easily quantified, such as the revenues that are generated by:

- Room Nights
- Commissions
- Sales and Catering Leads
- Restaurant/Room Service Reservations and Orders
- Other Sources of Revenue, such as Gift Shop Sales, Spa Bookings, etc.

REPORT WRITING

Report writing is a critical skill that can be developed by everyone and a powerful business tool. The following are a few helpful report writing "Dos and Taboos" that have been reprinted with the permission of their originator, Marjorie Silverman.

REPORT WRITING DOS AND TABOOS

Do:

- Adequately research and prepare.
- Use proper grammar and spelling.
- Use humor, when appropriate.
- Know the hotel's mission statement and how your report relates with it.
- Frame content in a positive manner.
- Present solutions.
- Use the facts.
- Keep it concise.

Don't:

- Express requests as demands.
- Fudge on the figures or present inaccurate information.
- Settle for sloppy or ill-considered work.
- Frame contents in a negative manner.
- Point the finger at another staff member or department.
- Make unreasonable requests.

ACCENTUATE THE POSITIVE – ELIMINATE THE NEGATIVE

As listed in the "Dos and Taboos," it's important to frame the contents of your reports in a positive way. Marjorie Silverman illustrates the contrast beautifully with these examples of a positively and negatively worded introduction, as well as a positively and negatively worded conclusion. Compare:

THE NEGATIVE vs. THE POSITIVE INTRODUCTION

From the Negative . . .

In an attempt to evaluate the Concierge Department, we feel professionalism and quality service provided to guests is impaired due to deficiency in these areas: current staffing issues, tools provided and hotel management support . . .
. . . A hotel is only as good as the Concierge Department . . . then our hotel is not very good due to these issues.

. . . To the Positive

We love our jobs! The hectic pace is part of the allure for the true concierge. The current staff is highly motivated, loyal and dedicated. The can-do attitude and the reluctance to say "no" is so much a part of the mindset of our concierges that we never have been very slow to call the attention of upper management to our situation. However, we care so much about the service level that mediocrity is something we cannot tolerate, nor do we believe that upper management would want us to slip below our own, as well as the hotel's high standards.

Fortunately, the problems we are experiencing are easy to fix. I sincerely believe that the changes we are proposing will vastly improve the guest perception not only of the concierge service but of the guest's entire hotel experience.

THE NEGATIVE vs. THE POSITIVE CONCLUSION

From the Negative . . .

I believe a lack of awareness and support has led us to a level of frustration and an inability to provide the level of service required not only by our standards but of hotel standards, as well. These are issues that can no longer be ignored if quality service for our guests is a priority. The staff at this point appears to be disappointed with the lack of attention to these matters. If we are to have quality staff and retain them, we must address these concerns promptly.

. . . To the Positive

I wrote a report shortly after opening the concierge desk in which I described our concierge service as "at one thoroughly efficient and warmly personal." I believe we are still very efficient and professional, but I regret to admit that we are less gracious and warmly personal than we used to be when we had more time to chat with our guests. When ten people are in line in front of you and both phones are ringing, we must dispatch guest request with the greatest efficiency possible. Unfortunately, it is inevitable that the service loses its graciousness.

I do not want to settle for less and neither does my staff. I would not request the additional expense if I did not sincerely believe that it was warranted and, indeed, necessary. I believe that in terms of public relations for the hotel, the goodwill for repeat guests, and the consistency at a time when management turns over on a one- or two-year cycle, we can significantly affect the hotel's profitability by attracting and keeping repeat business. We want the opportunity to do a better job.

Thank you for your consideration.

While both the negative and positive versions address the same issues, it's easy to see that the positively framed reports are more likely to invite positive responses.

The following is a comprehensive report developed by Jeanne Mills to dramatically communicate the revenues generated by the concierge team at MGM in Las Vegas. The numbers below have been fabricated, and it is only presented here to serve as an example of how powerful a reporting tool can be in establishing the concierge department as a valuable profit center.

More basic reports don't necessarily have to take the form of a spreadsheet, however, and can be sent as a simple, well-worded memo. It is still important to be very specific, however, by keeping accurate records and providing concrete information.

For example, instead of generalizing the volume of telephone traffic (e.g., "We're so busy.), it's much more powerful to provide hard numbers (e.g., "We received 329 calls in one day alone and dropped 200 of them, due to insufficient staffing.). Marjorie has provided the following example of stating the facts in a powerful and effective way:

> "By establishing good relations with Melanie Kersey, Associate Director of Tourism Services at the Art Institute, we were able to acquire VIP passes for our guests during the hugely successful Monet Show.
>
> "The museum advertised our options rate in their mailing, and we only sold our tickets to hotel guests. Of our 200 monthly allotments, approximately 20 were sold to meeting planners already booked in the hotel, upper management staff and sales designated

THE ULTIMATE SERVICE HOTEL, LLC
CONCIERGE EXECUTIVE SUMMARY
DECEMBER MONTH END 2009

Ticketing

Ticket Breakdown	
Cirque Theatre	8,946
Broadway Theatre	3,475
Kodak Theatre	1,376
Staples Arena	1,930
Total Tickets sold	**15,462**
Total Dollar Amount	$ 2,555,555.00
Gift Certificates	**506**
Total GC $	**$ 40,530.00**

*Actual Sales (Excludes Ticket Will Call)

Will Call Tickets	**2815**

*Will Call Tickets are for MGM Grand shows only

Restaurants

	Total Covers	Total $ Amount
Steak and Fish	1,700	$ 177,497.00
Taste of Mexico	455	$ 20,406.75
Tuscany Hills	304	$ 18,170.08
Paris on the Go	455	$ 56,661.15
Modern American	304	$ 23,325.92
East meets West	455	$ 39,243.75
French delight	304	$ 90,309.28
Ocean Tides	455	$ 37,018.80
The art of Japan	304	$ 21,723.84
Totals	**4,736**	**$ 484,356.57**

*Revenue of average check from P&L

Sister Properties

Reflection		**600**
Revenue	$	48,238.10
Life Mysteries		**456**
Revenue	$	44,218.55
The Musical		**303**
Revenue	$	61,162.98
Human Sences		**219**
Revenue	$	23,546.34
The Spectacle		**162**
Revenue	$	17,175.30
The Ventriloquist		**166**
Revenue	$	9,081.90
Imagine		**219**
Revenue	$	17,761.60
The Legend		**162**
Revenue	$	25,580.43
Total Tickets		**1,959**
Cross sell Revenue	**$**	**246,765.20**

*Actual Sales (Excludes Ticket Will Call)

Golf

	# of Rounds
Green Tee Golf	77
Waterfalls Golf	62
Desert Golf	144
Total Rounds	**283**

Night Life

Studio 54	402	$ 16,080.00
Tabu	60	$ 2,400.00
Total Night Life	**462**	**$ 18,480.00**

Room Service

Number of Orders	181
Total Revenue	$ 13,032.00

Floral

Number of Orders	181
Total Revenue	$ 10,127.85

Spa

	# of Resv.	$
Mas	620	$ 71,300.00
Fac	62	$ 9,300.00
Nail	310	$ 27,900.00
Scrub	45	$ 3,600.00
Bronz	12	$ 660.00
Total	**1,049**	**$112,760.00**

Monthly Conversion 36%

*Conversion comprised of calls to bookings

Total Revenue Generated from Concierge MTD	**$**	**3,481,606.62**
Total Concierge Expense MTD	**$**	**203,090.30**
Expense % to Revenue MTD		**5.8%**

The numbers have all been altered so as not to divulge any proprietary information. This is used here as an example and is not an actual document.

VIPs. The rest were reserved for guests who specifically booked rooms for the Monet exhibit.

"We were able to generate approximately 100 rooms per month for an average stay of two nights at an average $149 per night. For the four-month duration of the exhibit, the grand total was $119,200."

FOR UPPER MANAGEMENT

As I wrote this chapter, I realized that I needed to include a short section to help foster the understanding of those who manage those who are managing the concierge. It is important to note here that the career trajectory of the concierge is typically quite different from that of other hotel staff members. The position of concierge is their ultimate career, and they tend to remain – and grow – in the profession, rather than considering it a stepping-stone to other areas of responsibility. They are consummate professionals at what they do, which requires a unique and rare skill set and temperament that differs from other areas overseen by top management. As such, they need to be managed differently, with the understanding and appreciation that their job is unique and complex, therefore requiring a more open style of management than is indicated for other areas of the hotel.

THE PERILS OF OUTSOURCING

I feel very strongly that the trend of outsourcing hotel concierge services is a *disservice* to concierges, the concierge profession and the overall success of the hotel industry. This shortsighted trend is both unproductive and counterintuitive.

The core competency of any hotel is service, and the ambassador and epitome of service is the concierge. It is the concierge team that sets the standards for the service levels of every other department in the hotel. As such, I like to describe the concierge desk as the heartbeat of the hotel. To carry the analogy further, the idea of outsourcing this vital function is tantamount to giving a transplanted organ (seen as a foreign entity by the body) to a person who is thriving with a perfectly healthy, life-giving, heart.

While it might seem to be a money-saving proposition in the short term, outsourcing this centralized and vital function of the hotel simply is not a good business practice. In fact, it runs contrary to the proven axiom:

Employee Loyalty = Performance = Profit

I have devoted an entire chapter of this book to the importance of relationship – the cornerstone of the concierge profession. This includes the importance of the relationship of the concierge to the hotel itself. Typically, the loyalty of the outsourced concierge naturally falls to the company for which they work, rather than the hotel. On the other hand, the concierge who is employed by the hotel holds the interests of the hotel and its guests as his or her first and foremost priority.

As discussed in previous chapters, concierges must have close and cooperative relationships with every other department in the hotel. As employees, the concierge team are viewed and treated as members of the family, whereas individuals who are outsourced are seen quite differently. In the latter case, the level of rapport and cooperation simply isn't the same. The same holds true of the valuable relationships held outside of the hotel – including those with the city, the vendors and the community at large.

> *In desperation, the director of sales at another prominent hotel (which had outsourced their concierge desk) called our desk to illicit our help in getting one of their guests onto Pebble Beach. Knowing that their outsourced tour staff did not have the necessary relationships to make that happen, we were tempted to suggest he ask the folks at his concierge desk to take care of that for him.*

Finally, by outsourcing its concierges, hotel management sends the message that this vital function is not valued enough to be considered a part of the hotel. A small but significant example: Even if an outsourced concierge provides exemplary service, in most cases, he or she would not even be qualified to receive a service award for which only hotel personnel are qualified.

For these reasons, and many more, I strongly agree with the policy of Les Clefs d'Or, which opposes this practice and restricts its membership to hotel employees. Though outsourcing has become a recent trend, I believe time will tell, in terms of its limited benefits and long-term pitfalls.

THE LEGACY OF LEADERSHIP

ASSUMING THE ROLE of leadership in the concierge department requires the chief concierge to wear many hats – from teacher, to coach, to department advocate, to mentor. Fundamentally, however, it's important to remember that the underlying principle of all of these roles is to serve others, while staying focused on achieving results in line with the organization's values and integrity. It is a position that is as rewarding as it is challenging, affording all the joys and challenges of the concierge profession – and more.

Connecting Guests to Experiences Around the World

A FINAL THOUGHT

ONE of the greatest gifts of being a concierge is in being the ambassador of your destination and perfecting the ability to design experiences for people that create lasting memories. That is truly what it means to master "The Art and Science of the Hotel Concierge."

ACKNOWLEDGEMENTS

Or . . . My Four Favorite Words: "Thank You Very Much!"

I have heard it said that if the only prayer you ever said was "Thank You" that it would be enough. These powerful words of gratitude and appreciation shape our lives, for when we are in gratitude it is impossible to be in another more negative state such as fear, anxiety, or anger. Gratitude magically trumps everything else.

I have so much gratitude and appreciation for the many clients I have been privileged to work with as a consultant, speaker and trainer over these past twenty years. It is because of all of the love and support of my friends and colleagues, most especially through my relationship with Les Clefs d'Or that I want to take this opportunity to personally thank them for their enormous contributions to this book and to the unrelenting support of my message throughout my career. I could never have done this book or for that matter stayed in business without my concierge friends and most certainly would not have retained the passion for the profession for more than thirty years if it were not for the wonderful colleagues that I admire and have grown to love from around the world.

Thank You to Les Clefs d'Or, Thank you to every General Manager I have ever worked with, thank you to the Grand Hyatt San Francisco (formerly called The Hyatt on Union Square) where I learned the craft.

Thank You to each of you personally for helping me with focus groups, reading of the manuscripts, phone interviews, translations into Spanish and Japanese, bouncing off ideas, stories, advice and continued inspiration: Kathleen Fitzgerald, LeighAnne Dolecki, Jim McCasland, Charisse Fazzari, Michael Thorburn, Jack Nargil, Ginny Thomason, Robert Watson, Maite Foriasky, Karen Giobbia, Abigail Hart, Frederick Bigler, Maurice Dancer, Maria Wittorp de Jonge, Jon Adler, Michael Romei, Adam Isrow, Philip Bokan, Jossell Velazquez, Rick Burton, Lorley Musiol, Regena Falling, Julie Saunders, Domenic Alfonzetti, Michael McCleary, Michael Anderson, Charles Budden, Momoko Ono, Burak Aydin and Jeff Clavin (deceased).

A special "Thank You" to Jeanne Mills of the MGM Grand in las Vegas, you inspire me immensely and I praise you for the way you have elevated the profession, rethought it and proven that sales and service are inseparable.

Thank You for hiring me and recommending that I speak to your concierge associations, hotels, local businesses, corporate affiliations and for believing in my work enough to let me know, and helping to give me the stamina and commitment to keep doing it: Patricia Dreisezun, Laurie Gordon, Kate Anderson, Judy Kabler, Robert Marks, Shujaat Khan, Marco Milanez. Miguel Pena, Kay Cremeens, Diana Nelson, Patricia Clifton, Lisa Drahota Booher, Sylvia Rollins, John Winke, Bette Salemme, Jeanne Venn, Aldo Giaccomello, Inger Boudouris, Carmen Martin, Gloria Kennedy, Gunter Kleemann, Harold Mootz, Loida Diaz, Patricia Farman, Peter Rank, Susan Drosdzal, Mary LaMarche, Elizabeth Wilson, Muffin Spielman, Diane Dillon, Gerry Parent, Peter Johnson, Olga Pierce, Danelle Kensbock, Waldo Hernandez, Paula Kelly, John Sun Dong, Jerry Soh, Gregory Tan, Virginia Casale, Luc Lavoie, Tamas Ungar, Giorgio Durante, Etsuko Higashide, Kay Abe, Naoyuki Yoshimura and Carolina Avilara.

A very special "Thanks" to the staff at The Grand Hyatt San Francisco. Even after all of these years, I still pick up the phone and call them for directions and suggestions and they are always the utmost in fabulous. Ann, Liz, Elaine, Susan, John and Mark.

A special and heartfelt Thank You to Joanna Husk a senior member of the Grand Hyatt San Francisco team. Joanna is my muse. I call her and get together with her just to brainstorm and ask for her thoughts and ideas. She is such a font of creative information that I would never think about being in her presence without a paper and pen. Many of the excellent ideas in this book came directly from Joanna. "Surfing in the zone," "Style wizards of information management" and having a "Romance with your destination" to name a few. While Joanna is never at a loss for words the only word I can think of to describe her is wow!

Thank You to my friends in the hospitality industry that I share my values with and always look to for guidance, ideas and inspiration Nanci Sherman, Kathy "KO" Odsather, Michael Chaffin and Joe Kordsmeier.

Thank You to my mentor, Larry Allport (deceased), for showing me what a professional concierge truly is and for teaching me how to become one.

Thank You to Marjorie Silverman my friend and confidant. I have run every idea I have ever had about the concierge by Marjorie just to make sure it was "politically correct" and the appropriate thing to say and do. To me the "Concierge" and "Marjorie" are synonymous.

Thank You to Aimee Lyndon-Adams, my friend, business collaborator and spiritual growth advocate. Thank you for all that you taught me over the past 11 years. Many specific ideas made it into this book while others that are less quantifiable are evident throughout the text.

Because this is a textbook, the task of creating objectives was an important one. I needed an objective eye and a succinct mind. Thank You to my colleague at Talent Mondial, partner in seminar delivery and intrepid traveling buddy Dorothy van Hoorn for taking on the task and getting it right.

Thank You to George Glazer at the Educational Institute for holding my hand through the process and for finally believing that the time has come to invest in the concierge.

Thank You to Hall Kelley, designer extraordinaire, for the look and feel of a book that every concierge can be proud of. You designed each page with care and thoughtfulness.

A very heartfelt Thank You to Mr. William (Billy) S. Morris III of Morris Communications. Once again, *Where* Magazine is playing a significant role in ensuring that quality education about the profession reaches concierges around the globe. Your relentless support of the concierge is deeply appreciated.

Thank You to Lin Ivice, my coauthor. I "enrolled" Lin in the project in December of 2009. I told her it would be a big job to redo and rethink the old concierge text, but I don't think she realized just how big, "big" actually meant. By December of 2010 with two chapters left to go, she definitely knew that big really meant big. Imagine . . . taking on the task of co-authoring a book about a topic that you really don't know anything about especially when that topic is about a profession that is supposed to know everything. The real talent that Lin brings is being able to interpret what I am saying and make it professional, stellar, interesting and organized. I love the result and hope you do as well. Thank you Lin, you are a seriously talented person and I appreciate you.

And finally . . . to my precious, supportive, talented and beloved husband Bill Apton, Thank you for the photographs you contributed to this book, but mostly Thank You for the never ending support and the constant love and laughter.

Holly Stiel

About the Authors

In 1976, Holly Stiel became the first female hotel concierge in the U.S. when she created the desk at the Grand Hyatt Union Square in San Francisco. Two years later, she was the first American woman to be admitted to the exclusive Les Clefs d'Or Association for concierges. She has received the association's Honorary Member award for her broad contributions to the profession and was the first female and non-corporate executive to receive the "Distinguished Visiting Professor" Chair from Johnson and Wales University.

After 17 years as a concierge, Holly founded her own company, Thank You Very Much, Inc., to provide training for hotel concierges and customize concierge service philosophies and practices for all types of industries. Through partnering with producers, Holly also has been a pioneer in multi-media training, creating three award-winning interactive DVD programs. A philosopher, published author, keynote speaker, workshop leader and consultant, her programs have been delivered in 25 languages, to businesses ranging from The Bank of America to NASCAR. Holly lives in Mill Valley, California with her husband, Bill Apton.

in Ivice Holly Stiel

Lin Ivice is a published author and editor with 25 years experience in corporate communications, marketing, public relations and freelance writing and editing. She has collaborated on projects ranging from textbooks, books on women's spirituality, articles on health and wellness, newsletters, and a wide variety of marketing materials, including websites, blogs and radio advertising copy. Lin specializes in helping authors, speakers and consultants express their expertise with polished content, while creating an ongoing web presence to market their products and services. Lin resides in Sausalito, California.

Other Books by Holly Stiel

Ultimate Service, The Complete Handbook to the World of the Concierge

Thank You Very Much – A Book for Anyone Who Has Ever Said, "May I Help You?"

The Neon Signs of Service